D1570186

Peaceful Revolution

Peaceful Revolution

*Constitutional Change and
American Culture from
Progressivism to the New Deal*

Maxwell Bloomfield

HARVARD UNIVERSITY PRESS

Cambridge, Massachusetts, and London, England | 2000

Library of Congress Cataloging-in-Publication Data

Bloomfield, Maxwell H.
    Peaceful revolution : constitutional change and American culture from
Progressivism to the New Deal / Maxwell Bloomfield.
        p.   cm.
    Includes bibliographical references and index.
    ISBN 0-674-00304-7
    1. Constitutional history—United States.   2. United States—Social
conditions—1933–1945.   3. New Deal, 1933–1939.   I. Title.

KF4541 .B59   2000
306'0973—dc21   00-026108

To Helen

Contents

Preface

When I began the research for this book, I had the idea of exploring the ways in which supporters and opponents of the New Deal used the media to explain constitutional changes to depression audiences. The subject seemed made to order for critical inquiry, since the federal government sponsored a variety of cultural projects in the 1930s, to the dismay of conservative critics. And existing studies of New Deal culture provided merely a general survey of the period, with little attention to the constitutional aspects of governmental outreach programs.[1] I decided, therefore, that an assessment of cultural materials from a constitutional perspective would fill an important gap in the historical record.

As I immersed myself in the period and its background, however, it became clear that a separate volume would be needed to lay the cultural foundations for what many contemporaries termed the "constitutional revolution" of the 1930s. For one thing, the sheer bulk of the relevant, and largely neglected, material at the Library of Congress is overwhelming. Accordingly, this book will focus on the interplay between constitutional developments and media coverage from the turn of the century to the coming of the New Deal, with a backward glance at the beginning of Constitution worship in the early Republic. I do not attempt to discuss public reaction to every important constitutional issue that arose in those years. My aim is rather to demonstrate through representative examples the powerful appeal that constitutional values have always made to the American imagination. Novels, cartoons, plays, and movies, I argue, have often functioned as instruments of constitutional discourse, and both elite and marginalized groups in American society have employed such vehicles to promote constitutional agendas.

An introductory chapter describes the emergence of a popular cult of the Constitution in the Founding period, when the Federal Convention was hailed as a peaceful alternative to violent political upheaval. Issues of federalism and state rights dominated the popular consciousness in the antebellum years, as creative writers argued the merits of nullification, secession, and unionism to sectional audiences. Although constitutional solutions failed to resolve the moral dilemma of slavery, the Civil War—like the American Revolution a century earlier—was fought on constitutional grounds and resulted in the triumph of a more nationalist model of constitutionalism.

Chapters 2 through 6 explore the continuing importance of a constitutional legacy of "peaceful revolution" in modern America. Major themes include the Progressive critique of an outmoded Constitution at the turn of the century and fictional representations of an alternative constitutional order; the use of early silent films by suffragists and their opponents to influence the debate over a national woman suffrage amendment; the Wilson administration's mobilization of the media to promote a program of "war socialism" and the efforts of dissenters to convey their views to the American people; the revival of Constitution worship and its cultural consequences in the 1920s; and the effects of the early depression years in discrediting governmental authority and encouraging a renewed public interest in constitutional utopias. Chapter 7 examines the revolutionary rhetoric of Franklin D. Roosevelt's first inaugural address and relates his announcement of a New Deal to public demands for a peaceful revolution. In an Afterword I consider some implications of the study and of the use of popular culture materials as a supplement to more traditional approaches to problems of constitutional change in a pluralist democracy.

Portions of Chapters 1 and 2 previously appeared as articles in the *Journal of American Culture:* "Constitutional Values and the Literature of the Early Republic," *JAC* 11 (Winter 1988): 53–58, and "Constitutional Ideology and Progressive Fiction," *JAC* 18 (Spring 1995): 77–85. I am grateful to editor Ray B. Browne for permission to reprint this material.

The completion of the book has been greatly assisted by generous research and writing grants from the Columbus School of Law, whose faculty I joined in 1985. In particular, I would like to thank Dean Bernard Dobranski, former Dean Ralph J. Rohner, Associate Dean Veryl Miles, former Associate Dean George E. Garvey, and Assistant Dean Michael R. Kanne for their consistent support and encouragement. I am also indebted to my colleague in the History Department at the Catholic University of

America, Thomas R. West, who read the manuscript and offered valuable criticism. And special thanks to Gabrielle Fenlon, who typed the initial draft in its entirety, and to Judy Ann Blower and Darla Koenig, who typed successive revisions and additions. The staff at the Library of Congress deserves mention as well for helpful assistance over the years.

Peaceful Revolution

1

The Founders' Constitution and Republican Culture

> If from a vile assemblage of vagrants and rogues the wisest and most virtuous nation that ever existed deduced its origin, under the wise constitution and laws of Romulus—what may not be expected from an enlightened, virtuous and heroic people, . . . under a constitution formed by their free suffrages and the combined wisdom of all those who have gone before them?
>
> —ENOS HITCHCOCK (1788)

Americans profess to revere their Constitution, although relatively few have read it with care and fewer still have understood it in more than a superficial way.[1] Its real importance for the average citizen has been symbolic. Like its counterpart, the earlier Declaration of Independence, it serves as an enduring reminder of the moral vision that shaped the nation's founding. Successive generations, confronted with new political problems, have sought to reaffirm a sense of national identity and purpose by appealing to constitutional norms. Those norms in turn have been defined for the public as a result of publicity campaigns carried out on two distinct levels. On an official plane, congressional debates over pending legislation, Supreme Court decisions, and presidential messages convey an institutional perspective on issues of constitutional change. Public support for such change, however, may depend more on a second level of communication—the commentary provided by the popular media.

Although scholars have tended to neglect cartoons, poems, novels, movies, and television dramas as instruments of constitutional discourse, these agencies have clearly contributed to popular understanding of complex policy matters. By personalizing abstract constitutional doctrines, writers and artists have encouraged the general public to reflect on controversial measures and to participate in organized efforts to promote or oppose them. No causative link between media presentations and voter behavior can be scientifically established, of course; but if constitutional change grows out of changing social needs and values, the earliest warning signs of serious disaffection are likely to be found in the popular press.

1

The interplay between official action and popular response was already evident at the time of the American Revolution, when a native constitutional tradition first took shape. During the decade of controversy that preceded the outbreak of actual fighting, insurgent leaders defined the issues for the public through courtroom arguments, legislative speeches, and newspaper essays. Again and again they charged that the taxes and commercial restrictions lately imposed by the British government violated the rights of colonial Americans, which were guaranteed to them by the common law and by their royal or corporate charters. In response to this constitutional challenge, the loyalist bar developed counterarguments justifying parliamentary supremacy in equally legalistic terms. While patriot attorneys organized protest meetings and drafted petitions to Parliament, other opponents of British "tyranny" erected "liberty poles," published inflammatory broadsides and poems, preached libertarian sermons, and engaged in street demonstrations that often turned violent.[2] Since the revolutionary cause depended so strongly on constitutional grounds for its legitimacy, it is scarcely surprising that, when last-minute appeals for redress failed, the colonies took immediate action to regularize their new status as independent republics. A flurry of constitution-making on the state level succeeded the announcement of the Declaration of Independence, and the Continental Congress set up a committee to draft a written instrument of government for the new nation.[3]

This widespread resort to formal constitutions by the revolutionary generation had some deeper implications as well. Independence meant not only the absence of royal governors and parliamentary decrees but also the loss of unifying cultural symbols and traditions. Living in a pluralistic society that lacked ancient and authoritative folkways, Americans turned to the law to define themselves as a modern republican nation. Thomas Paine captured the ideal well in his rabble-rousing pamphlet, *Common Sense* (1776), when he observed that the rebellious colonists had no need of kings or other Old World icons of order because "in America THE LAW IS KING."[4] Through wise and humane laws, and especially through the fundamental principles established by their new constitutions, Americans hoped to create a model society based on reason and the consent of the governed.

Republican ideology called for a society of self-reliant freeholders, who should be encouraged to pursue wealth and status with a minimum of governmental interference. The most important function of law, according to the republican creed, was to facilitate economic growth and social mobility by releasing private entrepreneurial energies. Competition and self-help were to replace the colonial ideals of paternalism and security, as the nation moved from a ruler-subject model of social organization to one based on the principle of free exchange between equals. Philip Freneau echoed this libertarian ethic in a poem of the 1790s:

> COLUMBIA, hail! immortal be thy reign;
> Without a king, we till the smiling plain;
>
> . . . .
>
> Without a *king*, the laws maintain their sway,
> While honour bids each generous heart obey.
>
> . . . .
>
> So shall our nation, form'd on Virtue's plan,
> Remain the guardian of the Rights of Man,
> A vast Republic, famed through every clime,
> Without a king, to see the end of time.[5]

But responsible government proved difficult to achieve in practice. The first state constitutions adhered to a rigorous theory of separation of powers and conferred dominant authority upon the most popular branch of government, the legislature, at the expense of the executive and the judiciary. Within a few years this system of legislative supremacy came under sharp attack from creditor and propertied interests in almost every state. Populistic laws, these critics charged, were encouraging inflation and creating a dangerous climate of political unrest and instability. The outbreak of Shays's Rebellion in the fall of 1786 intensified conservative fears, as essayists and poets filled New England newspapers with denunciations of insurgent Daniel Shays and his ragtag army of impoverished Massachusetts farmers.

The Shaysites, protesting high taxes and a depressed economy, forcibly closed the courts in several Massachusetts counties to prevent further debt collections and mortgage foreclosures. Eventually they attacked the federal arsenal at Springfield, but the state militia quickly dispersed them and ended the rebellion. The episode, insignificant in itself, captured the popular imagination because it provided a dramatic illustration of the evils of unrestrained liberty.[6] "In a free government, the reality of grievances is no kind of justification of rebellion," commented Fisher Ames, writing for Boston's *Independent Chronicle*. "Besides," he added, "our constitution is the free act of the people; they stand solemnly pledged for its defense, and treason against such a constitution implies a high degree of moral depravity."[7]

Poets likewise condemned Shays and his followers for resorting to the violent tactics of the prerevolutionary years, and for attempting to replace a government of popularly enacted laws with mob rule. One anonymous versifier adopted the persona of a backwoods Shaysite to emphasize the anarchic individualism encouraged by the rebellion:

> Constitutions and oaths, sir, we mind not a rush,
> Such trifles must yield to us lads of the bush.[8]

The interstate press coverage of Shays's Rebellion stressed the general weakness of the new nation and helped to focus public attention on the need for sweeping constitutional changes in the national government. That government, formally established in 1781 under the Articles of Confederation, had institutionalized the revolutionary model of constitutionalism that prevailed in the states. A one-house Congress, to which each state elected delegates annually and in which each state had an equal vote, formulated all national policies. There were no countervailing executive or judicial branches, and democratic power-sharing was assured through a rotation requirement that prevented a delegate from serving more than three years in any six-year period. Fearful of creating a potentially oppressive American Parliament, the framers of the Articles left the most important legislative powers in the hands of the states. Congress could not tax, or regulate commerce, or guarantee that individual states would obey the treaties it negotiated with foreign powers. Under these conditions congressional prestige soon declined, and the genuine accomplishments of the central government in such areas as federal land policy were overshadowed by its mounting debts and ineffectual efforts at substantive reform. When delegates proposed amendments to increase congressional power, for example, they found they could never obtain the consent of all thirteen states, as required by the Articles.[9]

Jeremy Belknap, in a popular satire titled *The Foresters* (1792), traced the defects of the Confederation to a utopian ideology that grew out of the struggle for independence. Intoxicated by their newly won freedom, the American "families" (i.e., states) in Belknap's tale resolve to create a partnership of complete equality like that of the industrious beavers, who "carry on their operations with peace and unanimity, without even the appearance of a *master*." Unfortunately, humans prove to be less cooperative than beavers, and the "perfect republic" soon collapses for want of effective governmental sanctions. To illustrate the harmful effects of uncontrolled state power on national policy-making, Belknap employed an apt mechanical metaphor:

> In the club room, among a number of ingenious devices, there was a clock, of a most curious and intricate construction, by which all the common concerns of the partnership were to be regulated. It had *one* bell, on which *thirteen* distinct hammers struck the hours. Each hammer was moved by independent wheels and weights, each set of wheels and weights was enclosed in a separate case, the key of which was kept, not as it ought to have been, by the person who represented the family at club, but in each mansion house; and every family claimed a right either to keep the key at home or send it to club, when and by whom they pleased.

Such institutional arrangements in time cause a complete breakdown in the club's operations, as members "knew neither the hour of the day, nor the day of the month; they could not date their letters nor adjust their books, nor do business with any regularity."[10]

Belknap's humorous attack on the weakness of the Confederation government formed a late addition to a body of more sober constitutional criticism that appeared in newspapers and magazines in the 1780s. From the beginning of the Confederation, prominent businessmen, landowners, and professionals had urged the expansion of federal power as a means of strengthening public credit and preventing radical economic experimentation by the states. Through interstate commercial conferences, such as the Annapolis Convention of 1786, these nationalists publicized their views and finally proposed that the states send commissioners to a general meeting at Philadelphia to revise the Articles. A dispirited Congress issued a call for such an extraconstitutional gathering "for the sole and express purpose of revising the Articles of Confederation and reporting to Congress and the several legislatures such alterations and provisions therein as shall when agreed to in Congress and confirmed by the states render the federal Constitution adequate to the exigencies of government and the preservation of the Union."[11] Deliberations were scheduled to begin in May 1787.

The advocates of a strong central government employed a variety of popular literary forms to mobilize public support for the impending Philadelphia Convention. Royall Tyler linked constitutional reform to the survival of republican government in his play *The Contrast*. First performed in New York City on April 16, 1787, this comedy of manners—

the earliest commercially successful play by an American author—deftly contrasted the artificialities of the English caste system with the democratic mores of postrevolutionary America. Behind the witty dialogue and comic stereotypes, however, lay a serious political message. Tyler's hero, the virtuous Henry Manly, is a revolutionary patriot whose experience in helping to suppress Shays's Rebellion leads him to reflect at length on the future of the Confederation. Using historical analogy, a favorite device of eighteenth-century moralists, Manly draws an ominous parallel between the American Union and the Amphictyonic League of ancient Greece:

> The various [Greek] states engendered jealousies of each other; and, more unfortunately, growing jealous of their great federal council, the Amphictyons, they forgot that their common safety had existed, and would exist, in giving them an honourable extensive prerogative. The common good was lost in the pursuit of private interest; and that people who, by uniting, might have stood against the world in arms, by dividing, crumbled into ruin. . . . Oh! that America! Oh! that my country would, in this her day, learn the things that belong to her peace![12]

The implied endorsement of the approaching Philadelphia Convention could scarcely have escaped Tyler's audience.

Even more pointed were the recommendations for constitutional change made by Lemuel Hopkins and his fellow "Connecticut Wits" in *The Anarchiad*. Published in fourteen installments in the *New Haven Gazette* during 1786 and 1787, this mock-heroic poem celebrates an epic struggle between two primordial forces for the control of the New World. On one side stands the Anarch, the spirit of misrule and destruction; opposing him is Hesper, the godlike defender of order and rationality. As lawless mobs rise within the states, Hesper convenes his "principal counselors and sages" at Philadelphia to plan a constitutional counterattack. Invoking the spirits of the revolutionary dead, whose vision of a republican nation has been betrayed, Hesper calls for a new constitutional order that will be strong enough to check the "giddy rage of democratic States." His nationalistic prescriptions are quite explicit:

> But know, ye favor'd race, one potent head
> Must rule your States, and strike your foes with dread,
> The finance regulate, the trade control,
> Live through the empire, and accord the whole.[13]

The delegates who attended the actual Philadelphia Convention more than fulfilled the expectations of their literary well-wishers. Meeting in closed sessions, they early agreed to ignore their prescribed agenda and to frame a completely new constitutional system. In place of the rudimentary national Congress provided by the Articles, they constructed a central government composed of three separate, but interlocking, branches. Congress now had the power to tax individuals, to regulate interstate commerce, and to maintain its own military and naval forces. Although the states retained control over their internal affairs, they could no longer impair contractual obligations or engage in other specified inflationary practices. The framers provided that the new federal system should take effect when approved by nine states, acting through specially convened ratifying conventions.[14]

After some debate Congress transmitted the proposed constitution to the states without comment, and for ten months (September 1787 to July 1788) publicists argued the pros and cons of the document to a nationwide audience through the newspapers, the most popular medium of communication in the late eighteenth century. One series of essays—*The Federalist Papers*—became a classic of constitutional commentary. Written by Alexander Hamilton, James Madison, and John Jay under the collective pseudonym of "Publius," *The Federalist* defended the new constitution on logical and philosophical grounds that appealed to the rationalistic temper of the time.

The Philadelphia Convention had successfully reconciled power with liberty, Madison urged, by creating a self-regulating system of structural checks and balances.[15] Within the national government, each house of a bicameral legislature checked the other; the president checked Congress through his veto over legislation; and an independent judiciary checked both president and Congress through its interpretation of constitutional norms. Since the national government could exercise only those powers enumerated in the Constitution, the states provided a further external check against any federal encroachments on their sphere of sovereignty. Hamilton suggested that the overall arrangement resembled the Newtonian solar system, in which the states, like planets, revolved in their separate orbits around the central government as their sun.[16] The image, with its mechanistic overtones, aptly described for eighteenth-century readers a government of laws. For just as natural law—the law of gravitation—controlled the movement of celestial bodies, so did the Constitution—an equally transcendent law—define and limit the power of both nation and state.

Opponents of the new system, forced to adopt the label of "Antifederalists," were at an obvious disadvantage, since they had to defend an existing constitutional order that most of them agreed was defective. Lacking an alternative plan of their own, they sought to discredit the centralizing provisions of the proposed constitution by arguing that they would reestablish tyrannical government on the English model. As a South Carolinian critic put it:

> In five short years of Freedom weary grown
> We quit our plain republics for a throne;
> *Congress* and *President* full proof shall bring,
> A mere disguise for Parliament and King.[17]

In a related vein, other Antifederalists noted that the Constitution contained no Bill of Rights and thus left the federal government free to invade the most cherished liberties of the individual. They particularly deplored the absence of any federal guarantees of free speech and press or of jury trial in civil cases, and worried about the vaguely defined (and therefore menacing) power of the federal judiciary. Publicists not wedded to conspiracy theories feared that a powerful national government might destroy the pluralism of American society and encourage the development of an irresponsible federal bureaucracy, thanks to those intricate checks and balances so prized by the Federalists.[18]

While it is impossible to determine how many people read these newspaper polemics, they clearly did help to shape the thinking of those who attended the state ratifying conventions. The same issues tended to appear in debate after debate, and most of them had received prior consideration in the press. Coverage was far from evenhanded, however. From the beginning most papers favored the cause of constitutional revision and sought to "sell" the Philadelphia Convention to the public through adroit news management. Editors suppressed reports of conflict among the delegates, praised their patriotism and integrity, and urged readers to approve in advance whatever plan of government the group might devise. Once the details of the new Constitution became known, opponents often found it difficult to publish their arguments in major papers. Nevertheless, they did manage to communicate their objections, with sometimes striking results. The ratifying vote was close in such key states as Massachusetts, Virginia, and New York, where Antifederalists forced their adversaries to approve proposed amendments that would establish a federal Bill of

Rights. Gradually, as the ratification process gained momentum, the rancor and paranoia that had characterized debate on both sides tended to wane.[19]

By the end of July 1788, when the eleventh state had endorsed the new Constitution, it had already begun to assume the status of a sacred text, comparable in importance to the Declaration of Independence as a symbol of national unity. Parades and other civic rituals celebrated the accession of each new state to the Union, and the festivities grew in size with each announced ratification. A high point occurred with Philadelphia's "grand federal procession" on July 4, 1788, which brought together all social classes and occupational groups in a massive demonstration of support for the new system. One float, titled *The Constitution*, featured three judges of the state supreme court in their official robes, sitting "in a lofty ornamental car, in the form of a large eagle, drawn by six horses, bearing the constitution, framed, and fixed on a staff, crowned with the cap of liberty. The words, '*the people*,' in gold letters, on one staff, [appeared] immediately under the constitution."[20] Ministers from various faiths, including a rabbi, marched together in one division. The entire procession, noted Catherine Albanese, constituted "liturgy in the fullest sense," as Americans expressed a shared faith in the "religion of the republic and the Constitution, its most cherished sacrament."[21]

To Fourth-of-July orators, the adoption of the new Constitution provided an occasion for reassessing the legacy of the American Revolution. Populist violence was no longer a necessary or legitimate means of bringing about important political change, speakers now asserted. The work of the Philadelphia Convention offered an alternative model of "peaceful revolution" that better reflected the values of a free republican society. As Simeon Baldwin told a New Haven audience in 1788, the new system owed its establishment to an unprecedented exercise of popular sovereignty:

Revolutions in government have in general been the tumultuous exchange of one tyrant for another, or the elevation of a few aspiring nobles upon the ruins of a better system. Never before has the collected wisdom of any nation been permitted quietly to deliberate and determine upon the form of government best adapted to the genius, views and circumstances of the citizens. Never before have the people of any nation been permitted candidly to examine and then deliberately adopt or reject the Constitution proposed.[22]

Other speakers similarly applauded peaceful constitutional change as a remedy for social unrest, sounding a theme that had already appeared in some journals during the suppression of Shays's Rebellion.

The mood of euphoria that greeted the installation of the new federal government in 1789 proved short-lived, however. Divisive issues of domestic and foreign policy soon arose to spur the formation of political parties and to rekindle the old debate between Federalists and Antifederalists. From the 1790s to the Civil War two major groups of constitutional commentators sought to influence public opinion through their writings. Legally trained publicists from New England and the middle states espoused a national-will theory of government to justify the expansion of federal power, while southern lawyers and statesmen formed a state-compact school of constitutional interpretation that championed decentralization and state sovereignty. Each group approached constitutional issues in a formal and mechanistic way, and relied on close textual analysis to support its position.[23]

Joseph Story became the preeminent spokesman for the nationalists following the publication of his magisterial *Commentaries on the Constitution of the United States* in 1833. An associate justice of the United States Supreme Court, Story argued that the American people, acting collectively, had divided sovereign power between the nation and the states and established the Constitution as the supreme law of the land. While the states retained control of their internal affairs, Congress might properly draw upon a broad range of implied powers in carrying out its authorized functions. The Constitution, moreover, had created a permanent Union, whose basic features could be changed only by resort to a prescribed amending process. In the absence of such amendment, the Supreme Court remained the final arbiter of federal-state disputes through its power of judicial review. Story's nationalist model of constitutionalism, which influenced lawyers and judges through the rest of the century, reached a wider antebellum audience as well through several abridged editions aimed at students and general readers.[24]

By the time Story's *Commentaries* appeared, southern constitutionalists had refined and hardened their defense of state sovereignty. In their view, the Constitution was a compact entered into by equal and sovereign states for limited purposes. The federal government, as agent of the states, could exercise only those powers expressly granted to it. If Congress should enact a law that exceeded its constitutional authority, argued the South Carolinian statesman John C. Calhoun, a state might call a special convention of its citizens and declare the act null and void within its borders. Since each state remained the ultimate judge of constitutional issues affecting its sovereignty, a resort to nullification could not be challenged unless the other states adopted a constitutional amendment authorizing the contested federal action. In that case, the nullifying state might either agree to accept the amendment or withdraw from the compact through the exercise of its inherent right of secession.

For many constitutionalists after 1830, secession figured as an alternative form of peaceful revolution. "Instead of forcible resistance to the federal head," explained the philosophic jurist Frederick Grimké, a member of the Union "is at liberty quietly to depart, while others retain their position in the confederacy. This is one of the most important attributes of a federal government. Secession is the instrument happily substituted in the place of open hostility to the laws. So that in the confederate form of government, the law itself provides against those great emergencies which in other countries are said to make laws for themselves."[25]

These antithetical models of constitutional government collided with dramatic effect in the Nullification Crisis of 1832–1833. Angered by the recent imposition of extremely high tariffs on imported goods, the state of South Carolina put Calhoun's ideas into practical operation. A convention declared the federal tariff laws unconstitutional and passed a nullification ordinance that forbade their enforcement within the state. If the federal government should attempt to collect the duties by force, warned the ordinance, the people of South Carolina would consider such action as "inconsistent with the longer continuance of South Carolina in the Union."[26]

In response, President Andrew Jackson drew upon the nationalist tradition of constitutional commentary. "The Constitution of the United States . . . forms a *government*, not a league," Jackson affirmed in a ringing proclamation of December 10, 1832, addressed to the people of South Carolina.[27] The states had created a single nation by relinquishing some of their sovereign powers to the federal government, he insisted, and the Union could not be destroyed thereafter by any kind of unilateral state action. To signal his determination to preserve the Union at all costs, Jackson further induced Congress to pass a Force Bill that empowered him to use whatever civil or military means might be needed to resolve the standoff and execute the laws.

The threat of armed conflict did not materialize, however. Congress quickly passed a compromise tariff bill that substantially reduced current rates and appeased the nullifiers. In March 1833 another convention assembled in South Carolina to rescind the original nullification ordinance, while purporting at the same time to nullify the Force Bill in a final empty gesture of defiance. The entire nullification episode lasted only five months, but its implications for the future were ominous. If nullification had failed as a constitutional remedy, there remained the untried option of secession. And a more intractable problem—slavery—continued to feed southern fears of encroaching federal power. By midcentury the inherent contradiction between republican rhetoric and constitutionally protected slavery had become insupportable to many northerners, and all efforts to resolve the dilemma peacefully—from the Compromise of 1850 to the Dred Scott decision of 1857—proved unavailing.[28]

Cartoonists and novelists found imaginative ways to dramatize the constitutional issues behind nullification and secession for their audiences. Particularly noteworthy is an 1833 cartoon that shows Calhoun climbing to the top of a pyramidlike structure whose ascending steps bear the notations: "Nullification," "S.C. Ordinance," "Treason," "Civil War," "Deception," and "Disunion." Calhoun stands just below the top step, stretching upward to grasp a crown ("Despotism") that floats in the air above him. At the foot of the pyramid lie two slain male figures: one clutches a banner ("Constitution"), the other is covered with a similar banner ("E Pluribus Unum"). On one side Jackson pulls at the coattails of a Calhoun supporter, while speech balloon above him proclaims, "Stop! you have gone too far. Or by the Eternal, I'll hang you all." The design skillfully drives home the message that nullification is both unconstitutional and antirepublican.[29]

An equally impressive attack on nullification occurred in Asa Greene's genial satire, *A Yankee among the Nullifiers* (1833). Greene, a New York journalist, had visited South Carolina and drew upon firsthand impressions in crafting his tale. His hero, Elnathan Elmwood, is a transplanted New Englander who runs for Congress against a "red-hot Nullifier," Major Harebrain Harrington. In a stump speech before a cheering crowd, Harrington indulges in the kind of rhetorical bombast favored by some southern firebrands:

> The Tariff, gentlemen, is unconstitutional. . . . Any law that operates more oppressively upon one portion of the community than another is unconstitutional. . . . Shall the democracy of the South look tamely on and see themselves despoiled by the tories of the North? Shall we who produce cotton and rice be taxed for the sole benefit of those who consume pork and molasses? Shall we submit to be ruled forever

by cotton spinners, pedlers, and pedagogues? . . . Perish the whole Union first! Perish the Constitution and the laws! . . .

What then shall we do, gentlemen and Fellow-citizens? . . . NUL-LIFY; I say NULLIFY! *(Nullify! nullify! responded from a hundred voices.)* . . . We must refuse to pay duties. What! shall Congress have a right to enact a law which South Carolina has not an equal right to abrogate? Heaven forfend! This right is clearly guaranteed by the Constitution. It is among our *reserved rights;* and we will blow the Union to atoms sooner than we will yield one jot or tittle of it.[30]

Harrington wins the election on this fire-eating platform, and the nullifiers sweep to victory throughout Elnathan's district.

In related subplots, a learned professor devises a set of mathematical tables by which anyone may calculate the value of the Union "to the thousandth part of a mill, in the short space of one minute and three seconds"; a gray mare named Union wins a hotly contested race over its competitor, Nullifier, after losing the first heat; and Harebrain Harrington and his friends lead a mob to "nullify" Elnathan's cotton mill, which is employing a workforce of "Africans." Greene brings his story to a rousing climax by describing the efforts of local slaves to put their version of nullification into practice.

As their leader, Caesar Johnson, explains to the other slaves at a secret meeting on Harrington's plantation:

A Nulliflier be a man wat does cisely as he please, and no tanks to nobody. . . . Wateber he don't like, he Nullify. . . . [S]hall the sassy wite man nullify the Guberment? and shall not we, de color men, nullify de wite ones? Wat has Guberment done to Messer McDuffle, and Curnil Hayne, and Docker Crooper, and all de ress of the Nullifliers, compared wid wat dese same Nullifliers hab done to us? . . . And wat, I ax you, should hinner us from nulliflyin de Nullifliers?

. . . [W]en de oberseer, he order you to go to work in de mornin, merely fole up your hans and stan on your *zarve rights.* Dis is a peaceable remery; and sure as you lib it will pose him. Den, spose he offer to flog you, or raise a han to make you work, take to your heel and run as if de dibble was after you. Dis, if I no mistake de word, gemmen, de Nullifliers call de right of *Fleesessium.*[31]

The next day the slaves follow Caesar's instructions and stage a work stoppage, only to receive a flogging for their insubordination. At night, "fearful of being utterly nullified, if they should persevere in their former mode of proceeding,"[32] they resolve to secede and sneak off to a nearby cane brake, taking with them a plentiful supply of hams and hens. Rumors of a bloody slave revolt immediately circulate among the whites, and unionists join nullifiers in tracking down the fugitives. A burlesque battle of the cane brake ensues, from which the whites emerge victorious. Elnathan distinguishes himself in the fighting and wins the hand of a planter's daughter in marriage. The tale ends with a plea for better sectional understanding, as Elnathan becomes an adopted son of the South and announces plans for a new mill to be manned exclusively by Yankee laborers.

Constitutional apologists for state rights also employed satire to attack the policies of the Jackson administration. A striking lithograph of the early 1830s, titled "Born to Command: King Andrew I," presents Jackson as a tyrannical monarch. In a full-length portrait the president wears royal robes, with crown and scepter, as he tramples the Constitution underfoot. The drawing was aimed specifically at Jackson's alleged abuse of the veto power, but its symbolism well captured the mood of the nullifiers.[33] Jackson came in for further criticism in *Memoirs of a Nullifier,* a polemical fantasy published in 1832 at the height of the nullification controversy. According to the anonymous author, the president sold his soul to the devil when he "threatened his native State with the bayonet, in case she attempted to defend her liberty." In this version of current history, Congress authorizes the president to use the army and navy to enforce a new law that requires all Americans to buy and use only one spelling book—the *American Spelling Book* by New Englander Noah Webster. Anyone who violates this protectionist measure shall, by its terms, "be considered guilty of treason against the United States and be punished accordingly." The bill's sponsor, Daniel Webster, sees it as the beginning of a broad policy that will soon ban all books and writings imported from England and other countries, for the benefit of our "home productions."[34]

The case for secession received its most compelling fictional treatment in Nathaniel Beverley Tucker's *The Partisan Leader* (1836). A professor of law at William and Mary and the son of a distinguished Virginia jurist, Tucker used his hastily written novel to attack the evils of Jacksonian nationalism in a presidential election year. The story opens in 1849, as Martin Van Buren, Jackson's handpicked successor, enters upon his fourth term as president of the United States. Vain, unscrupulous, and despotic, Van Buren rules over an increasingly consolidated American empire from a "presidential palace" in Washington. Although he preserves the forms of constitutional government, he destroys any meaningful checks and balances by aggrandizing presidential power at the expense of Congress, the courts, and the states. To accomplish his acts of "usurpation"—the exact nature of which Tucker leaves conveniently vague—Van Buren relies on an inner circle of corrupt officeholders, whose loyalty he ensures through bribes and other perquisites. His policies, which are popular in the North and West, involve the economic exploitation of the cotton-growing South—a minority section—for the benefit of northern manufacturers. The statesmen of the Cotton Kingdom gradually recognize that the Constitution affords them no effective remedy against the oppression of a fixed sectional majority. When Van Buren is reelected for the fourth time in a pro forma contest, virtually every southern state, by prearrangement, secedes from the Union to form an independent Southern Confederacy.

The separation is peaceful, despite Van Buren's desire to retaliate: "The disposition of the usurper, at first, was to treat them as revolted provinces; and to take measures for putting down, by force, their resistance to his authority."[35] Such a course proves impracticable, since the Confederacy has signed a prearranged treaty of commerce and friendship with Great Britain and can count on her support. A policy of free trade goes into effect at once and restores prosperity to the South within months. The new Confederate Constitution, which mirrors that of the Union in most respects, expressly prohibits protective tariffs. It also guards against "the danger to liberty from excessive revenue" by requiring that impost duties be assessed annually, so that they will cover only the projected operating expenses of the federal government.

Virginia alone fails to benefit from the new constitutional order, since Van Buren's henchmen control the state legislature and prevent any moves toward secession. Determined to retain the state's allegiance at all costs, the wily president orders federal troops to the area, ostensibly to protect its borders from Confederate aggression. An "army of observation" remains in Richmond to oversee the deliberations of the legislature, which Van Buren plans to abolish in time as an "absurd relic of *imperium in imperio*": "We can then restore them all the benefits of real and efficient local legislation, by erecting these degraded sovereignties into what they ought always to have been—municipal corporations, exercising such powers as we choose to grant."[36] The struggle of patriotic Virginians to reassert their republican ideals in the face of mounting federal tyranny forms the dramatic core of Tucker's novel.

To personalize the case for secession, Tucker employs a narrative device—the use of a "wavering hero"—familiar to readers of Walter Scott's popular border romances. Douglas Trevor, a West Point graduate and the son of a distinguished Virginia unionist, supports the existing constitutional system as a matter of principle. Even when he becomes the target of a malicious persecution directed by one of Van Buren's cronies, he does not question the value of a perpetual Union. As the president's arbitrary actions multiply, however, Douglas comes, willy-nilly, to espouse the radical secessionist views of his uncle Bernard Trevor, who warns: "We are on the eve of what you will call rebellion. I shall call it a war of right and liberty. . . . Would you support the constitution by taking part with those who trampled it under foot . . . ?"[37] When the president sends federal troops to control elections to the state legislature, Douglas's remaining doubts vanish. He joins his uncle and others in forcibly reopening the local polling place, an action that results in their being charged with treason and summoned to appear before a newly created executive court—the Court of High Commission—in Washington. Instead, they escape to North Carolina, from which Douglas soon returns to rally the mountaineers of western Virginia (an "honest, brave, hardy, and high-spirited peasantry") to the cause of independence and southern nationhood.

Tucker offers his readers some exciting scenes of guerrilla warfare while constantly reminding them of Virginia's leadership role during an earlier constitutional crisis: the colonial struggle against British tyranny that culminated in the American Revolution. The grievances of the antebellum South arise from the same kinds of governmental oppression that afflicted the American colonies, he insists. In the late eighteenth century an unrepresentative Parliament imposed discriminatory taxes and trade restrictions that violated the constitutional rights of Americans: "By coming between the manufacturer and the farmer, and interrupting this exchange by perverse legislation, the Government broke the tie which bound the colonies to the mother country."[38] Under Jackson and Van Buren, a Yankee Congress has passed equally unjust commercial regulations that have jeopardized the freedom and property of southern planters. By defying a malevolent federal government, antebellum secessionists are merely reclaiming their natural rights, as defined in the Declaration of Independence.

While Tucker's appeal to the revolutionary tradition conceded the inherently radical character of secession, it also enabled him to link constitutional legitimacy to the needs of distinctive regional cultures. Virginia, like other slaveholding areas, is a traditional society, in which custom and personal loyalty bind all classes together in an organic unity. The freedom-loving mountaineers defer to Douglas Trevor because they recognize his superior leadership abilities. Similarly, the slaves are content with their lot because they rely on their paternalistic masters for necessary guidance and protection. When Bernard Trevor flees to North Carolina, he takes only an armed workforce—his "black watch"—to protect himself and his family from federal pursuers. Northerners will never understand the "disinterested devotion" of the slave, Tucker comments through his alter ego, the statesmanlike Mr. B——: "They know no more of the feelings of our slaves, than their fathers could comprehend of the loyalty of the gallant cavaliers from whom we spring; and for the same reason. The generous and self-renouncing must ever be a riddle to the selfish."[39]

Since Yankees and Virginians have espoused different and antagonistic value systems, it is useless to pretend that a single Constitution can adequately satisfy their respective demands. A homogeneous region like the slaveholding South requires its own constitutional system in order to preserve its unique institutions and identity. Even northern sectionalists can perceive the wisdom of carving one or more new nation-states out of the unwieldy carcass of the old Union. "My country is to me . . . what yours is to you," confides Van Buren's chief minister to a southern rebel, as he launches a palace revolt to establish a Northern Confederacy in the concluding pages of Tucker's work.[40]

Although *The Partisan Leader* ends abruptly on a cliff-hanging note—with Douglas Trevor a prisoner in Van Buren's hands—Tucker assured his readers that the eventual outcome of the "glorious struggle" would be Virginia's independence. In this respect he proved a poor prophet. The real War for Southern Independence, fought a quarter century later, led to a crushing defeat for the Confederacy and the abolition of slavery by a constitutional amendment. The seceding states did, however, take some steps that were consistent with Tucker's vision. Their legislatures passed ordinances of secession that drew upon the rhetoric of eighteenth-century revolutionists to justify the dissolution of the federal compact. Then, having declared their independence, the insurgent states quickly combined to form a new federal government, whose constitution guaranteed the rights of slaveholders but otherwise reaffirmed, with little change, the provisions of the United States Constitution. Finally, toward the end of the war, some prominent civilian and military leaders seriously urged the arming of slaves for military service, much as Bernard Trevor had trusted his faithful servants to resist the detested Yankees.

The prolonged and bloody conflict also helped to create the kind of leviathan state that many southerners had feared for generations. Under the pressure of wartime need, the Union government imposed a military draft, levied a federal income tax, made newly issued "greenbacks" legal tender for all commercial transactions, and authorized northern military commanders to seize and imprison suspected civilian disloyalists without a trial. Such actions would have been unthinkable before the war, when Washington seemed to the average American a distant—almost a foreign—capital, whose power seldom intruded in any dramatic fashion on a person's daily life. Even more alarming for defenders of traditional federal-state relations was the ratification of the Fourteenth Amendment in 1868. The new measure defined national citizenship as paramount and made the federal government for the first time the monitor of state practices affecting the basic rights of the individual.[41]

Some contemporary observers, including Herman Melville, predicted from the outset that the war might bring permanent changes to the constitutional system:

> Power unanointed may come —
> Dominion (unsought by the free)
> And the Iron Dome,
> Stronger for stress and strain,
> Fling her huge shadow athwart the main;
> But the Founders' dream shall flee.[42]

He was right. Although it would take decades for the wartime model of national power to become broadly institutionalized and approved in public opinion, the contours of the future regulatory state were clearly discernible by the end of the fighting. The old Republic of the Founders—decentralized, agrarian, suspicious of federal authority—could not survive the onslaughts of a triumphant Union.

2

Modern Constitutionalism and Progressive Reform

> A constitution which fixedly restrains a people from correcting their actual evils, becomes associated in the popular mind with the evils themselves.
>
> —JUDGE CHARLES F. AMIDON (1907)

Encouraged by the production demands of the Civil War, the United States became a powerful industrial nation in the late nineteenth century. Transcontinental railroads linked the Atlantic and Pacific coasts; giant corporations manufactured and shipped products to consumers nationwide; and national labor organizations arose to mobilize workers for large-scale strikes that often turned into bloody class confrontations. Federal and state governments seldom intervened in this industrial warfare, except to send in troops as a last resort.

Reform movements—from the Grangers in the 1870s to the Populists in the 1890s—urged the expansion of government power to control the economy in the public interest. Although advocates of such constitutional change achieved some important success at the state level, they made slow progress in securing federal legislation. Congress took the first steps since the Civil War toward the creation of the modern federal regulatory state with the passage of the Interstate Commerce Act of 1887 and the Sherman Antitrust Act of 1890. But it was only after the Spanish-American War, as the nation entered a period of relative prosperity and calm, that a confident middle-class public lent its support to a latter-day "peaceful revolution." Within twenty years four new amendments—the first since Reconstruction—were added to the Constitution, and Congress enacted a number of measures that significantly enlarged federal power and established new administrative agencies to oversee regulatory programs. As in the antebellum years, the media contributed to the process of change in a variety of ways: through constitutional commentary addressed to a general audience, through utopian fiction, topical novels and poems, plays, and cartoons, and through a powerful new vehicle of mass communication—the movies.

By the early twentieth century an information explosion in American law coincided with the rise of revolutionary new technologies for the shaping of public opinion. Mechanical improvements reduced the cost of publishing magazines and newspapers and encouraged the creation of mass audiences undreamed of in earlier generations. Movies, a new medium of communication, brought enhanced social awareness to millions of unskilled workers, especially those recently arrived immigrants who crowded into the nation's ghettos. A new generation of writers, often young and college-educated, rebelled against the romanticism and prudery of nineteenth-century literary conventions and called for an American literature more responsive to the problems of a modern industrial society. Through factual articles and problem-centered fiction, these writers—derisively termed "muckrakers" by their critics—sought to document the wasteful and inhumane practices of a mature capitalist order. At the height of their popularity from 1902 to 1914, they contributed significantly to a middle-class ethos that favored political and economic reform.[1]

One of the major obstacles to such reform lay in the conservative constitutional jurisprudence of the late nineteenth century. In an effort to make American law more "scientific" and predictable, jurists after the Civil War sought to create a system of authoritative legal rules that might be applied to recurring fact situations in a mechanical fashion. Fearful of class warfare and the possible redistribution of wealth through legislative action, courts developed new doctrines, such as "liberty of contract," to protect the property rights of individuals and corporations from the threat of government regulation. At the same time, advocates of mainstream jurisprudence professed to draw a sharp line between law and politics. Judges were learned technicians, not policymakers, they argued, and the law was a closed system of logical principles that had to be obeyed, regardless of the consequences for society.[2]

Not all judges agreed, of course. Even before 1900 many courts, especially at the state level, had begun to turn away from this laissez-faire jurisprudence and to consider social facts when assessing the constitutionality of proposed economic regulations. Roscoe Pound, a young law professor, provided an intellectual rationale for this trend in an influential article that appeared in *The Green Bag*, a popular legal journal, in 1907. Deploring the public's perceived gap between "legal justice" and "social justice," Pound

warned that the law must confront the urgent problems of modern industrialism by utilizing the hard data supplied by the social sciences. "The
modern teacher of law should be a student of sociology, economics, and
politics as well," he urged.

> He should know not only what the courts decide and the principles
> by which they decide, but quite as much the circumstances and con-
> ditions, social and economic, to which these principles are to be ap-
> plied; he should know the state of popular thought and feeling which
> makes the environment in which the principles must operate in prac-
> tice. Legal monks who pass their lives in an atmosphere of pure law,
> from which every worldly and human element is excluded, cannot
> shape practical principles to be applied to a restless world of flesh and
> blood.[3]

In practical terms, Pound's call for a "sociological jurisprudence" found
an answer in the famous Brandeis brief of 1908. Louis D. Brandeis, a reform-minded Boston attorney, introduced the brief in *Muller v. Oregon*[4] to
persuade the United States Supreme Court that Oregon might constitutionally regulate the working hours of laundresses within the state. De-
voting only two pages to legal precedents, Brandeis relied instead on more
than one hundred pages of statistics and other factual data drawn from a
mass of medical reports, psychological treatises, reports of factory inspec-
tors, and published assessments of the effects of comparable legislation in
the United States and abroad. Such extralegal sources of information, he
argued, demonstrated that the Oregon lawmakers had acted reasonably in
legislating to protect the health of their women workers. Impressed by
such reasoning, the Supreme Court unanimously upheld Oregon's maxi-
mum-hours law. While the *Muller* decision scarcely inaugurated a revolution in judicial thinking—it proved to be merely an exception to the still
prevailing doctrine of freedom of contract—other lawyers began to follow
Brandeis's example and to interject an unprecedented quantity of factual
information into the judicial process. Brandeis himself furthered this trend
after his appointment to the Supreme Court in 1916 by citing such extralegal sources in his opinions.[5]

The heightened importance of factual inquiry in both law and literature
resulted in a major revision of constitutional ideology before World War I.
To most Americans of the nineteenth century—both before and after the
Civil War—the Constitution had seemed the embodiment of fixity and
fairness, a "sacred charter" whose enlightened principles promoted the

well-being of every citizen. "We have as a people deeply reverenced our Constitution," observed Senator Henry Cabot Lodge in 1911, recalling the patriotic centennial celebrations of a quarter century earlier.

> Those celebrations of the framing of the Constitution and of the inauguration of the government have been almost forgotten. More than twenty years have come and gone since the cheers of the crowds which then filled the streets of New York and Philadelphia—since the reverberations of the cannon and the eloquent voices of the orators died away into silence. And with those years, not very many after all, a change seems to have come in the spirit which at that time pervaded the American people from the President down to the humblest citizen in the land. Instead of the universal chorus of praise and gratitude to the framers of the Constitution the air is now rent with harsh voices of criticism and attack. . . . [E]very one who is in distress, or in debt, or discontented, now assails the Constitution.[6]

Indeed, since the 1890s increasing numbers of Americans—workers, farmers, consumers, racial and ethnic minorities—had begun to question the wisdom and neutrality of the constitutional order created by the Founding Fathers. The cumbersome machinery of checks and balances, designed for a simpler society of small farmers and tradesmen, threatened to block effective government control of a dangerously unstable economy. Deep-seated popular suspicion of laissez-faire constitutionalism received impressive scholarly reinforcement in 1913 with the publication of Charles A. Beard's influential study, *An Economic Interpretation of the Constitution of the United States.* Using previously neglected Treasury and census records, Beard presented the Founding Fathers as a conspiratorial elite who had devised an undemocratic Constitution to protect their property from the attacks of popular legislative majorities. Many other turn-of-the-century commentators agreed that an "invisible government" of wealth and privilege ruled America through the forms of constitutional democracy. Middle-class readers of magazines and books learned the details of such "machine rule" through a host of investigatory works that bore such titles as *Our Dishonest Constitution, Our Judicial Oligarchy,* and *The Treason of the Senate.*[7]

For working-class audiences, alternative presses and distribution networks carried the constitutional critique to the farms and small towns of the Midwest and Southwest. Oscar Ameringer's satirical history of the United States, *Life and Deeds of Uncle Sam* (1909), enjoyed immense popularity in labor and socialist circles. An Oklahoma humorist and news-paper editor known as "the Mark Twain of American Socialism," Amer-inger emphasized the persistence of economic inequality and capitalist domination in American history. Noting that no genuine workingman or small farmer had attended the Philadelphia Convention, he proceeded to debunk the resulting undemocratic Constitution, over which "so many high-school graduates, Thanksgiving-day orators, and Fourth-of-July spielers have slobbered":

> In monarchies, when the monarch becomes crazy and has to be re-moved to a padded cell, he retains his royal title, but a prince regent is appointed to sit on the throne and read the typewritten speeches handed to him by the Prime Minister. Well, the fathers of the Consti-tution persuaded the *sovereign people* that while they were sovereign, all right, they needed a prince regent to do the governing for them. And since we had no thorough-bred princes, they invented the checks of the Senate, the President, and the Supreme Court.[8]

Ameringer's caustic little book sold half a million copies by 1917, despite the absence of reviews in mainstream journals and newspapers. His fre-quent travels and speeches at socialist meetings in several states introduced him to a large grassroots audience, which promoted his work by word of mouth. Translated into fifteen languages, *Life and Deeds* remained suf-ficiently popular to justify its republication in the 1930s. "No history book until Charles and Mary Beard's *Rise of American Civilization* reached so many readers," noted historian Paul Buhle.[9]

In fiction, writers applied the new constitutional thinking most strik-ingly in a number of utopian novels that offered blueprints for the con-struction of more democratic institutions. While the authors differed in their prescriptions for change, most championed some type of majori-tarian democracy as a remedy for the abuses of the modern capitalist state. More important, they generally insisted on following established legal procedures in dismantling the old order, and thus carried forward the antebellum vision of a "peaceful revolution" into the new industrial age. Edward Bellamy's collectivist romance, *Looking Backward: 2000–1887* (1888), was the prototype for most American literary utopias of the early twentieth century.[10]

Bellamy's hero, Julian West, awakens from a century-long hypnotic sleep to find himself in a future world of technological marvels from which class conflict and economic insecurity have been eliminated. All industry has been consolidated and nationalized, so that every citizen now receives an equal share of the nation's wealth. As Doctor Leete, Julian's mentor, explains, "No man any more has any care for the morrow, either for himself or his children, for the nation guarantees the nurture, education, and comfortable maintenance of every citizen from the cradle to the grave."[11] In return for these benefits, every person must serve in the nation's workforce—the "industrial army" or one of the professional guilds—from the age of twenty-one until retirement at age forty-five. Through periodic aptitude tests individuals are matched with jobs, and department heads make every effort to accommodate individual preferences. The entire system resembles an elaborate meritocracy, since even the highest managerial posts are elective and depend on a candidate's previous record of competence and commitment to unselfish public service.

In this egalitarian and consensus society, politics in any meaningful sense has virtually ceased to exist. Administrators and social planners have replaced nineteenth-century lawmakers, and the traditional institutions of government have shrunk to negligible proportions. Although there is still a president, elected for a five-year term from the ranks of retired department heads, his function is merely to oversee the smooth operation of the economy. He also appoints a few national judges—mature individuals with no formal training in law—to resolve minor disputes within the workforce and to preside on rare occasions over a criminal prosecution. All state governments have disappeared, and Congress meets only once every five years to receive a report on the state of the economy from the outgoing president. With the abolition of private property and other forms of special privilege, observes Doctor Leete, "[W]e have nothing to make laws about. . . . It is rarely that Congress, even when it meets, considers any new laws of consequence, and then it only has power to commend them to the following Congress, lest anything be done hastily."[12]

Bellamy regarded the Constitution of the late nineteenth century as a major obstacle to democratic change, and excluded law schools and lawyers from his utopian society. Yet he insisted that the transition from a ruthless capitalist order to an egalitarian paradise had occurred "with absolutely no violence" and with a scrupulous regard for legal procedures. In *Looking Backward* he explains the transformation by referring vaguely to the irresistible force of an enlightened public opinion, but in a sequel, *Equality* (1897), he outlines in some detail the successive stages by which a "peaceful revolution" has been accomplished.

First, the "revolutionary party," committed to the immediate nationalization of the interstate railroad system, the telephone and telegraph network, and other quasi-public industries, achieves a major political victory through the ballot box. The extension of government power over such businesses provokes little outcry, for, as Doctor Leete notes, "This whole class of natural or legal monopolies might . . . have been taken under public management without logically involving an assault on the system of private capitalism as a whole."[13] Next, the government establishes a network of public service stores, in which the growing class of public employees can use government scrip to buy food and manufactured goods at cost. Public ownership of distribution facilities then expands to include productive enterprises as well, as the government takes control of farms and factories to supply its stores.

At this point the cost of compensating the owners of expropriated properties, as required by the Fifth Amendment, might seem to be prohibitive. Bellamy argues, however, that depressed farmers were happy to turn over their lands voluntarily to the government in exchange for a secure income as new members of the public workforce. In the case of factories, the government commandeers only the "thousands" of idle plants that have already shut down due to hard times. The owners of these moribund enterprises do receive "some allowance, equal to a very low rate of interest, for the use of their property."[14]

Gradually, as workers in the private sector become aware of the advantages of a system of nonprofit production and distribution, they clamor for admission to the public workforce. The government expands its economic operations; the private money supply loses its value, since it cannot match the purchasing power of government scrip; and the remaining capitalist holdouts, finding that they can no longer recruit workers or even purchase basic necessities in the dwindling private markets, at last capitulate, turn over their properties to the state, and join the public service. They cannot be reimbursed for their losses, explains Doctor Leete: "To have compensated the capitalists in any practical way—that is, any way which would have preserved to them under the new order any economic equivalent for their former holdings—would have necessarily been to set up private capitalism over again in the very act of destroying it, thus defeating and stultifying the Revolution in the moment of its triumph."[15] On the other hand, the people inflict no punishment on their former masters, but welcome them into the new democratic order.

Although Bellamy nods on occasion in the direction of constitutional government, his utopia rather derives from the Declaration of Independence—"the true American constitution—the one written on the people's hearts"[16]—with its assertion of the equality of all men. The symbol of the new dispensation is, appropriately enough, a windmill: "It represents the modern ideal of a proper system of government. The mill stands for the machinery of administration, the wind that drives it symbolizes the public will, and the rudder that always keeps the vane of the mill before the wind, however suddenly or completely the wind may change, stands for the method by which the administration is kept at all times responsive and obedient to every mandate of the people, though it be but a breath."[17] In *Looking Backward* Congress had met infrequently and passed little legislation; in the revised model of pure democracy that Bellamy sketches in *Equality*, Congress appears to sit in continuous session under constant popular scrutiny. The voters may recall any of their representatives at a moment's notice, and all measures of more than a routine nature must be submitted to a popular referendum before they take effect. Through the telephone system instantaneous voting has become possible, so that the entire nation may act as a lawmaking body: "We vote a hundred times perhaps in a year, on all manner of questions, from the temperature of the public baths or the plan to be selected for a public building, to the greatest questions of the world union, and find the exercise at once as exhilarating as it is in the highest sense educational."[18]

The underside of this democratic system relates to its treatment of dissenters. In the absence of constitutionally protected rights, criminals and "vicious" individuals face life imprisonment and sterilization in mental hospitals, while those who refuse to work at their assigned jobs can look forward to banishment to remote frontier areas that resemble nineteenth-century Indian reservations. Although Bellamy insists that the fairness of his institutional arrangements and the shared idealism of public service will prevent the development of any significant discontent, the prospect for nonconformists seems oppressive, to say the least. Nor does economic equality necessarily guarantee full gender or racial equality. Women in *Looking Backward* participate in the workforce as a special branch of the industrial army and cannot vote. (Under pressure from feminist critics, Bellamy later modified his position. In *Equality*, women do have the vote and are fully integrated at last into the workforce.) Blacks, on the other hand, never achieve social equality with whites but continue to occupy a "separate but equal" status in Bellamy's utopia.[19]

Despite its limitations, *Looking Backward* soon captured the imagination of readers around the globe and became one of the best-selling American novels of the nineteenth century.[20] Its influence even penetrated to the United States Supreme Court, where conservative Justice David J. Brewer commented in a dissenting opinion of 1892, "The paternal theory of government is to me odious. The utmost possible liberty to the individual, and the fullest possible protection to him and his property, is both the limitation and the duty of government. If it may regulate the price of one service, which is not a public service, or the compensation for the use of one kind of property which is not devoted to a public use, why may it not with equal degree regulate the price of all service and the compensation to be paid for the use of all property? And if so, *Looking Backward* is nearer than a dream."[21] From the opposite end of the political spectrum, Oscar Ameringer recalled his reaction to Bellamy's narrative: "A great book. A very great book. One of the greatest, most prophetic books this country has produced. It didn't make me look backward, it made me look forward, and I haven't got over looking forward since I read *Looking Backward*."[22]

No later utopian novelist advocated as radical a model of democratic socialism as Bellamy proposed. By the turn of the century many writers stopped short of urging the complete overthrow of capitalism[23] and imagined instead its transformation into a more humane and socially responsible order. Unlike Bellamy, they also looked toward a new constitution as the capstone of their legal revolution and sometimes included its complete text as part of their story line. Firm believers in social engineering, they shared the pragmatic and moralistic values of Progressivism, a bipartisan reform movement that called for significant government intervention in the economy to promote the general welfare. Two of their narratives—Samuel Merwin's *The Citadel* and Edward M. House's *Philip Dru: Administrator*—exposed the philosophy and unresolved tensions of Progressivism with special clarity. Both works appeared at the height of the movement's popularity in 1912, when the Democratic and Republican party platforms each endorsed Progressive principles.[24]

Merwin's title refers to the Constitution, which his hero John Garwood, a Progressive young congressman from Illinois, considers "the citadel of reaction and restraint." In a fiery speech before the House of Representatives, Garwood assails the Constitution in Beardian terms as an undemocratic document whose rigidity prevents the federal government from confronting the urgent problems of the modern age. "[L]et us . . . examine that paper very carefully to find out how nearly or how remotely it squares with present-day facts," he concludes. "It is quite conceivable that we may need a new one; or that we might get along better under modern conditions with no Constitution at all."[25]

Denounced as a dangerous radical by Chicago's business leaders and the conservative wing of the Republican Party, Garwood seeks reelection as an independent candidate and takes his case for constitutional reform directly to the people. The remedy he proposes is a constitutional amendment to permit future popular majorities to change the Constitution at will through a simplified amending process. "The real problem," he explains, "is to break down the rigidity, the fixed character of our government, and open it to influence from the same laws of continued change and growth that govern the development of the individual and of industry. Of course we shan't bring about this great reform until we have succeeded in making both the Constitution and the courts secondary to Congress. For the people, or their representatives, must dominate . . . absolutely."[26]

In this version of "pure" democracy, the people will determine the nature and timing of constitutional change through an easy amendment process. Garwood anticipates a gradual transition to a socially responsible and egalitarian society as the electorate enacts more and more Progressive measures, from woman suffrage and old age and mothers' pensions to the nationalization of monopolistic enterprises. The alternative to such a peaceful revolution, he fears, will be violent class warfare. Although the voters of Illinois give his proposal strong support, he loses a close election through voting frauds sanctioned by the business elite who oppose him. Still, Garwood remains confident that his campaign has educated the public to the need for further critical scrutiny of an antiquated Constitution. "The change has begun—the change to modernity," he tells his sweetheart Margaret Lansing, a biologist in the Department of Agriculture and a representative "new woman." "And it really begins to look as if we had come close to making the whole United States think about the Constitution."[27]

Merwin, a veteran political reporter and muckraking editor, idealized "the people" in a dangerously naive way. Absent from his narrative is any concern for minority rights. Apparently, like other reform-minded writers of the time, he assumed that the masses would recognize and support a true "public interest" that could transcend the divisions of class, race, and ethnicity. But sentimental appeals to brotherhood and cooperation cannot conceal the potential for majoritarian tyranny that inheres in Garwood's scheme. Nor do frequent references to the building of a nobler race reassure the reader that blacks and ethnics will have an easy time of it in the new constitutional order.

Even more disturbing in its darker implications is the story of *Philip*

Dru: Administrator. Where John Garwood was at least content to let popular majorities shape the constitutional system, Philip Dru imposes a model constitution on the American people after seizing supreme power through a military coup. The brainchild of Colonel Edward Mandell House, an experienced political consultant, Dru represents the bureaucratic and efficiency-minded side of Progressivism. After an eye injury forces him to abandon a promising military career, Dru becomes a social worker on Manhattan's East Side and experiences the suffering caused by a ruthless industrialism. In several widely read articles, he condemns the injustices perpetuated by existing social structures:

> *In a direct and forceful manner, he pointed out that our civilization was fundamentally wrong inasmuch as among other things, it restricts efficiency; that if society were properly organized, there would be none who were not sufficiently clothed and fed; that the laws, habits and ethical training in vogue were alike responsible for the difference between the few and the many; that the result of such conditions was to render inefficient a large part of the population, the percentage differing in each country in the ratio that education and enlightened and unselfish laws bore to ignorance, bigotry and selfish laws.*[28]

When the newspapers obtain an incriminating dictaphone record that reveals how financiers, industrialists, and their political spokesmen control both major parties, a public outcry ensues. To maintain its power, the incumbent administration uses the army to prevent free elections. Thereupon civil war breaks out, pitting the very rich and the very poor against the middle class—a scenario of mass violence that fed the deepest fears of middle-class audiences. Dru takes command of the Western Army of sturdy middle-class patriots, defeats the government forces in a single decisive battle, and marches on Washington. There he announces the end of the old constitutional system and proclaims himself dictator, or "Administrator of the Republic," with the approval of the army and a majority of civilian supporters. This drastic step is necessary, he argues, in order to effect fundamental changes in the "defective machinery" of government. Once his reforms are achieved, he promises to restore democratic rule under a new constitution.

To a modern reader, this flouting of constitutional norms seems protofascist at best, but turn-of-the-century audiences found it relatively easy to regard benevolent despots like Dru as democratic heroes. Like Napoleon Bonaparte, whose organizational genius made him the object of an admiring cult in America during the 1890s, Dru embodied character traits familiar to Americans as part of a cherished cultural heritage. A self-made man who rises from obscurity to power through his own talent and force of will, he represents an Americanized version of Nietzsche's superman—a heroic leader who shares the democratic values of the masses.[29]

In institutionalizing these values, however, Dru ignores grassroots opinion and relies instead on professional advice. He appoints boards of experts to study specific social problems and recommend remedial legislation. On a more general level, he establishes legal commissions to revise and modernize the state and federal codes by eliminating obsolete and contradictory laws and by incorporating the policies newly formulated by other expert groups. He insists that these legal changes must precede the drafting of new constitutions, so that their adaptability to existing conditions may be tested in practice. The constitutions, when framed, will thus conform to a radically restructured legal environment, whose machinery will be run "absolutely in the interest of the people."

Some of the reforms that Dru introduces in his role of supreme lawgiver merely make the system more efficient and economical: uniform divorce laws and simplified land registration procedures in all states, for example. Others look toward a major redistribution of wealth, accompanied by a vast increase in the power of the federal government. Dru approves a graduated income tax whose rates rise sharply at the upper levels, to a maximum of 70 percent on all incomes of $10 million or more; a comparable inheritance tax; universal suffrage; old age pensions and workmen's compensation; and a cooperative marketing and loan system for small farmers and businessmen. He also seeks to curb corporate abuses through federal incorporation and franchise laws, which require businesses to file semiannual reports of their activities and to seat a representative of the state or national government on their boards of directors. While he orders the nationalization of a few public service corporations, including the telephone and telegraph companies, his commitment to managerial efficiency leads him to endorse continued private direction in most instances: "The people were asked to curb their prejudice against corporations. It was promised that in the future corporations should be honestly run, and in the interest of the stockholders and the public."[30]

The conservative aspects of Dru's "legal revolution" appear most strikingly in his labor policies. To alleviate working-class discontent, his franchise laws reserve one seat on corporate directorates for a labor representative; establish an eight-hour day and a maximum work week of six days;

and guarantee workers a share of surplus profits in addition to their wages. As the price of these concessions, workers are forbidden to strike and must submit all grievances to a government arbitration board. Furthermore, their wages may be legally reduced in "dull" times. Through the elimination of class conflict Dru hopes to enhance productivity and the distribution of goods throughout society. But his effort to create a partnership between capital and labor offers little promise of democratizing economic relationships, since business hierarchies will continue to dominate the workplace and to determine corporate policy.

In fact, real democratic empowerment of any kind seems secondary to Dru's overriding interest in scientific social planning. Although the national constitution, like those in other turn-of-the-century utopias, vests dominant political power in a popularly elected House of Representatives, the task of that body will be to manage the model institutions already established by Dru and his experts. To be sure, the formal machinery of the new government appears to authorize extensive popular lawmaking, since all traditional checks and balances have virtually disappeared. The federal judiciary, drastically reduced in size, can no longer review the constitutionality of legislative acts; the president has become a purely ceremonial figure, with no veto power; and, while the Senate may still reject a measure passed by the House, such action will cause the contested law to be submitted to the electorate for a final vote on its constitutionality. All legislation must originate in the House, which has been restructured along English lines, with an executive chosen by the House now introducing and defending bills, much like a British prime minister. But these bills must conform to the enlightened constitutional principles laid down by Dru, who neglected to provide for amendments. Despite the machinery of democratic decisionmaking, then, the citizens of Dru's utopia will be limited to tinkering about the edges of a near-perfect system. In the last analysis, Colonel House believed as fervently as the Founding Fathers in the need for social order, and the best government, he agreed, should operate like a well-oiled machine.[31]

The plot of *Philip Dru* departs from the "peaceful revolution" formula in bringing its hero to power through military force. But House makes clear to his readers that Dru exercises his extraconstitutional authority with the consent of "the people." Once a new national constitution has been drafted, the "Administrator of the Republic" steps down, "amidst the plaudits of a triumphant democracy." National elections resume, and Dru resists all efforts to make him the first executive under the new system. Fearing that his continued presence may provoke other attempts in the future, he sails off to an "obscure portion of the world where I cannot be found and importuned to return."[32]

While Merwin, House, and other utopian novelists projected a new constitutional universe,[33] some literary "reformers" used fiction to justify the continued suppression of minority rights guaranteed by the existing Constitution. Just as the national government had been slow to exercise its power in economic matters, so the civil rights "revolution" promised by the trio of Reconstruction amendments did not materialize to any appreciable degree in the late nineteenth century. The Supreme Court interpreted the provisions of the amendments narrowly and ruled in the *Civil Rights Cases* (1883)[34] that Congress could protect African Americans only against racially discriminatory practices carried out by state governments, not by private individuals. Even when there was state action, moreover, African-American litigants could not prevail if a segregation measure purported to require "separate but equal" facilities for the white and colored races. Such was the lesson of *Plessy v. Ferguson* (1896),[35] which upheld Louisiana's "separate coach" law as a reasonable exercise of the state's power to protect public order. The *Plessy* decision encouraged the construction of a full-fledged caste system in the southern states around the turn of the century.

But some conservative southern authors demanded even more: the disfranchisement of African-American voters. Confronted with the positive command of the Fifteenth Amendment—"The right of citizens of the United States to vote shall not be denied or abridged by the United States or by any State on account of race, color, or previous condition of servitude"—these writers appealed to a higher law of racial inequality. Thomas Dixon Jr.'s immensely popular novel, *The Leopard's Spots* (1902), established the narrative conventions that guided other advocates of white supremacy in the first two decades of the twentieth century. A Baptist minister and law school graduate, Dixon had earned an impressive reputation as a spokesman for New York City's poor before he discovered his true calling: to defend Anglo-Saxon civilization from the destructive assaults of African Americans and other minorities unfit for the responsibilities of republican government.

The novel's melodramatic plot, which spans the years from 1865 to 1900, paints a lurid picture of the excesses of black rule in North Carolina. Whenever blacks gain political power, Dixon argues, they threaten the lives and property of "civilized" white men and carry out brutal attacks on white women in the name of social equality. A true reign of terror had existed under the black-and-tan Reconstruction governments until the Ku Klux Klan arose to reestablish Anglo-Saxon dominance. Now, in the 1890s, African Americans are again filling public offices, thanks to their alliance with the small white farmers of the state. To restore responsible government once and for all, young Charles Gaston urges his fellow citizens in the town of Independence to reaffirm their Revolutionary heritage. At a mass meeting chaired by Gaston, the townsmen adopt a second Declaration of Independence, aimed this time at local tyranny:

> Resolved, that we issue a second Declaration of Independence from the infamy of corrupt and degraded government. The day of Negro domination over the Anglo-Saxon race shall close, now, once and forever. The government of North Carolina was established by a race of pioneer white freemen for white men and it shall remain in the hands of freemen.[36]

The document ends by calling for the immediate resignation of all black officeholders and their white allies. After a brief show of resistance by a black mob, Gaston and his supporters take over the town and legalize their coup through an election in which only white males are permitted to vote.

When the rest of the state learns of Gaston's initiative, his political popularity soars. At the state Democratic convention he electrifies the audience by demanding that the party endorse black disfranchisement as the major plank in its platform. "The Anglo-Saxon race is united and has entered upon its world mission," he declares.

> We believe that God has raised up our race, as he ordained Israel of old, . . . to establish and maintain for weaker races, as a trust for civilization, the principles of civil and religious Liberty and the forms of Constitutional Government. . . . So long as the Negro is a factor in our political life, will violence and corruption stain our history. . . . We will take from an unprofitable servant the ballot he has abused. . . . It is the law of nature. It is the law of God.[37]

An enthusiastic convention adopts Gaston's policy and nominates him for governor. In the ensuing election a united white democracy scores a stunning victory at the polls and prepares to carry out its campaign pledge "to nullify the Fourteenth and Fifteenth Amendments to the Constitution of the Republic."

Dixon, unlike some of his imitators, does not describe the specific forms of legal discrimination, such as poll taxes and literacy tests, that were imposed by southern legislatures.[38] But he displays an unrivaled ability to popularize his racist agenda by appealing to the raw emotions of his readers. Again and again he insists that the African American is little more than a jungle beast, given political power by a vindictive Congress to punish the defeated South. His white characters, proud descendants of colonial frontiersmen, are engaged in an epic struggle for racial survival that will determine the future of the nation: "One drop of Negro blood makes a Negro. It kinks the hair, flattens the nose, thickens the lip, puts out the light of intellect, and lights the fires of brutal passions. The beginning of Negro equality as a vital fact is the beginning of the end of this nation's life."[39] Only a system of strict apartheid can preserve the heritage of Washington and Jefferson in the modern South.

If constitutional reform for Dixon and his supporters thus meant the reassertion of state control over race relations, African-American authors called instead on the federal government to protect the constitutional rights of the black population. In contrast to Dixon's arguments, such representative novelists as Charles W. Chesnutt and Sutton E. Griggs created alternative fictions that told quite a different story of victimization and lawlessness. Their works describe a caste society in which whites wield dominant political and economic power and ruthlessly suppress all efforts by blacks to claim the rights of American citizens.

Chesnutt's *The Marrow of Tradition* (1901), also set in a North Carolina town, presents the disfranchisement movement as a racist conspiracy led by demagogic newspaper editors and politicians. Instead of restoring order, as in Dixon's tale, disfranchisement encourages the white majority to further acts of terrorism and violence against a defenseless black community. Once stripped of the vote, African Americans have no recourse against state-sanctioned violence, since prevailing doctrines of federalism prohibit national interference in local affairs. "The [federal] government can only intervene under certain conditions, of which it must be informed through designated channels," explains a black lawyer. "It never sees anything that is not officially called to its attention. The whole Negro population of the South might be slaughtered before the necessary red tape could be spun out to inform the President that a state of anarchy prevailed. There's no hope there."[40] Unwilling to encourage armed resistance to white aggression, black professionals stand helplessly by as the town's leaders instigate a bloody race riot, which forms the climax of Chesnutt's powerful story. "Our time will come," reflects William Miller, the community's only black physician—"the time when we can command respect for our rights; but it is not yet in sight."[41]

Black professionals—a group that Dixon either ignored or ridiculed—also play central roles in Sutton Griggs's *Imperium in Imperio* (1899), a remarkable fantasy of black power and alienation. The plot chronicles the parallel careers of two young African Americans, Belton Piedmont and Bernard Belgrave. Schooled from boyhood in the libertarian principles of the American Revolution, each becomes a notable example of the college-educated and rights-conscious "New Negro." As southern legislatures pass repressive segregation laws in the 1890s, Bernard, a lawyer, receives an urgent summons to meet his friend at the Thomas Jefferson College in Waco, Texas, where Belton teaches. On his arrival, Bernard learns that the ostensible college is really the capital of the Imperium, a secret government established by blacks to protect their civil rights.

"[You] know," Belton observes, "that there is one serious flaw in the Constitution of the United States, which has already caused a world of trouble, and there is evidently a great deal more to come. . . . This flaw or defect in the Constitution of the United States is the relation of the General Government to the individual state."[42] Although the General Government claims ultimate sovereignty over blacks and other citizens of the United States, it is powerless to protect them against lynchings and other outrages committed within a state. To remedy this situation, Belton and his associates have created a separate government to provide the kind of equal justice that blacks cannot obtain under existing institutions.

The Imperium represents yet another version of the constitutional utopias so characteristic of the early twentieth century. Its constitution, modeled on that of the United States, contains some recognizably Progressive features, such as a one-house Congress elected by popular vote. The members serve for an indefinite term but may be recalled at any time by their constituents. Other provisions highlight the racial foundations of the new order:

> This Congress passes laws relating to the general welfare of our people, and whenever a bill is introduced in the Congress of the United States affecting our race it is also introduced and debated here.
>
> Every race question submitted to the United States judiciary, is also submitted to our own. A record of our decisions is kept side by side with the decisions of the United States.[43]

Bernard soon learns that he has been elected the first president of the Imperium and sets out to compile a record of every fresh assault on African-

American liberties committed throughout the nation. When the United States Congress meets to declare war on Spain in 1898, Bernard calls an emergency session of his Congress to determine the Imperium's future relations with Anglo-Saxon America. Observing that black political rights have been curtailed in most states through violence, fraud, or statute, he urges his listeners to rise up against their oppressors, overthrow the government of Texas through a well-planned coup, and convert the state into an independent black republic. The audience responds enthusiastically to this war policy until Belton rises to plead for moderation.

Before resorting to force, Belton argues, an effort should be made to convince whites that they are dealing with a new generation of black freemen, who have absorbed Anglo-Saxon political values in their schools and are prepared to die, if need be, to defend their liberty. If this educational strategy fails, the Imperium should secretly order all African Americans to emigrate to Texas, where their superior numbers will enable them to control the government peacefully through the political process. (In fact, Texas did not impose a poll tax until 1902, three years after Griggs published his novel.) Swayed at first by Belton's eloquence, the Congress nevertheless decides to support Bernard's program of militant black nationalism. Unwilling to join the treasonous conspiracy, Belton resigns from the Imperium, an action that costs him his life. Before the threatened race war can begin, however, another member of the Imperium betrays the plot to the authorities. In a last testament the repentant conspirator pleads for interracial understanding and warns that the continued denial of equal rights to African Americans will only produce new forms of black resistance: "I urge this because love of liberty is such an inventive genius, that if you destroy one device it at once constructs another more powerful."[44]

Like other Progressive writers, Griggs and Chesnutt hoped that their works would help to generate public support for remedial government action. Both men also participated in grassroots efforts to protect black civil rights. Chesnutt, a Cleveland attorney as well as a literary artist of national prominence, largely abandoned the writing of fiction after 1905, out of frustration with the poor sales of his serious protest novels. Thereafter he argued for racial justice through lectures and pamphlets and helped to found the National Association for the Advancement of Colored People in 1909.[45] A biracial reform organization, the NAACP collected data on civil rights violations and sought to combat them through legislative lobbying and constitutional litigation in the courts.

Although Griggs, a Baptist preacher, lacked the literary craftsmanship of

Chesnutt, he was equally committed to the civil rights movement and enjoyed great influence within the African-American community. As one perceptive critic has noted, "Griggs not only operated his own publishing company [the Orion Publishing Company of Nashville, Tennessee] but also, during his travels as a prominent minister and orator, promoted an extensive sale of his works among the black masses of the country. Though virtually unknown to white American readers, his novels were probably more popular among the rank and file of Negroes than the fiction of Chesnutt and [Paul Laurence] Dunbar."[46] Like Chesnutt, Griggs welcomed the establishment of the NAACP, which was prefigured in some ways by the "Imperium," and he included as a supplement to the third edition of his novel *The Hindered Hand* (1905) a lengthy attack on the vicious racism of Thomas Dixon.[47]

As Chesnutt and Griggs encouraged a resurgent civil rights movement through their novels, so the advocates of woman suffrage made effective use of fictional narratives to advance their cause. The suffrage issue figured in a number of novels and plays of the early twentieth century,[48] but it was through the movies that it finally attracted the attention of mass audiences. Both of the national suffrage organizations—the National American Woman Suffrage Association (NAWSA) and its more militant offshoot, the Congressional Union (CU)—turned to films by 1912 to achieve maximum publicity for the enfranchisement of women. The movies they made linked suffrage to other Progressive reforms but also exposed deep class and racial divisions within the movement. Together with a much larger body of antisuffrage films, they provide a valuable record of the conflicting cultural demands that underlie constitutional change.

Filmmakers discovered the box office potential of suffrage films as early as 1898, with the release of a short film, *The Lady Barber*, which caricatured a woman suffragist who takes over a barber shop and intimidates the male customers with her aggressive style of hair cutting. Thereafter scores of antisuffrage comedies pandered to popular fears of a sex revolution and urged audiences to preserve traditional family values and gender roles. The scenarios presented a "veritable arsenal of antisuffrage arguments," comments historian Kay Sloan,[49] as masculine and unattractive women tyrannized over their husbands and boyfriends, neglected their children, and threw society into chaos by attempting to fill political posts for which they were unqualified. In one representative two-reeler, *When the Men Left Town* (1914), the women win every political office in a town election and immediately ban all smoking and drinking. Disgruntled, the men move away, leaving their wives and sweethearts to deal with such municipal problems as garbage collection and the running of the trolley system. Unable to cope with these responsibilities, the women invite the men back and resign their offices amid general rejoicing. The message was clear: women should stick to their household duties and not meddle in public life.[50]

Other comedies portrayed the breakdown of romances and the neglect of family responsibilities that resulted from women's obsessive efforts to gain the vote. Children suffer abandonment in *A Cure for Suffragettes* (1912), as mothers park their baby buggies outside a meeting hall and go in alone to plan new suffrage strategy. Hearing the screams of the infants, a kindly policeman pulls the line of buggies to the station house, where other men look after the babies until the frightened mothers rush in to retrieve their offspring. Although the screenplay implies that the women have learned a valuable lesson and will now abandon their foolish campaign, the last title card leaves matters in some doubt by reminding viewers "but even a suffragette can be a mother."[51]

No such ambiguity characterized most antisuffrage films, however, especially those that featured physical combat between men and women. In such offerings as *A Day in the Life of a Suffragette* (1908), female militants display the aggressive frenzy of a Parisian mob in the French Revolution. According to an extant synopsis:

Women are as good as men, they are often better than men: why should they stand the cruel oppression of the stronger sex? Thus a crowd of common women are making speeches and drunk with their own words and getting up to battle pitch, they start forth into the street armed with banners rapidly made and screaming revolutionary songs. They march against a police patrol, who are endeavoring to bar the way. The female onslaught is so powerful that the poor policemen fall sprawling on the ground, and as the female wave sweeps over their prostrate bodies they have reason to regret their rash attempt. Encouraged by their first success, our suffragettes go on their way, their numbers getting bigger at every street turn, until things take an alarming aspect; the militia is called out, and after a comic struggle between women and soldiers, the whole female force is marched into custody and locked up for the night. The next morning, the subdued women are seen coming out of the jail and meekly following their husbands on their way back to their domestic duties.[52]

The reassuring ending does little to dispel the impression of feminine irrationality and violence created by the preceding images.

To combat these harmful stereotypes, the leaders of NAWSA ventured into filmmaking themselves in 1912. Approached by Reliance Films, one of many small prewar production companies, Anna Shaw and Jane Addams agreed to appear in a two-reel prosuffrage melodrama, *Votes for Women*. The film employed some of the documentary techniques favored by Progressive authors and tied the suffrage movement to other ongoing reform efforts. After some initial footage of Addams and Shaw addressing a labor meeting, the camera records their visit to a filthy tenement, in which poor women slave for sweatshop operators. When the heroines learn that a senator owns the tenement, they prevail on his fiancée to convert him to the suffrage cause. Through the influence of his sweetheart, the senator becomes an enthusiastic reformer, and the movie ends with newsreel shots of a recent mammoth suffrage parade in New York City.

According to NAWSA records, *Votes for Women* received wide distribution and figured in campaigns to amend the suffrage provisions of constitutions in New Jersey and several other states. Suffrage organizations arranged for showings in movie houses, churches, public parks, and other popular meeting places. Demand for the film was reportedly so high that both reels had worn out in two years—a circumstance that encouraged suffragists to engage in further moviemaking efforts.[53] In Chicago, where women enjoyed limited voting rights, local groups sponsored short films that taught women how to register and vote and encouraged their participation in the spring elections of 1914.[54] In addition, the national organizations participated in the production of two more substantial melodramas, which they planned to use in their continuing campaigns on both the state and national levels.

These later films followed the narrative conventions already established in *Votes for Women*. They combined romance with propaganda by featuring an attractive young suffragette as the central character, and suggested that morally concerned women voters would help to clean up a corrupt, male-dominated political system. In *Eighty Million Women Want—?* (1913), produced by the Congressional Union, the heroine rescues her lawyer sweetheart from the clutches of a powerful political boss and uncovers a voting fraud scheme in the process. By the end of the movie, the boss has been tried and convicted for his crimes, the suffragists have won a stunning victory at the polls, and the young lovers have agreed to marry. While the romantic subplot reconciled suffrage agitation with Victorian norms of feminine propriety, other aspects of the film appealed to the class and racial prejudices of viewers. The boss's henchmen are lower-class thugs, and one scene of the gang's leaders includes a sleek black politician, the boss's personal aide, who wears a stovepipe hat and tails and smokes a cigar. The scenario suggests that such male voters are responsible for corrupting politics, while honest women are denied the vote. The same argument appeared in more explicit terms in an earlier CU comedy, *Suffrage and the Man* (1912), in which the heroine's father comments, "My butler and my bootblack may vote—why not my wife and daughter?"[55]

Suffragists combined showings of *Eighty Million Women Want—?* with lectures, as they had done with *Votes for Women,* and again attracted large audiences. But their dream of creating a commercially successful film that could be exhibited in movie houses across the nation collapsed with the release of *Your Girl and Mine* (1914). This ambitious NAWSA production, seven reels in length, chronicles the misfortunes of a wealthy heiress who marries a drunken and abusive husband and experiences the injustice of patriarchal property and child custody laws. A white-robed figure, the "Goddess of Suffrage," appears at intervals to point the moral: women must have the vote to protect their rights. *Your Girl and Mine* opened to enthusiastic reviews at special screenings in Chicago and New York, but the World Film Company canceled its national tour after a dispute arose with NAWSA leaders. Its only commercial showing proved to be a financial disaster and discouraged suffragists from engaging in any further moviemaking efforts.[56]

To what extent the suffrage films may have influenced voter behavior remains an open question. At the least, they brought the issue to the attention of mass audiences and exposed gender-related fears and anxieties that resurfaced in state and federal legislative debates. When the movement stalled in the states, Alice Paul's Congressional Union concentrated exclusively on securing a federal suffrage amendment. Adopting the more militant tactics of British suffragettes, Paul's followers (renamed the Woman's Party in 1916) organized huge parades and other demonstrations, picketed the White House, engaged in hunger strikes, and endured arrest and imprisonment for their peaceful protest activities. Some conservative congressmen denounced them as the "Bolsheviki of America" and deplored their unladylike behavior. Others, including Mississippi Senator John Sharp Williams, voiced racial concerns not unlike those raised in CU films. Williams sought to limit the coverage of any federal suffrage amendment to white citizens of the United States, leaving the individual states free to decide for themselves whether to enfranchise "Japanese, Chinese, or Negro" women, "who are not of our race, who are not of our aspirations, who are not of our ideals, who are not of anything that makes an essential part of us."[57]

In a similar vein, Representative Frank Clark of Florida argued that giving southern black women the vote would undermine the caste system that ensured racial peace in the South:

> While the great masses of the Negroes in the South are contented with existing conditions, some of the alleged leaders of the race are agitators and disturbers and are constantly seeking to embroil their people in trouble with the white people by making demands for social recognition which will never be accorded them; and the real leaders in these matters are the Negro women, who are much more insistent and vicious along these lines than are the men of their race.
>
> Make this amendment a part of the federal Constitution and the Negro women of the southern states, under the tutelage of the fast-growing socialistic element of our common country, will become fanatical on the subject of voting and will reawaken in the Negro men an intense and not easily quenched desire to again become a political factor.[58]

The diehard opposition of southern senators and other state rights advocates successfully blocked passage of the amendment even after the onset of World War I. Although Woodrow Wilson personally lobbied for the measure as an important component of the national war effort, Congress did not capitulate until the spring of 1919. Thereafter the requisite number of states quickly ratified, and the Nineteenth Amendment took effect on August 26, 1920, in time for women to vote in the November presidential election. Charlotte Perkins Gilman, a leading spokesperson for women's rights, hailed the victory in terms that echoed the optimistic endings of prosuffrage films:

> Gone are the ages that have led us bound
> Beneath a master, now we stand as he,
> Free for world-service unto all humankind,
> Free of the dragging chains that used to bind.
> No longer pets or slaves are we, for lo!
> Women are free at last in all the land![59]

As the tortuous progress of the suffrage movement suggests, fictional narrative and constitutional law seldom interact in any clear-cut fashion. The media normally play an important, but complementary, role in the process of constitutional change. Proponents of a federal income tax amendment, for example, began their campaign as soon as the United States Supreme Court, by a narrow 5–4 vote, struck down a popular income tax statute in 1895. The Democratic Party denounced *Pollock v. Farmers' Loan and Trust Co.* in its 1896 platform, and members of Congress sought to overturn the decision through a constitutional amendment. Of the 357 amendments proposed between 1897 and 1909, more dealt with the income tax than with any other subject in five different years.[60]

During that same time period the media kept the issue before the general public in a variety of ways. Utopian novels with a constitutional agenda—from *President John Smith* (1897) and *Waiting for the Signal* (1897) to *The Citadel* and *Philip Dru*—either specifically endorsed a graduated income tax or left that matter to be decided, like all others, by a majority vote of "the people." Muckraking journalists exposed the corrupt methods by which some great American fortunes had been amassed and condemned the lavish lifestyle of the idle rich. *Cosmopolitan* magazine, which claimed almost half a million subscribers in 1906, added to its popularity that year by conducting a symposium on the topic, "Are Great Fortunes Great Dangers?" A panel of prominent figures, representing all shades of public opinion, wrestled with such questions as "Does the possession of a billion of dollars in the hands of an individual constitute a menace to the republic?" Not surprisingly, most contributors agreed that great wealth did threaten democratic institutions, and recommended income and inheritance taxes as a remedy.[61]

The debate over the merits of a federal income tax received coverage in conservative and independent journals, as well as the muckraking *Cosmopolitan*.[62] Sober discussions of government power in the "respectable" press sometimes gave way to alarmist visions of an impending social revolution. Thus, the usually staid *North American Review* carried "An Appeal to Our Millionaires" as its lead article in June 1906. The anonymous author—described in an editorial note as "the most profound philosopher living in the United States"—suggested that no American should be permitted to earn more than $50,000 a year. Unless the wealthy agreed to some voluntary curtailment of their privileges, he warned, they faced the twin dangers of a violent class upheaval on the order of the French Revolution or "very extreme" legislation that could sweep away their property rights as effectively as dynamite bombs.[63] Fear of revolutionary violence, which had largely dissipated since the turn of the century, nevertheless served as a stimulus to both the income tax campaign and other major

Progressive reform efforts. Allusions to the threat of renewed class warfare may be found in much popular art of the time,[64] in many reform novels, including *The Citadel,* and in the comments of political theorists and statesmen.[65]

After more than a decade of agitation in Congress and the media, the Senate at last approved an income tax amendment in July 1909. Later that month the House of Representatives overwhelmingly endorsed the amendment, which became law on February 3, 1913, when the thirty-sixth state ratified it. Passage of the Sixteenth Amendment—the first since Reconstruction—reinvigorated the constitutional amending process, which many informed observers had long considered moribund. In addition, it answered two important Progressive goals: by providing a source of new federal revenue, it encouraged the expansion of the regulatory state; and by authorizing a tax that might be used to redistribute wealth, it reduced the danger of violent class conflict.[66]

Progressive ideals similarly inspired repeated efforts to secure the popular election of United States senators through a constitutional amendment. The issue was a long-standing one. Such an amendment had first been proposed in 1826, but the movement did not receive widespread support until the late nineteenth century. By that time the Senate had become known as a "millionaires' club," whose wealthy members served the interests of powerful corporations rather than the public. In the 1890s Populists and Democrats launched a determined drive to make the upper house more accountable to "the people," and Progressives in both major parties carried on the struggle in the early twentieth century. At stake was nothing less than a radical alteration in the structure of the government established by the Founders.

Those who framed the Constitution thought of the Senate as a council of wise men, an elite body of elder statesmen who should serve as a necessary check on the democratic House of Representatives. House members held their seats by virtue of popular elections; senators, who represented their respective states, were chosen by state legislatures. Critics charged that an institution unresponsive to the popular will had no place in a modern democratic state. Major corporations sometimes interfered in senatorial elections on behalf of a favored candidate, they pointed out; bribery and fraud had become commonplace in some states; legislative deadlocks occasionally left some senatorial vacancies unfilled; and, worst of all, senators often blocked important reform measures at the behest of their corporate benefactors. The only remedy lay in a constitutional amendment to permit the direct election of senators by the people. Between 1894 and 1911 the House passed such an amendment four times, only to see it rejected each time by the Senate.[67]

As in the income tax campaign, the media kept the issue before the public through cartoons, essays, and novels that attacked senatorial corruption. David Graham Phillips's series of muckraking articles, "The Treason of the Senate," was particularly effective in stirring national indignation over the abuses of the existing system. In nine monthly installments that appeared in *Cosmopolitan* magazine from March through November 1906, Phillips traced the influence of corporate contributions on the voting record and personal wealth of twenty-one sitting senators. Although he presented few facts that were not already a matter of public record, he embellished his account with some eye-catching invective that reputable journalists seldom employed. Thus, senators collectively were "treacherous" and "traitorous," "bribers," "perjurers," and "change-pocket thieves."

In response, President Theodore Roosevelt condemned "the man with the muckrake" in a public speech delivered in April; Senator Joseph W. Bailey of Texas defended himself at length against Phillips's charges on the floor of the Senate; and popular interest in the "Treason" series soared. Although the Senate continued to reject amendment proposals for another five years, Phillips's muckraking brought new life to the debate and encouraged reformers to redouble their efforts.[68] On May 13, 1912, both the House and the Senate agreed to the final version of an amendment that had been introduced the previous year. The states were quick to approve the proposal, which provided "The Senate of the United States shall be composed of two Senators from each State, elected by the people thereof, for six years." On April 8, 1913, Connecticut became the thirty-sixth state to ratify, and the Seventeenth Amendment went into effect.[69]

These twentieth-century amendments brought fundamental and lasting changes to the constitutional system. Unlike the Reconstruction amendments, which had been imposed on the defeated southern states as part of a wartime settlement, the Progressive amendments represented a peaceful revolution in popular thinking about the nature and obligations of government. (The Eighteenth Amendment, which established national prohibition, proved abortive and will be discussed in a later chapter.) Several major statutes further increased the regulatory power of the federal government at the expense of the states, and the media again contributed to such constitutional change. Upton Sinclair's novel *The Jungle* (1906), a classic indictment of working conditions in Chicago's meatpacking plants, influenced the passage of the Meat Inspection Act of 1906. Samuel Hopkins Adams's nonfiction articles on patent medicine fraud in *Collier's* magazine stirred congressional interest in regulation and provided valuable support for the Pure Food and Drug Act of 1906. And attacks on the evil of child labor in *The Saturday Evening Post, Cosmopolitan,* and other magazines and newspapers encouraged Senator Albert J. Beveridge of Indiana to launch a crusade for federal regulation that led in time to the passage of the Keating-Owen Child Labor Act of 1916.[70]

Constitutional commentators, whether Progressives or conservatives, had little doubt that they were living in a time of profound and unsettling change. Respected journals of opinion, including the *North American Review, Forum,* and *Outlook,* opened their pages to a spirited debate over the nature and significance of the "new federalism." Advocates on both sides recalled the troubled years that had preceded the calling of the Philadelphia Convention, and advanced arguments that echoed those made by Federalists and Antifederalists—by strict and broad constructionists—in the late eighteenth century.

The American people again faced a constitutional crisis comparable to that experienced by the Founding generation, asserted Charles F. Amidon, a federal district judge in North Dakota:

> The political revolution of 1776 required the creation of a central political power because it gave rise to great political concerns that could not be provided for by the several States. Today, as the result of an economic revolution quite as fundamental and far-reaching, there are certain great business interests that have become National in their character and extent which cannot be left to conflicting State authority. It is as unwise to stand timidly shrinking from the exercise of economic control now as it would have been a century ago to hold back from the exercise of political power through the fears of those who dreaded an adequate National government. . . . [O]ur choice . . . lies between the single authority of the Nation and the anarchy of the different States in combination with partial National control.[71]

Amidon argued that an expansive reading of the interstate commerce clause would empower the federal government to control every aspect of interstate business activity and thus bring the Constitution into line with modern economic conditions. Other publicists looked instead to the general welfare clause as a vast reservoir of untapped congressional power that might be used to remedy any "matter of national concern."[72] Still others carried the Founding analogy to its logical conclusion by urging that a new federal convention be called to redefine for the twentieth century the proper boundaries between state and national power.[73]

Opponents of the "new federalism" countered the arguments of the neo-Federalists by appealing to doctrines of strict construction, state rights, and traditional republican government. If Congress had been given the power "to do all that it may conceive to be for the 'general welfare' of the country," declared George Harvey, editor of the *North American Review*, the rest of the Constitution would be meaningless. Like Jefferson and Madison, Harvey insisted that Congress could claim only those implied powers that were essential for carrying out some express constitutional grant.[74] Similarly, the dean of Yale Law School warned that an overly broad reading of the interstate commerce clause could destroy any meaningful distinction between federal and state authority and bring virtually all economic activity under the control of the federal government.[75]

In broader terms, some critics voiced fears that the democratizing reforms introduced by Progressives would bring an end to republican government. David Jayne Hill, a lawyer and diplomat, worried that a new ethic of social justice was undermining individual initiative and respect for the Founders' vision of limited government. Americans were no longer satisfied to compete with others under a regime of neutral laws, Hill complained: "What is demanded is not 'equal laws' but 'laws of equalization.'" This tendency could only lead to an increase in "class legislation" and to the eventual collapse of republican institutions.[76]

"The habit of undue interference by government in private affairs breeds the habit of undue reliance upon government in private affairs," agreed former Secretary of State Elihu Root. "Weaken individual character among a people by comfortable reliance upon paternal government and a nation soon becomes incapable of free self-government and fit only to be governed; the higher and nobler qualities of national life that make for ideals and effort and achievement become atrophied and the nation is decadent."[77] Other writers drew ominous parallels with ancient Athens, whose government had succumbed to the evils of excessive democracy. They quoted with approval Aristotle's lurid description of government by "the multitude," in which the Greek philosopher remarked that flattering demagogues controlled the votes of the people, "who are too ready to listen to them." Was not twentieth-century America moving in a similar direction? they asked. Proposals for the direct election of senators, the recall of judges, and the initiative and referendum signaled a dangerous willingness on the part of "the people" to abandon republican principles in favor of "pure democracy."[78]

In fact, the constitutional changes inspired by Progressivism stopped far short of creating a "mobocracy." Although muckraking journals hailed the passage of each new regulatory measure as a victory for "the people," lobbyists for major industries often helped to draft such legislation and to blunt its intended effects. Investigative reporters were similarly vulnerable to economic pressures from publishers and advertisers, and the muckraking movement began to wane after 1910, as crusading magazines came under more conservative management and business advertisers threatened to cut off needed revenue.[79] Yet contemporary observers were not wrong in believing that a fundamental transformation in the philosophy and functions of government was taking place. Americans were living in the midst of a genuine revolution, whether they realized it or not, argued Walter Weyl in an influential study published in 1911. "This revolution . . . is a revolution not of blood and iron, but of votes, judicial decisions, and points of view," Weyl noted, and he cited a lengthy list of regulatory laws to prove that the nation was gradually evolving into a full-fledged welfare state.[80]

Progressive fiction helped to shape the public's response to this ongoing constitutional process. By describing, in however sentimentalized a fashion, the conditions of life in the corporate state, writers created a compelling argument for government control of the economy. Their moralistic narratives complemented the speeches of constitutional reformers and sometimes made a lasting impact on audiences. Thus, when Franklin K. Lane, Woodrow Wilson's secretary of the interior, contemplated the constitutional changes that had taken place during Wilson's presidency, he was quick to give credit to Colonel House, the president's close friend and adviser. "[W]ilson likes the idea of personal party-leadership," Lane observed in his wartime diary of 1918; "Cabinet responsibility is still in his mind. Colonel House's book, *Philip Dru*, favors it, and all that book has said should be, comes about slowly, even woman suffrage. The President comes to *Philip Dru* in the end."[81]

While Lane undoubtedly exaggerated House's influence, his point remains valid in a general sense: the media *do* play a significant role in promoting constitutional discussion. As the nation entered World War I, however, any criticism of Wilson's "war socialism" through the media became increasingly dangerous.

3

The Selling of War Socialism

> In times of peace the sense of the State flags in a republic that is not militarized. For war is essentially the health of the State. The ideal of the State is that within its territory its power and influence should be universal. . . . And it is precisely in war that the urgency for union seems greatest, and the necessity for universality seems most unquestioned. The State is the organization of the herd to act offensively or defensively against another herd similarly organized.
>
> —RANDOLPH BOURNE (1918)

The Progressive "revolution" lost momentum with the onset of a general European war in 1914, as public attention increasingly shifted to matters of foreign policy and national defense. Although Congress did pass several more regulatory measures, including the Keating-Owen Child Labor Act, voters took less interest in such reforms than in the prospect of being drawn into the international conflict. Once Congress declared war, however, the nation underwent a political and economic transformation that had no parallel in its previous history. Overnight the federal government took charge of a vast mobilization of men and resources, and Progressive dreams of national planning came to brief, but spectacular, fulfillment. As William Leuchtenburg has noted, "Under a form of war socialism not unlike that which had been found necessary by European governments, federal agencies directed every major sector of the economy."[1] The war likewise enhanced the influence of the media, though at the expense of the kind of investigative reporting that had characterized the Progressive years. Most wartime writers abandoned serious fact-finding and constitutional criticism to embrace the rousing patriotic slogans churned out by the Wilsonian war machine. Those who voiced dissenting views faced a challenge from federal authorities for which their prewar experience had not prepared them.

The unprecedented centralization of power in wartime Washington raised serious constitutional questions concerning federalism and the allocation of power between Congress and the president. The Lever Food and Fuel

Control Act of August 10, 1917, delegated vast lawmaking authority to the president, without any meaningful guidelines or other restraints on its use. To ensure the production and distribution of essential fuels and foodstuffs during the wartime emergency, the statute empowered Woodrow Wilson to buy and sell such necessary products, to regulate markets and exchanges, to take over and operate factories and mines, and, in extreme circumstances, to fix prices in any industry. Although Wilson did not in fact exercise many of these powers, he did create new federal agencies, including a Food Administration and a Fuel Administration, to develop immediate programs of national conservation. As Food Administrator, Herbert Hoover proclaimed meatless and wheatless days and established high minimum prices to encourage wheat production. Harry A. Garfield, the Fuel Administrator, doled out supplies of oil and coal and ordered nonessential factories closed one day each week. Federal power likewise intruded into areas normally reserved for state control through other wartime measures, from the Selective Service Act to the nationalization of the country's railroads.[2]

The regimentation of society under federal auspices provoked little significant opposition. Unlike Abraham Lincoln, who had often acted unilaterally during the Civil War crisis, Wilson considered himself a parliamentary president along the lines of Philip Dru's proposed "Executive," and therefore sought prior congressional approval for most of his actions. The sweeping provisions of the Lever Act dismayed some congressmen, to be sure. Representative George M. Young of North Dakota, a Republican, denounced the measure for creating a presidential dictatorship, and some Democrats, including Senator Thomas W. Hardwick of Georgia, agreed that the price-fixing portions of the proposed law represented an unconstitutional delegation of lawmaking power to the executive branch. "It would turn over the business of our country to one individual," warned Senator Thomas P. Gore of Oklahoma, who insisted that constitutional restraints on executive power must be observed, even in wartime. The Constitution may be needed in future crises, Gore added, to prevent dictatorship and "to protect us against [the] subserviency of a Congress that might be willing to lick the dust at the feet of such a dictator."[3]

Most congressmen argued, however, that the federal government, in the exercise of its war powers, might take any action that was reasonably related to the war effort. Illinois Senator J. Hamilton Lewis, a Democrat, advanced the most extreme defense of unfettered national authority, contending that the Constitution was "more or less suspended" in wartime.

In words that might have been lifted from Samuel Merwin's *The Citadel* and other Progressive reform novels, Lewis observed, "The time has gone by when the people of this country are so much concerned about the Constitution as they are about their institutions; and I for myself announce as my creed that I will not permit the obsolete provisions of a paper constitution to prevent the preservation of the human constitution."[4] Despite some acrimonious debate, the Lever Act eventually passed both houses of Congress with substantial majorities.

More troubling to the Wilson administration than the threat of congressional opposition was the uncertain state of public opinion in the early days of the war. In the close presidential race of 1916, Wilson had won reelection on a peace platform, and pacifist sentiment remained strong on the eve of hostilities. American efforts at mediation failed, however, and the German government's resumption of unrestricted submarine warfare upon neutral vessels in early 1917 drove the president at last to seek a declaration of war from Congress. Wilson's war message of April 2, 1917, appealed for national unity by defining American objectives in idealistic and Progressive terms. "[W]e shall fight for the things we have always carried nearest our hearts," he affirmed—"for democracy, for the right of those who submit to authority to have a voice in their own governments, for a universal dominion of right."[5] The eloquent phrases, which implied that the war might strengthen Progressivism at home while extending its influence overseas, produced a favorable response nationwide and brought many antiwar advocates into the Wilsonian camp.

To mobilize popular support behind his wartime programs, Wilson created a national publicity bureau, the Committee on Public Information (CPI), a week after Congress formally declared war. The new agency, based solely on an executive order, controlled the flow of government news and shielded the president from direct contact with potentially hostile reporters. To head the CPI, Wilson chose forty-one-year-old George Creel, a talented muckraking journalist and loyal supporter. True to his Progressive background, Creel endorsed the official philosophy of the CPI, which emphasized "faith in democracy . . . faith in the fact." He set up a News Division to supply the press with purportedly accurate information on the progress of the war, and most papers adopted a policy of voluntary censorship in return for these government handouts. The administration's virtual monopoly of war news assumed its most systematic form with the CPI's publication of a daily *Official Bulletin,* beginning May 10, 1917. The first comprehensive guide to the day-to-day proceedings of every federal agency, the *Bulletin* satisfied both Creel's desire for open disclosure and Wilson's insistence on "neutral" facts.[6]

Although Creel genuinely believed in the need for "objective" news reporting, even in wartime, he soon recognized that his top priority was the promotion of the Wilsonian war program. With characteristic energy he mobilized all forms of mass media for what he called "the world's greatest adventure in advertising."[7] In the absence of commercial radio, he organized a force of 75,000 "Four-Minute Men" to deliver patriotic speeches on war-related subjects to nationwide audiences. The group's designation called up images of the heroic minutemen of the American Revolution, while also emphasizing the assembly-line techniques of modern warfare. (In contrast to their latter-day counterparts, of course, the Revolutionary minutemen had fought against the kind of centralizing and intrusive government policies that the Four-Minute Men were attempting to defend.)

The CPI supplied its volunteer speakers with periodic *Bulletins* that contained a standardized four-minute script and the date (or dates) on which it was to be delivered. A favorite forum was the local movie theater, which had outgrown its working-class origins to become a center of middle-class entertainment. Newspapers advertised both the current feature film and the name of a designated four-minute speaker as part of an evening's program. Pursuant to CPI guidelines, the speakers kept within their respective time slots, with the effect of sending identical messages simultaneously to audiences around the country. Although critics dubbed these amateur orators the "Stentorian Guard," the public tended to respond favorably to their patriotic appeals.

The early talks were rather low-key and factual, with the aim of influencing intelligent middle-class opinion. By 1918, however, the CPI scripts had become blatantly propagandistic and rabble-rousing. Speakers now relied on official atrocity stories as a matter of course, and the *Bulletin* of September 1918 introduced "Four-Minute Singing" to keep morale at "white heat." Movie theaters used special slides to project the lyrics of these songs onto their screens. A typical program might include standard patriotic melodies ("America," "The Star-Spangled Banner"), sentimental favorites ("There's a Long, Long Trail," "Keep the Home Fires Burning"), and new songs pledging compliance with federal wartime directives ("Saving Food," "Helping On").[8]

In the first major public relations campaign of the war, the CPI collaborated with local elites to enlist popular support for a policy of conscription. The issue was deeply divisive, since it threatened long-standing traditions of voluntarism and decentralization. Congressional opponents of a draft law, many of them Democrats from the South and West, argued that it would "Prussianize America," "destroy democracy at home while fighting for it abroad," and create a "sulky, unwilling, indifferent army." When the measure nevertheless passed under strong presidential pressure, critics predicted a wave of violent grassroots resistance. "You will have the streets of our American cities running red with blood on Registration Day," Senator James Reed, a Democrat from Missouri, warned the Secretary of War, Newton D. Baker.[9] Such fears were not wholly imaginary. On the only other occasion that the federal government had resorted to conscription, the results had been disastrous. The drafting of men into the Union army during the Civil War had provoked three days of bloody rioting in New York City, and the military authorities who enforced the draft had been widely criticized for unjust and high-handed behavior.

To prevent a recurrence of such problems, Secretary Baker relied on local civilian boards to administer the system and to lend it the sanction of community approval. More important, he launched an intensive propaganda drive weeks ahead of the registration date to persuade Americans that conscription was merely one more aspect of the Progressive reform impulse in wartime. As he informed the president,

> I am exceedingly anxious to have the registration and selection by draft . . . conducted under such circumstances as to create a strong patriotic feeling and relieve as far as possible the prejudice which remains to some extent in the popular mind against the draft. With this end in view, I am using a vast number of agencies throughout the country to make the day of registration a festival and patriotic occasion. Several Governors and some mayors of cities are entering already heartily into this plan, and the Chamber of Commerce of the United States is taking it up through its affiliated bodies.[10]

In practice, Baker's strategy called on local clergymen, businessmen, public officials, newspaper editors, and Four-Minute Men to redefine the meaning of "conscription" in accordance with the administration's idealistic policy statements. Chief among these was a presidential proclamation that accompanied the signing of the draft bill on May 18, 1917. Here Wilson characterized the approaching registration day as a "great day of patriotic devotion and obligation," on which young men between the ages of twenty-one and thirty would fulfill a solemn public duty by signing these "lists of honor."[11] The language spoke of voluntary action on the part of draftees and gave no hint of the criminal penalties that would follow non-compliance.

A similar effort to minimize the coercive aspects of conscription lay behind the official designation of the new draft law as the "Selective Service Act." Progressives had long preached an ethic of disinterested public service as a means of reconciling the individualistic values of the nineteenth century with the demands of the modern regulatory state. They sought, as Herbert Croly noted in his influential study, *The Promise of American Life* (1909), to apply Hamiltonian means to Jeffersonian ends. By advertising the draft as a call to honorable public service, Wilsonian spokesmen preserved the fiction of voluntary choice while relying on punitive law enforcement agencies to deal with "slackers."[12]

In fact, no repressive action by the Wilsonian war machine proved necessary to keep the peace on Registration Day. Nearly 10 million men signed up quietly for military duty on June 5 in a remarkable demonstration of the effectiveness of modern techniques of mass persuasion. To be sure, dissenting voices continued to be raised. Hundreds of conscientious objectors and civil libertarians found themselves in jails by the end of the war, and draft evaders totaled roughly 337,000 persons by one official estimate, or about 12 percent of those inducted.[13] Still, the only large-scale organized opposition to the draft took the form of the abortive Green Corn Rebellion of August 1917. For many participants this hopeless venture pitted an older vision of limited government against the Wilson administration's all-encompassing nationalism.

Centered in the farm areas of western Oklahoma, the Green Corn Rebellion followed a well-established tradition of grassroots resistance to the exploitive practices of landlords, bankers, and merchants in nearby "electric light towns." Local grievances meshed with national concerns by the early summer of 1917, as rumors circulated that federal authorities were about to seize young farmers for overseas military duty while forcing older men to work on large government farms. In response, several hundred dirt-poor sharecroppers and tenant farmers, including some blacks and a few Indians, organized for a projected march on Washington. According to one of their leaders, a radical labor organizer, their departure would spark a nationwide mass movement that could stop the war, end the draft, and replace Wilson—the "Big Slick"—and his associates with a true people's government of workers and farmers. As matters turned out, however, the marchers never left Oklahoma. A posse of seventy armed men, with information supplied by an informer, descended on the main rebel camp at

Spears' Bluff on August 3, before any marching orders had been given. Unwilling to fire on their neighbors and elected officials, most of the insurgents fled, bringing the rebellion to a speedy and ignominious end. For the next week posses rounded up and arrested 450 suspected rebels. Of these, grand juries later indicted 184. In the end, about 75 men received prison sentences for their part in organized draft resistance.[14]

The episode illustrates both the strength of socialist antiwar sentiment in Oklahoma and the persistence of a Jeffersonian tradition of decentralized government and individual rights. While many of the rebels were militant left-wing socialists unwilling to accept the Socialist Party's policy of nonviolent constitutional protest, others joined the movement mainly to protect their local folkways against the threat of federal interference. For these latter-day Jeffersonians, socialist ideology was less important than traditional doctrines of self-help and resistance to governmental tyranny. As rebel Walter Strong later recalled:

> We decided we wasn't gonna fight somebody else's war for 'em and we refused to go. We didn't volunteer and we didn't answer the draft. Most of us had wives and kids and we didn't wanna leave them here to do all the work of harvestin' and have us go over to France and fight people we didn't have anything against. We didn't have any bands and uniforms and that stuff down there in the sandhills so that crap about the Germans comin' over here when they finished up the English and French didn't go over with us.[15]

With the easy suppression of the only substantial uprising against the draft, antiwar activists looked to the courts as their last hope for relief. But on January 7, 1918, the United States Supreme Court unanimously upheld the constitutionality of the Selective Service Act as a valid exercise of congressional power to raise and support armies. To the argument that conscription violates individual liberty, Chief Justice Edward Douglass White responded that "the very conception of a just government and its duty to the citizen includes the reciprocal obligation of the citizen to render military service in case of need and the right to compel it."[16] Public opinion generally welcomed the decision in the *Selective Draft Law Cases* as a matter of course. "Every patriotic citizen expected" the result, reported the *New York Times;* some publications, including the *Michigan Law Review,* even suggested that the antidraft litigants might have been part of an enemy plot to spread "treacherous hostile propaganda."[17]

The successful campaign to promote conscription served as a model for later wartime drives to sell Liberty Bonds and to ensure compliance with other federal programs by mobilizing grassroots opinion. To reach the largest possible audience, Creel and the CPI enlisted the services of authors, scholars, artists, cartoonists, and movie producers in a massive ideological crusade that further demonstrated the effectiveness of modern advertising techniques. The Division of Syndicate Features, established in August 1917, recruited fifty of the nation's most popular writers, including Booth Tarkington, Owen Wister, Gertrude Atherton, Samuel Hopkins Adams, Meredith Nicholson, Ida Tarbell, Fannie Hurst, Edna Ferber, Mary Roberts Rinehart, Rex Beach, and William Allen White. Some of these volunteers were former muckrakers, like Creel; all were familiar to readers of mass circulation journals and newspapers. They popularized the war effort in syndicated columns that reached an estimated audience of 12 million Americans every week, and Creel also distributed their work to publications in foreign countries.[18]

An overlapping group of wartime novelists produced ideological fiction that made skillful use of democratic symbols to justify wartime controls. While the CPI did not commission these novels, it welcomed them as an important addition to its consensus-building efforts. Most of the authors had achieved popular celebrity in the prewar years and drew upon the conventions of Progressive fiction in fashioning their plots. Aiming at a broad middle-class readership, they carried forward the Progressive concern with healing the deep class, racial, and gender divisions within American society. The logic of their argument pushed them toward an ultimate endorsement of the war as a means of furthering the kind of peaceful constitutional revolution that had figured so prominently in Progressive literature.

Three works in particular—Mary Roberts Rinehart's *Dangerous Days* (1919), Ida M. Tarbell's *The Rising of the Tide* (1919), and Arthur Train's *The Earthquake* (1918)—provide valuable insights into the construction of wartime propaganda. Each focuses on middle-class or elite protagonists and their reactions to the Wilsonian war program. In Rinehart's *Dangerous Days*, wealthy Clayton Spencer converts his steel mill into a munitions factory at the request of the government and offers to supply shells for the war effort at a nominal profit. As he tells his son Graham, "There were times when big profits were allowable. There was always the risk to invested capital to consider." But Clayton "did not want to grow fat on the nation's misfortunes."[19] For Graham, too, the wartime crisis provokes a belated commitment to altruistic public service, as the callow young college graduate joins the army and quickly develops into a heroic soldier. In fact, most of Clayton Spencer's friends strongly support the war, despite high taxes "directed primarily against the rich" and food and fuel quotas. The only exceptions are a few selfish parasites, including Clayton's wife Natalie and her opportunistic lover.

Although Rinehart concentrates on a small group of upper-class characters, she emphasizes the democratizing effects that Wilson's war measures will have for all of American society. "This is every man's war," observes one of Clayton's rich friends in voicing approval of the draft,[20] and in officers' training camp Graham finds himself taking orders from the family's former chauffeur, now a competent noncommissioned officer. The limits of such wartime fraternization are readily apparent in the narrative, however. Despite Rinehart's suggestion that the war may end the "absurd" class system in America, she leaves little doubt that Graham and other sons of the well-to-do will occupy the higher leadership posts in the military forces.

Similarly, to judge from the novel's heroine, Audrey Valentine, women can expect little change in their traditional status as a result of wartime service. An idle socialite before the war, Audrey joins the workforce out of patriotic duty, becoming first a munitions worker and later a war correspondent. As the end of the war approaches, however, she acknowledges the temporary nature of her public role:

> The old Audrey was gone; and in her place was a quiet woman, whose hands had known service and would never again be content to be idle. Yet she knew that, with the war, the world call would be gone. Not again, for her, detached, impersonal service. . . . What she wanted, quite simply, was the service of love. To have her own and to care for them. She hoped, very earnestly, that she would be able to look beyond her own four walls, to see distress and to help it, but she knew, as she knew herself, that the real call to her would always be love.[21]

In contrast to Rinehart's protagonists, whose support for the war is never in doubt, the characters in *The Rising of the Tide* remain divided and lukewarm in their attitudes, even after the nation enters the conflict. Ida Tarbell, a former muckraking journalist, uses Sabinsport, a small midwestern town, as the setting for a narrative of community involvement in the war effort. Her principal characters are middle-class professionals who take opposing positions on the merits of American intervention. Ralph Gardner, a crusading newspaper editor, fears that the war will divert public attention from unfinished domestic reforms, with especially disastrous consequences for the working class. "There won't be a law protecting labor left in the country if this goes on," he complains. "Who's going to think about hours and wages and safety and social insurance with that thing going on over there?"[22] Initially sympathetic to Germany because of its progressive social welfare programs, he is slow to abandon his pacifist views.

Ralph's friend, Dick Ingraham, on the other hand, favors the Allied cause from the beginning. A liberal clergyman, Dick thinks of the war in Wilsonian terms as a call to aid the forces of democratic self-government abroad. And he labors to persuade Ralph that American participation will further benefit the reform movement at home. "What's going on in England and France?" he queries. "The recognition of the necessity of accepting as government practices many a thing you've been turning Sabinsport upside down to get. This war is righteous in aim, and all righteousness will be shoved ahead as it goes on. . . . Governments and parties are admitting, without contention, the need and the justice of measures they've fought for years."[23] Convinced at last, Ralph recants his pacifism, joins the army, and dies on the battlefield in France.

Antiwar sentiment persists in the community, however, as dissenters protest the introduction of each new federal measure and rumors of governmental inefficiency and corruption circulate widely. The citizens of Sabinsport do not become enthusiastic supporters of the war effort until the struggle touches them personally, through the establishment of a neighboring army camp and through published lists of local battlefield casualties. As in Rinehart's narrative, military and civilian forms of public service break down class barriers and unite all Americans in "the consciousness of a great cause." The only holdouts are a handful of cranks and German sympathizers, and these agitators, it turns out, are responsible for the false rumors and criticisms that have temporarily impeded popular acceptance of the war program. By equating dissent with enemy propaganda, Tarbell strips it of legitimacy and prepares her readers to endorse Sabinsport's new policy of suppressing any "criticism of the Government, any doubt of a war enterprise, [or] any reluctance to accept at full face value any request of the Government."[24]

While the novels of Tarbell and Rinehart received generally favorable reviews, they did not appear until some months after the war had ended. More immediate and measurable in its impact was the wartime fiction of Arthur Train. *The Earthquake* ran as a serial in the immensely popular *Saturday Evening Post* before its publication in book form in March 1918, and went quickly through three reprintings.[25] Train's first-person narrative records the impressions of a Wall Street broker, John Stanton, as he observes the effects of the wartime crisis—"the earthquake"—on his family and friends. The theme of shared sacrifice under government direction, which dominated the novels of Rinehart and Tarbell, reappears here; but Train, a former New York attorney, makes a special case for the rehabilitation of the wealthy class through wartime service.

In response to the national emergency, Stanton's pampered wife dismisses her servants and volunteers for canteen duty and other relief work; his daughter enters business college to learn the clerical skills needed for a government job; and his son, a Harvard undergraduate, enlists in the army. His friends, too, display an uncharacteristic zeal for public service, as prominent lawyers, businessmen, and doctors either join the armed forces or take dollar-a-year jobs with the federal government in Washington. Unfit for military duty because of a bad heart, Stanton aids the war effort by undertaking a publicity campaign to persuade the well-to-do to sacrifice their remaining luxuries, so that chauffeurs and other nonessential employees may be pushed into war work. If such appeals for further voluntary retrenchment and economy should fail, he does not blink at federal conscription of civilian labor to fill the nation's production needs. The war has already revolutionized popular thinking about the reach of federal power, he urges:

> We observe with satisfaction that our form of government is sufficiently elastic to enable us not only to carry on a great war without breaking down . . ., but to make the world safe for democracy by an exhibition of autocracy that might well have astonished Thomas Jefferson. Socialists, republicans, liberals, conservatives, populists, and reactionaries—our Bolsheviki and our Minimalists—are all gratified equally. . . . It is a somewhat quaint experience to sit in a club window with a plutocrat who has spent most of his life in cursing the government and complaining of congressional interference with his business affairs, and listen to him talk about what "we," i.e., the government of which he now forms a part, are going to do. It is equally refreshing to hear a railroad president bewailing the hesitation of the government in taking over control of the railroads.[26]

Although Train praises the public spirit of the millionaires and predicts an end to class distinctions in the postwar world, his discussion of the draft reveals a much more conservative bias than either Tarbell or Rinehart

demonstrated in their novels. To begin with, John Stanton attributes the
leadership qualities of his son and his Harvard classmates to racial inheritance: "Probably there is an inherited gift for leadership in the Anglo-
Saxon that has made it easier for us."[27] Instead of celebrating the democratic aspects of a conscript army, moreover, he notes the importance of
conscription as a mechanism for the social control of the lower classes.
Young draftees will return from military duty with a new respect for law
and order, he affirms, and with ingrained habits of obedience to authority.
Or, as his son Jack puts it, "When Ikey and Abie go back to the East Side,
if any greasy anarchist attempts to put anything over on them, Ikey and
Abie will stand him up against the wall and say: 'See here, old sport! Have
you ever had any dealing with the United States Government? Well, *we
have!* Uncle Sam's all right! Get out!'"[28] To discipline future troublemak-
ers in the ways of "true Americanism," Stanton favors the retention of
compulsory military service as a permanent national policy.

Wartime movies reproduced these themes for still larger audiences. The
Division of Film, which Creel set up within the CPI, brought the federal
government for the first time into a close working relationship with the
film industry. Movie producers willingly churned out a spate of war-related films designed to boost public morale. Feature films that promoted
some aspect of the war effort averaged five a month in 1917, and double
that number the following year. Production peaked in the closing months
of the war, with more than twenty new releases announced in September
1918.[29] While some of these films were standard melodramas dealing with
spy-catching at home or German atrocities abroad, others sought to mobilize popular support behind specific federal programs, including conscription and the conservation of food and fuel.

Typical of a group of draft narratives is *The Pride of New York* (Fox,
1917), which carries the theme of democratic leveling to its logical conclusion. The script follows the wartime adventures of three major characters: a wealthy playboy, a workingman named George, and a millionaire's
daughter who develops a romantic interest in them both. When the men
find themselves drafted into the army, the girl joins the Red Cross. Soon
the three meet again in Europe, where, in the words of a trade journal review, the girl discovers that class distinctions no longer matter:

> George, genial, smiling, continues to improve in her estimation,
> while the rich man's son, still a snob and disliked by his fellow sol-
> diers, fades from her esteem. When George, battling for all he is

worth, fearing nothing in his fight to uphold the honor of his country, saves this girl from death at the hands of the Germans, she places her hand and heart in George's keeping.

When the rich man's son sees that his idleness and his snobbish ways have caused him to lose this girl, whose real worth he never appreciated, his whole disposition changes. He patterns his acts and his conduct after George's and becomes a credit to himself, to his family, and to his country.[30]

While the film thus celebrates the democratizing effects of military service more unequivocally than most wartime novels, it poses no real challenge to existing social structures. The class system can readily accommodate occasional marriages across class lines, and one important function of movies like *The Pride of New York* is to reinforce the social position of wealthy Americans. George's rival, the rich ne'er-do-well, achieves moral regeneration through his military duty and can therefore claim his property rights with a greater sense of legitimacy in the postwar world. The only true villains in conscription films are the cowards and pacifist dupes who resist the draft, and even they often change their minds and join the Wilsonian crusade as the plot unfolds. The hero of *The Slacker* (Rolfe-Metro, 1917), for example, marries at first in a cowardly attempt to escape the draft. Under the influence of his patriotic wife, however, he reforms and eventually enlists in the army. The film ends with some newsreel footage of President Wilson appealing for military volunteers. To aid the recruitment effort, theater owners allowed enlistment booths to be set up in their lobbies during showings of *The Slacker* and several other conscription movies.[31]

As with the draft law, some filmmakers used movies to encourage public compliance with federal directives that limited the consumption of essential foodstuffs and fuels. *The Patriot* (Metro, 1917) dealt with one family's bumbling efforts to conserve food. "[I]n spite of its comedy, it carries a real lesson," commented an industry publication.[32] On a more serious level, *The Food Gamblers* (Eastern Triangle, 1917) promoted wartime austerity by attacking commodities speculators as traitors, a theme that reappeared in *The Profiteers* (Astra-Pathé, 1919). During the last months of the war the federal government, anxious to prevent further coal shortages, commissioned several film companies to produce short documentaries on the continuing need for fuel conservation. Based on scripts and suggestions supplied by the CPI, these message-laden one-reelers, with such titles as *A Day in the Coal Fields* and *The Cost of Careless Firing*, circulated primarily in the nation's war plants. A more ambitious four-reel feature, *Keep the Home Fires Burning,* made under the auspices of the Fuel Administration, reached larger audiences following its official adoption by the American Defense Society, an influential patriotic group. Collaboration between the government and the film industry culminated in a six-week drive for coal conservation in the northeast United States at the end of 1918. During the entire campaign, filmmakers added promotional trailers to their weekly newsreels at the request of the Fuel Administration.[33]

The conservation films formed part of a larger group of wartime documentaries, through which the federal government sought to publicize the work of its agencies. Besides controlling the content of these productions, by 1918 CPI officials also censored commercial films through the denial of lucrative export licenses to any movies that dealt with crime, adultery, political corruption, strikes, or any other theme that, in Creel's view, might give foreign audiences "a false impression of American life."[34] The government's preferred vision of American society emphasized class harmony and popular faith in the workings of a beneficent democratic order.

As the war came to an end, Wilsonian bureaucrats put increasing pressure on production companies to assist postwar adjustment by condemning labor violence and all forms of radicalism in their films. According to David Niles, head of the Motion Picture Section of the Labor Department, movies with a labor theme should preach obedience to law and should portray the hero as "a strong, virile American, a believer of American institutions and ideals."[35] Niles urged directors and producers in November 1918 to consult him before making any new films dealing with labor problems or socialism. Failure to do so, he warned, might lead to federal censorship.

With government spokesmen controlling the channels of mass communication, opponents of the Wilsonian program had increasing difficulty in making their voices heard. Congress did much to suppress dissenting views by passing the Espionage Act of June 15, 1917, and its sequel, the Sedition Act of May 16, 1918. Under the Espionage Act, anyone who obstructed the recruitment and training of United States troops might be imprisoned for a maximum term of twenty years and fined as much as $10,000. The Sedition Act imposed the same heavy penalties on persons convicted of willfully using "any disloyal, profane, scurrilous, or abusive language" about the government, the Constitution, the flag, or the armed forces.[36] Despite the vagueness of such provisions and their obvious interference with First Amendment guarantees of free speech and a free press, the United States Supreme Court upheld the constitutionality of both measures. "[T]he character of every act depends upon the circumstances in which it is done," observed Justice Oliver Wendell Holmes for a unanimous Court in *Schenck v. United States* (1919):

> The most stringent protection of free speech would not protect a man in falsely shouting fire in a theatre and causing a panic. . . . The question in every case is whether the words used are used in such circumstances and are of such a nature as to create a clear and present danger that they will bring about the substantive evils that Congress has a right to prevent. . . . When a nation is at war many things that might be said in time of peace are such a hindrance to its effort that their utterance will not be endured so long as men fight and that no Court could regard them as protected by any constitutional right.[37]

The Justice Department zealously enforced both statutes, launching nearly two thousand prosecutions that yielded some nine hundred convictions. Postmaster General Albert S. Burleson aided the cause of repression by denying second-class mailing privileges to magazines that he deemed "subversive." The consequent rise in distribution costs drove many antiwar journals, including the prestigious *Masses,* out of business.[38] Yet dissidents often found new ways to reach their audiences, and their surviving wartime publications offer a valuable corrective to the mainstream propaganda of the Wilson administration.

One group that aroused the suspicion of federal authorities from the start was the African-American press corps. Although most black editors and journalists supported the war, they continued to protest all forms of racial discrimination and to demand federal enforcement of the civil rights guaranteed by the Thirteenth, Fourteenth, and Fifteenth Amendments. In this way they carried on the muckraking tradition throughout the war and pointed out for their readers the great gap that separated Wilson's democratic rhetoric from the treatment blacks actually received in the military forces and in the larger American society. African-American soldiers at first could look forward only to jobs as stevedores or common laborers in segregated units commanded by white officers. Few black officers existed, and the Army had no plans to train others. Outbreaks of racial violence were also increasing, especially in the southern states, where lynchings sometimes took the form of ghastly public burnings.[39]

To combat such wartime racism, many African-American newspapers followed the lead of the Chicago *Defender,* the nation's most successful black weekly. Under the direction of Robert S. Abbott, the *Defender* after 1910 became a powerful champion of the civil rights movement. Borrowing from the yellow journalism of William Randolph Hearst and Joseph Pulitzer, Abbott appealed to the black masses through the use of banner headlines, graphic illustrations, and the sensational reporting of racial incidents. A nine-point "platform" below the paper's masthead began with the uncompromising assertion: "American race prejudice must be destroyed."[40] The *Defender*'s militant stance attracted a growing list of subscribers, especially in the war years. Blacks from around the country wrote to Abbott to report local violations of civil rights and to ask for advice and assistance; the paper's staff provided legal aid on some occasions.

Not surprisingly, the *Defender* encountered intense opposition from white southerners in its efforts to reach black readers below the Mason-Dixon line. Some communities confiscated the papers before they could be delivered to a local agent; the Mississippi legislature passed "An act to make it a misdemeanor to print or circulate or publish appeals or presentations or arguments or suggestions favoring equality or marriage between the white and Negro race"; and disgruntled individuals complained to the Justice Department that the *Defender* was a tool of German propaganda and should be barred from the mails and suppressed.[41] In response to such actions, Abbott developed an alternative distribution network that relied on Pullman porters, dining-car waiters, and traveling black entertainers to carry the *Defender* through the southern states. The railroad employees dropped off their papers at designated sites on a regular basis, while the singers and musicians left complimentary copies at the concert halls where they performed. These tactics helped to increase individual subscriptions, despite continued acts of repression by local authorities.[42]

As Abbott found new ways to deliver his message, so did the NAACP and other black organizations engage in new forms of peaceful constitutional protest during the war. In response to a recent brutal lynching in Memphis, Tennessee, and a bloody race riot in East St. Louis, Illinois, James Weldon Johnson of the NAACP and a group of African-American ministers and other race leaders in New York City planned one of the first mass demonstrations of black people in the twentieth century. On Saturday afternoon, July 28, 1917, between 9,000 and 10,000 African-American men, women, and children marched down Fifth Avenue in a "silent protest parade." The women and children wore white; the men, bringing up the rear, dressed in dark clothes. Muffled drums added to the solemnity of the march and directed attention to the many banners that called for

federal protection of civil rights. "MR. PRESIDENT, WHY NOT MAKE AMER-
ICA SAFE FOR DEMOCRACY?" read one such banner.[43]

Along the line of the parade, black Boy Scouts handed out leaflets that
clearly described for onlookers the civil rights agenda of the marchers:

> We march because we want to make impossible a repetition of Waco,
> Memphis, and East St. Louis, by rousing the conscience of the coun-
> try and bringing the murderers of our brothers, sisters, and innocent
> children to justice.
>
> We march because we deem it a crime to be silent in the face of
> such barbaric acts.
>
> We march because we are thoroughly opposed to Jim-Crow Cars,
> Segregation, Discrimination, Disfranchisement, LYNCHING, and the
> host of evils that are forced on us. It is time that the Spirit of Christ
> should be manifested in the making and execution of laws.[44]

The dramatic silent demonstration received national press coverage, as its
sponsors had hoped. Like the advocates of a woman suffrage amendment,
whose own large-scale marches continued during the war, black civil rights
activists found an effective way of tying their demands for constitutional
protection to the democratic rhetoric of the wartime emergency.

Prodded by NAACP lobbyists and a militant black press, the Wilson
administration made some limited, but important, concessions. In May
1917 the War Department agreed to establish a separate training camp for
black officers in Des Moines, Iowa, from which 639 men received commissions the following October. Several black infantry regiments saw combat service, and members of the 93rd Division distinguished themselves
on the battlefields of France. For most black enlisted men, however, military service still meant some sort of manual labor, and black officers encountered racial slurs and contemptuous behavior from their white counterparts on both sides of the Atlantic. (Cartoonist Leslie Rogers of the
Chicago *Defender* once triggered a federal investigation of the paper by
picturing black troops fighting the Germans while white American soldiers
shot the black heroes in the back.)[45]

To improve the continued low morale of African Americans, Secretary
of War Baker appointed Emmett J. Scott in the fall of 1917 to be his
special assistant for matters affecting blacks. Scott, a former secretary of
Booker T. Washington, proved adept at public relations and worked to
ease racial tensions within the Army. At his suggestion, George Creel
agreed to the calling of a national conference of prominent African Ameri-

cans, especially journalists, to ensure "that Negro public opinion should be led along helpful lines rather than along lines that make for discontentment and unrest."[46] The conference, jointly sponsored by the War Department and the Committee on Public Information, met in Washington from June 19 to 21, 1918, and included thirty-one black editors. Government representatives listened to the complaints and suggestions of the African-American participants and remedied some grievances promptly. Ralph W. Tyler, an experienced newsman from Columbus, Ohio, for example, became the first regularly commissioned black war correspondent, with orders to cover military operations on the western front in France. In return, the editors pledged in a concluding statement to try to keep black public opinion "at the highest pitch, not simply of passive loyalty but of active, enthusiastic and self-sacrificing participation in the war."[47]

Whether influenced by appeals for wartime solidarity or by threats of federal prosecution, most editors did tone down their rhetoric during the last months of the war. Once the fighting ended, however, they renewed their campaign for equal rights with all their old aggressiveness. "We are returning from war!" wrote W. E. B. Du Bois in *The Crisis,* the NAACP's official magazine:

> THE CRISIS and tens of thousands of black men were drafted into a great struggle. . . . But today we return! . . . We stand again to look America squarely in the face and call a spade a spade. . . .
>
> Make way for Democracy! We saved it in France, and by the Great Jehovah, we will save it in the United States of America, or know the reason why.[48]

Like African-American journalists, Wobblies and socialists also faced repeated wartime investigations for their dissident views and actions. As members of the Industrial Workers of the World (IWW), the nation's only radical labor union, Wobblies threatened the war effort through their workplace militancy and support of disruptive strikes. Committed to industrial democracy and class struggle, the IWW worked to organize and empower migrant laborers, unskilled immigrants, and others ignored by the conservative American Federation of Labor. Wobbly tactics included "sabotage," a vague term that suggested violent acts of terrorism, although union spokesmen insisted that it generally meant no more in practice than sit-downs or slow-downs on the job. Still, the IWW's militant rhetoric played into the hands of its enemies. Consider, for example, the revolutionary thrust of a poem that appeared in the union's weekly newspaper, *Solidarity,* in August 1917. It commemorates the recent death of Frank Little, a Wobbly organizer, at the hands of local vigilantes:

> Traitor and demagogue,
> Wanton breeder of Discontent—
> That is what they call you—
> Those cowards, who condemn sabotage
> But hide themselves
> Not only behind masks and cloaks
> But behind all the armored positions
> Of property and prejudice and the law.
>
> . . . .
>
> Within our hearts is smoldering a heat
> Fiercer than that which parches fields and plains;
> Your memory, like a torch, shall light the flames
> Of Revolution. We shall not forget.[49]

Wilsonian propagandists used such imagery to stigmatize the Wobblies as dangerous firebrands and paid agents of the German government. Mary Roberts Rinehart, for one, portrayed sinister Wobbly characters in her wartime fiction. But the most extensive treatment of an imagined Wobbly conspiracy occurred in Zane Grey's western, *The Desert of Wheat* (1919). A popular author with two earlier best-selling novels to his credit, Grey constructed a fast-paced narrative in which patriotic Washington farmers battle a Wobbly gang bent on destroying the wheat crop before it can be harvested for shipment to Europe. "The I.W.W. do not intend to accomplish their treacherous aims by anything so feeble as speech," explains a prominent rancher; "they scorn the ballot box. They are against the war, and their method of making known their protest is by burning our grain, destroying our lumber, and blowing up freight-trains."[50] To stop such acts of sabotage, the farmers resort to speedy vigilante justice. They hang the captured gang leader from a railroad bridge, arrest all suspicious persons on sight, and deport them from the area in open cattle cars. Grey justified these actions by reminding his readers that frontiersmen had long used informal methods of law enforcement in emergency situations.

While the Justice Department did not officially countenance vigilantism, its own campaign against the IWW made a mockery of the Bill of Rights. On September 5, 1917, federal agents simultaneously raided IWW offices, union halls, and homes around the country, arrested 184 men and women, and illegally seized tons of evidence, from official records to private letters. This material formed the basis for several major prosecutions under the Espionage Act. The largest trial took place in Chicago, where 101 Wobblies—virtually the entire leadership group—faced charges of criminally conspiring to obstruct the war effort. The government's case rested on IWW theories about capitalism and the use of "direct action" by workers in industrial disputes, and prosecutors introduced statements made in Wobbly songs, stories, and poems to prove the conspiratorial nature of the group. After listening to five months of testimony and looking at hundreds of exhibits, a jury deliberated only one hour before finding all the defendants guilty. Wobbly Ralph Chaplin, one of the prisoners, believed that the wartime culture had a lot to do with the jury's quick verdict:

> The band in the lobby of the Federal Building was blaring "Hail Columbia" as we started for the North Side, and electric lights in the cheap movie theater across the street still alternated with "The Menace of the I.W.W." and "The Red Viper." That was old stuff also—old not only to us but to the jury, which had been listening to the patriotic airs and marching out to lunch under the damning sign for five full months.[51]

The imprisonment of the IWW's best organizers and publicists seriously weakened the organization, which faced further lawsuits brought by state authorities in the postwar years. But those behind bars, who regarded themselves as "class-war prisoners," remained adamant and continued their attacks on capitalism from their prison cells. Sometimes they opened new channels of communication with the outside world. Wobblies awaiting trial for months in Chicago's Cook County jail, for example, put out a weekly four-page newspaper called the *Can Opener*. Drawn in pencil, this production contained original articles, poems, and cartoons, including a version of the "sab-cat," a black cat that Wobbly artists had made a symbol of sabotage. Supporters raised funds for the local defense of arrested Wobblies by auctioning copies of the *Can Opener* at public meetings. In addition, prisoners serving long sentences wrote hundreds of essays, songs, and poems by the mid-1920s, many of which appeared in IWW defense bulletins and in such national magazines as *Outlook, Survey, The Liberator, New Masses,* and *The Nation*.[52]

Socialists likewise managed to continue their antiwar argument despite federal repression. The most extraordinary example of perseverance occurred in Milwaukee, where government officials tried every expedient to shut down the Milwaukee *Leader*, an influential socialist newspaper. After revoking the journal's mailing privileges, imprisoning its editor-in-chief, and seizing its files, Wilsonian authorities brought pressure to bear on its remaining advertisers. As Oscar Ameringer, who had joined the editorial staff during the crackdown, later recalled, "The Fuel Administration gave business concerns who advertised in the *Leader* to understand that if they didn't withdraw their patronage, they couldn't secure fuel. The Food Administration hinted to breweries who still employed the *Leader* as an advertising medium that unless they ceased they might experience difficulties in securing malt, hops and sugar."[53] Although advertising revenues dwindled, the paper continued to appear, thanks to contributions from supporters around the country as well as the loyal German-American community of Milwaukee.

The *Leader*'s survival was exceptional; most socialist journals had to suspend publication during the war. But intimidation and imprisonment did not silence the Socialist Party's antiwar spokespersons. Like their Wobbly counterparts, they turned courtroom trials into a form of popular theater through which they sought to indict the capitalist system and its legal underpinnings. "I believe in the Constitution," Eugene V. Debs assured a jury in September 1918 in answer to charges that he had violated the Espionage Act by delivering an allegedly seditious speech.

> In what I had to say . . . my purpose was to have the people understand something about the social system in which we live and to prepare them to change this system by perfectly peaceable and orderly means into what I, as a Socialist, conceive to be a real democracy. . . . Isn't it strange that we Socialists stand almost alone today in upholding and defending the Constitution of the United States? The revolutionary fathers who had been oppressed under king rule understood that free speech, a free press and the right of free assemblage by the people were fundamental principles in democratic government. . . . I would not, under any circumstances, suppress free speech. . . . If the Espionage Act finally stands, then the Constitution of the United States is dead.[54]

Unimpressed, the jury found Debs guilty, and he began serving a ten-year prison term at Atlanta Penitentiary in April 1919. The following year he entered the presidential race as the candidate of the Socialist Party and received over 900,000 votes. His campaign buttons read "Vote for Prisoner 9653."[55] For him, and for all others who did not conform to a wartime ideology of "100% Americanism," the Progressive vision of a majoritarian constitutional utopia turned into a recurring nightmare that lasted through most of the postwar decade.

Wilson's war socialism, on the other hand, did not survive. In the 1920s conservative politicians largely succeeded in curbing federal power and in reviving the kind of Constitution worship that had prevailed in the nineteenth century. As wartime economic controls were lifted, there developed a constitutional discourse that redirected attention to issues of limited government, traditional federalism, and state rights.

4

Constitutional Conservatism
in a Decade of Normalcy

It is as true now as when it was first uttered that the people are
governed best who are governed least. This country has not grown
to be the greatest, most powerful and happiest in the world through
the activities of boards or bureaus, but only through the efforts of its
virile, strong and intelligent people, with the assurance given by the
Constitution that they shall enjoy the fruits of their labor. . . . The
wise men who wrote the Constitution did not intend to place the
citizens in leading strings.

—CORDENIO A. SEVERANCE, PRESIDENT OF THE AMERICAN
BAR ASSOCIATION (1922)

If World War I enlarged federal regulatory power in unparalleled ways,
the postwar decade witnessed a kind of constitutional counterrevolution.
Some signs of disaffection were becoming evident even while the fighting
continued. Congress voiced increasing criticism of President Wilson's
"dictatorship" by the spring of 1918, and in June the Supreme Court reaffirmed constitutional limitations on federal power by striking down the
Keating-Owen Child Labor Act. That measure, the product of a decade of
agitation by congressional reformers, barred from interstate commerce
any goods coming from establishments that employed young workers
more than a prescribed number of hours each week. In *Hammer v.
Dagenhart,* Associate Justice William R. Day condemned the law for attempting to regulate the conditions of manufacture, an activity reserved
for state control by the Tenth Amendment. "[I]f Congress can thus regulate matters entrusted to local authority," Day warned, "all freedom of
commerce will be at an end, and the power of the states over local matters
may be eliminated, and thus our system of government be practically destroyed."[1] Although the law in question was not a war measure, its demise
suggested that the Court would take a hard look at any further efforts to
expand federal power once the fighting ended. "We may well wonder in
view of the precedents now established," wrote former Justice Charles Evans Hughes in 1920, "whether constitutional government as heretofore

maintained in this Republic could survive another great war even victoriously waged."[2]

Such sentiments echoed in the popular media during the immediate postwar period. The *Saturday Evening Post,* which reached more than two million subscribers weekly, had long been considered a reliable indicator of middle-class opinion. Editor George Horace Lorimer prided himself on his "frank Americanism," which appealed to legions of loyal readers schooled in the values of an older WASP America. So when Lorimer published a two-page editorial on the weakening of those values under a paternalistic wartime government, he could be sure of a large and respectful audience. "We have really been living in a semi-socialist state, and it has half ruined us," he asserted.

> To finish the job we have only to perfect our socialistic system of confiscatory taxation; to further increase our governmental activities in restraint of trade and liberty, so that nobody can do anything without a license and a passport and a permit; to continue our policy of regarding destructive alien reds as wronged innocents, and constructive American businessmen as suspicious characters. . . . If the United States is going to remain a going concern, it must discard this soft, lie-abed, sugar-teat socialism, this asking-papa-for-anything-you-want theory of life, and begin to practice self-denial and self-help.[3]

Lorimer considered this message so important that he turned to some of the *Post*'s best known authors for supporting pieces. Corra Harris supplied a short story set in an idyllic small town, whose inhabitants have grown too accustomed to government controls and handouts. Now that the emergency is over, she concludes, they must cast off such dependency and resume their normal lives as responsible and self-reliant adults. In a similar vein, the narrator in Booth Tarkington's "Saving the Country" consults in turn a railroad brakeman, a radical intellectual, and a Civil War veteran in an effort to determine the best approach to postwar reconstruction. Both the worker and the radical favor the continuance of some aspects of war socialism, such as heavy federal taxation of the wealthy, but the old veteran calls instead for a return to limited government, noting: "If you will study the liberty conceived by the fathers of this country you will find that it is a liberty for every man to seek and earn and keep, in peace and under protection of the law, whatever reward his energy and his intelligence can get for himself and his family." The narrator finds the veteran's reasoning persuasive, especially since the other two reconstructionists "seem to feel that they can scatter my earnings so much better than I can."[4]

Popular disillusionment with Wilsonian idealism and the flawed work of the Paris Peace Conference led to stunning Republican victories in the elections of 1920, in which successful presidential candidate Warren G. Harding pledged an end to "nostrums" and a return to "normalcy."[5] One important aspect of "normalcy" proved to be a revival of Constitution worship in the postwar decade. While this grew naturally out of the patriotic fervor of the wartime experience, it also responded to postwar fears of communist subversion. Americans had welcomed the Russian Revolution of March 1917 with its promise of liberal democracy, but the subsequent Bolshevik uprising in November threatened to destroy both the capitalist economy and the constitutional system that supported it. After the Third International announced a program of world revolution in March 1919, the "Red menace" became a subject of major concern in the American media. Plays, movies, and novels replaced German spies and Wobbly saboteurs with villainous agents of the Comintern, who plotted to overthrow democratic governments and to trample on the Bill of Rights. Collectively, these propaganda efforts helped to create a climate of continuing suspicion and paranoia that affected immigrants, workers, and racial minorities throughout the 1920s.[6]

George Kibbe Turner's novel *Red Friday* (1919) purported to show in some detail how a prolongation of Wilson's war socialism could lead to a Bolshevik takeover of the United States. Plangonev, "the brain of the proletariat," arrives in New York with a plan to bankrupt the nation and plunge society into anarchy. The war created an enormous public debt, he reasons, thanks in part to the wasteful practices of federal agencies: "But at bottom this great waste came certainly because it was popular—as it will be always—this general division of capital in war to all in a democracy—the small bourgeois as well as the large, the farmer, the proletariat—by wages, great profits, steady work for the workers." If costly government management of American industry could be maintained and expanded, along with the continued imposition of high income, inheritance, and corporation taxes on the wealthy, the capitalist economy would self-destruct in a few years. As Plangonev explains to his American confederate, a gullible Christian socialist, the key to Bolshevik success in the United States lies in the voting power of the masses: "The power creating public debt—of destroying and confiscating private property by popular vote. . . . The great, broad, safe highway to socialism . . . a revolution of perfect peace and quiet!"[7]

To carry out his scheme, Plangonev enlists the help of Stephen Black, a powerful Wall Street speculator who sees a chance to become fabulously wealthy by ruining the other great bourgeois financiers. Through Black's influence, Wall Street does not object to the permanent nationalization of the railroads, a popular measure that ensures the continuance of high operating costs and increased taxes to pay for them. Government competition for labor and materials soon depletes the revenues of private corporations, and Black reaps huge profits by selling stocks short on the New York exchange. By the spring of 1922 private industry is in a shambles; most stocks are worthless; federal and local governments have taken over many more businesses; the public debt continues to rise; and taxes, having consumed the capital of the very rich, are beginning to affect the rest of society. Class warfare seems imminent, as farmers and small capitalists organize an Anti-Confiscation League to resist further government exactions, and city workers, stirred up by Plangonev's agents, grow angry and violent in the face of prospective wage cuts and unemployment.

Plangonev plans to destroy the remaining bond market and force the nation into universal bankruptcy on "Red Friday," but his infatuation with Black's daughter wrecks his scheme. At the eleventh hour Charlotte flatters the Russian into showing her written proof of the conspiracy, then kills him, reveals the plot to the police, and saves the country from impending catastrophe: "There was but one thing concededly that did or could release the nation from its danger—a sudden general emotional impulse; a great appeal to the traditional emotions of the people, driving them to action. For every one well knows to-day it was just this outburst of Plangonev's detested and, I believe, always feared emotions of property—the emotions of family and nation and religion—which finally overthrew the Russian and his plans." Chastened by their narrow brush with anarchy, all classes now cooperate to hasten the return of "old conditions in the supremely individualistic United States."[8]

Critics had few kind words for *Red Friday.* "It deserves to be bound with those fairy stories for the feebleminded which described what took place when a million Huns invaded New York," commented a reviewer in *The Dial.*[9] Even those who approved Turner's anticommunist message found fault with his purple prose and wooden characters. Despite its obvious flaws, however, *Red Friday* offered a more compelling picture of communist subversion than any competing narratives, which included such plays as Thomas Dixon's *The Red Dawn* and Booth Tarkington's *Poldekin,* along with a string of alarmist movies with such titles as *Bolshevism on Trial, The World Aflame, Look Out for the Snake, Common Property, The*

Red Virgin, and *The Face at Your Window.*[10] Turner had been a prominent muckraking journalist before the war and still understood the concerns of middle-class readers. The themes that he developed in *Red Friday* responded to genuine popular anxieties: fear of radical labor and foreign-born agitators; suspicion of big government and Wilsonian regulatory programs; and alarm at the decline of traditional moral values. These issues continued to attract public attention throughout the 1920s, long after the Red Scare of 1919–1920 had run its course. And equally prescient was Turner's implied call for a revival of "sound" constitutional government, which would protect the personal and property rights of all citizens against invasion by the state.

Several organizations had already begun to mobilize public support for such a constitutional revival by the time of *Red Friday*'s publication. As early as 1916 the Sons of the American Revolution proposed to make "Constitution Day"—September 17, the day on which the Philadelphia Convention of 1787 had completed its work and adjourned—a national holiday. The idea first attracted widespread attention in 1919, when the National Security League, the American Defense Society, the Boy Scouts of America, and other patriotic groups joined in a nationwide campaign to celebrate the anniversary with appropriate speeches and other ceremonies. Although Congress declined to create another official holiday, the popular observance of Constitution Day drew large crowds until the late 1920s. When attendance at these public ceremonies started to dwindle, the new medium of radio brought the message of Constitution Day orators to mass audiences in homes across the country.[11]

That message tended to be deeply conservative, as most speakers extolled the Constitution in such reverential terms as "our holy of holies, an instrument of sacred import" and "the best and only effective antidote against bolshevism and the other alien cults which are attacking the foundations of our institutions."[12] Congress furthered the process of Constitution worship by allocating $12,000 in 1922 for the storage and public exhibition of the document and its companion, the Declaration of Independence, at the Library of Congress. (The two artifacts had previously lain in a steel vault at the State Department.) On February 28, 1924, President and Mrs. Calvin Coolidge opened the "Shrine of the Constitution and the Declaration of Independence" to the public after a formal dedication ceremony. Framed in bronze and illuminated by soft incandescent lamps, the fragile documents invited the veneration of the masses.[13]

In a related move, the American Bar Association and the National Education Association spearheaded an aggressive campaign to instill a proper respect for the Constitution in the nation's youth. "The schools of America must save America!" reported a special committee of the ABA in 1922. "The schools of America should no more consider graduating a student who lacks faith in our government than a school of theology should consider graduating a minister who lacks faith in God."[14] Prodded by the ABA, the NEA, and the National Security League, twenty-three states passed laws by 1923 that required constitutional instruction in their public and private schools; an additional twenty states enacted such legislation by 1931.[15]

The new civics courses and revamped offerings in American history and "social sciences" sought, above all, to promote "patriotism" and loyalty to established institutions. Proponents of constitutional orthodoxy borrowed from the propaganda techniques of World War I by denouncing "subversive" textbooks and attacking nonconformist teachers. The American Legion urged school boards to adopt its own model history text, Charles F. Horne's *The Story of Our American People,* which had been commissioned to "preach on every page a vivid love of America and preserve the old patriotic legends." Although few schools in fact adopted Horne's book, its pietistic approach to the nation's past differed only in degree from that endorsed by all too many educators in the 1920s.[16]

For example, in their pioneering sociological study of "Middletown"—postwar Muncie, Indiana—Robert and Helen Lynd found evidence of a strong conservative bias in the history and civics courses being offered in the local schools. The State Manual for Elementary Schools instructed teachers that "[t]he right of revolution does not exist in America."

> We had a revolution 140 years ago which made it unnecessary to have any other revolution in this country. . . . No man can be a sound and sterling American who believes that force is necessary to effectuate the popular will. . . . Americanism . . . emphatically means . . . that we have repudiated the old European methods of settling domestic questions, and have evolved for ourselves machinery by which revolution as a method of changing our life is outgrown, abandoned, outlawed.

High school instructors received a similar directive to emphasize "respect for law" and for "the fundamental institutions of society: private property, guaranteed privileges, contracts, personal liberty, [and the] right to establish private enterprises."[17]

Students apparently absorbed the conservative message with little difficulty. On a questionnaire administered to 556 juniors and seniors in Middletown's high school, 70 percent of the boys and 75 percent of the girls answered "false" to the statement "A citizen of the United States should be allowed to say anything he pleases, even to advocate violent revolution, if he does no violent act itself." And an equally impressive majority—70 percent of the boys, 62 percent of the girls—rejected any hint of a redistribution of wealth: "The fact that some men have so much more money than others shows that there is an unjust condition in this country which ought to be changed."[18]

The most widely read constitutional study of the postwar decade likewise abandoned critical analysis in favor of flag-waving nostalgia. James M. Beck's *The Constitution of the United States* reflected the temper of its time as effectively as Beard's earlier work had embodied the spirit of prewar Progressivism. Beck, a conservative Republican lawyer who served as solicitor general from 1921 to 1925, praised the Constitution in nineteenth-century terms for establishing a limited government that protected property and other individual rights from the assaults of democratic majorities. While he devoted most of his book to a worshipful recreation of the work of the Federal Convention, his concluding chapters assumed a darker tone as he contemplated the state of "constitutional morality" in contemporary America.

In "A Rising or a Setting Sun?" he wonders how Benjamin Franklin would react to the changed political conditions of 1924. Undoubtedly, Franklin would be impressed by the enormous technological changes that have occurred since the eighteenth century. But he would soon discover that such material "progress" has been accompanied by widespread corruption and lawlessness, the decay of political leadership, and dangerous deviations from the constitutional principles of the Founding Fathers. In specific terms, Beck denounced the centralizing tendencies of recent federal regulation, which threatened the "substantial destruction of the rights of the States"; deplored the inadequate protection given to property rights, which "have been impaired by many socialistic measures"; and reserved his strongest condemnation for the federal tax system: "The adequate defense of the Constitution against the spirit of Socialism ended with the progressive income tax, whose excessive graded taxes often effectually confiscate the wealth of the few for the benefit of the many." Because of popular apathy and indifference to such violations of basic principles, he warned, "the Constitution is in graver danger today than at any other time in the history of America."[19]

Yet responsible government might still be preserved if the masses redis-covered and embraced the constitutional vision of the Fathers. For Beck, constitutional conservatism was almost a matter of religious faith, and he liberally sprinkled his text with uplifting metaphors for his readers. At vari-ous times he described the Constitution as a "Gothic cathedral," an "an-chor" that "holds the ship of state to its ancient moorings," a "great light-house," a "rudder," and a "temple of Liberty and Justice."[20] But his most memorable imagery occurred in a passage in which he tried to explain how a fixed Constitution, grounded in immutable moral values, could never-theless adapt to changing social needs:

> The Constitution is neither, on the one hand, a Gibraltar rock, which wholly resists the ceaseless washing of time or circumstance, nor is it, on the other hand, a sandy beach, which is slowly destroyed by the erosion of the waves. It is rather to be likened to a floating dock, which, while firmly attached to its moorings, and not therefore [at] the caprice of the waves, yet rises and falls with the tide of time and circumstance.[21]

Although some liberal reviewers took wicked delight in deconstructing such ponderous pronouncements—"His idea seems to be that while [the Constitution] does not move forward or backward, it jiggles up and down," commented Harvard law professor Thomas Reed Powell[22]—Beck's book quickly achieved wide circulation and popularity. Based at first on three lectures that he delivered at Gray's Inn, London, in 1922, the work underwent substantial revision and expansion in 1924, by which time it had already gone through several printings. Andrew W. Mellon, secretary of the Treasury, subsidized the distribution of two thousand cop-ies to libraries around the country; Eldridge R. Johnson, president of the Victor Talking Machine Company, provided an additional ten thousand copies for schools and libraries; and Beck's publisher brought out an abridged version in 1927 for use in elementary schools. By September 1928 over 50,000 copies of *The Constitution of the United States* had been sold, including French and German editions.[23]

As a constitutional conservative, Beck strongly opposed federal efforts to enforce the Eighteenth Amendment. That amendment, which prohib-ited the "manufacture, sale, or transportation of intoxicating liquors" within the United States, represented the most significant expansion of federal power in the postwar decade. A Progressive reform that achieved some popular success at the state level in the early twentieth century, prohibition became a matter of national concern during World War I when Congress forbade the manufacture of distilled spirits as a food control measure. By December 1917 wartime patriotism, inflamed by the Anti-Saloon League's attacks on German brewers and distillers, led to the passage of a prohibition amendment that thirty-six state legislatures quickly ratified. The "noble experiment" went into operation on January 16, 1920, pursuant to the terms of an enforcement measure—the Volstead Act— that vested administration of the law in a special unit of the Treasury Department.[24]

From the beginning, Beck and other strict constructionists condemned the new legislation on two grounds: it violated the basic freedom of the individual and it infringed on the lawful police power of the states. "That the federal government should prescribe to the peoples of the States what they should drink would have been unthinkable to the framers of the Constitution," wrote Beck in 1919.[25] Although the Eighteenth Amendment might claim to be part of the Constitution in a formal sense, it lacked true legitimacy, he insisted; Congress might properly refuse to allocate funds for its implementation. Other opponents went even further and called for a new amendment to repeal the "unconstitutional" prohibition measure.

Leading the fight for repeal throughout the 1920s was the Association Against the Prohibition Amendment (AAPA), headed by Captain William H. Stayton, a lobbyist for the Navy League. Stayton had helped to organize the publicity campaign for military preparedness before World War I and now turned his propaganda skills to the cause of constitutional reform. The AAPA struggled along on a shoestring budget until 1926, when several wealthy businessmen, including Pierre Du Pont and John J. Raskob, joined the movement. Thereafter ample funds were available for disseminating the repeal message, and the results were impressive. According to the AAPA's annual report for 1930:

> [S]ix hundred millions of copies of newspapers, containing conspicuous publication of our news, were read . . . 153,617,704 copies of magazines and periodicals containing articles and editorials attacking prohibition have been read . . . more than 4,000,000 copies of books, pamphlets, reports, reprints, letters and leaflets were distributed from our office in 1930 . . . [and] with the cooperation and consent of the newspapers and artists concerned, a collection of cartoons attacking and ridiculing prohibition was published and widely distributed.[26]

Cartoonists in fact found prohibition an irresistible subject for satire. Rollin Kirby of the New York *World* created the most popular symbol of the "dry decade" in "Mr. Dry," a stern puritanical figure dressed in nineteenth-century style, with a long swallow-tailed coat, top hat, black gloves, and a tightly furled umbrella. In one of his earliest appearances in 1920, Mr. Dry leads an unseen audience in singing "My Country, 'Tis of Thee!" On the lecture platform beside him stands a table holding a huge seltzer bottle filled with water. The image brilliantly conveys the loss of personal freedom that accompanied prohibition, and suggests the cultural vision that inspired its supporters.[27] Prohibitionists tended to be old-stock Americans, fearful of an unruly immigrant workforce and committed to the preservation of the Protestant republic and traditional values. Their opponents, on the other hand, preached resistance to government tyranny, itself a venerable American tradition. Thus, the masthead of *The Minute Man,* a monthly publication of the AAPA's New Jersey branch, quoted the Fourth Amendment against "unreasonable searches and seizures," and the editor often printed extracts from Beck's book on the Constitution.[28]

Official corruption under the Volstead Act became an increasingly popular topic for cartoonists as the decade progressed. Enforcement of the law remained spotty at best. A sizable minority, especially in big cities, always opposed it; the Prohibition Unit lacked manpower and money; and the continuing public demand for bootleg liquor encouraged the rise of powerful criminal gangs led by such notorious figures as "Scarface" Al Capone in Chicago and Dutch Schultz in New York. Often local police and politicians connived with the bootleggers in return for handsome payoffs. Growing popular cynicism over such reported venality found effective representation in Clive Weed's cartoon, "The National Gesture," which appeared in the humor magazine *Judge* in 1926. Weed pictured a string of respectable enforcement officials—Prohibition Agent, Police Officer, Politician, Magistrate, Petty Official, Clerk—standing as in a police lineup. Each man slyly holds one hand out behind him, ready to receive an expected bribe. The hypocrisy that so often characterized the enforcement process attracted many other cartoonists, including Daniel Fitzpatrick, whose "Samuel" showed the familiar image of Uncle Sam with a flask of whiskey protruding from his back pocket.[29] Cartoonists who supported prohibition approached the enforcement issue from a more sober perspective that drew upon the Constitution worship of the "Dry Decade." Typical was a 1922 cartoon that pictured "The Constitution" as a massive seawall protecting the American people from the raging waters of "Lawlessness" and "Anarchy." A middle-aged "Law Abiding Citizen" is shown atop a ladder, hammering holes in one large block marked "18th Amendment." Above him a speech balloon declares, "I'll just break this one!" As water spurts from several openings, the caption below points the moral: "But It Weakens the Whole Structure."[30]

After the Wall Street crash of 1929, the repeal movement gained increased support, as proponents urged that legalizing the manufacture and sale of liquor would insure needed federal tax revenue during a period of economic depression. Several new organizations, including the Voluntary Committee of Lawyers, sprang up to aid the AAPA's repeal campaign. Headed by Joseph Hodges Choate, Jr., and other eminent bar leaders, the lawyers' committee pledged to "preserve the spirit of the Constitution of the United States" and, more immediately, "to bring about the repeal of the Eighteenth Amendment."[31] Through the lobbying efforts of its members, the American Bar Association went on record in 1930 as favoring repeal, and state and local bar associations around the country passed similar antiprohibition resolutions. When Congress at last submitted a repeal amendment to the states in February 1933, it stipulated that ratification should be carried out through special state conventions—the first time such a procedure had been used. To prevent confusion and delay, the lawyers' committee prepared a model legislative measure to guide state lawmakers in setting up such conventions. As a result, the ratification process proceeded smoothly, and the Twenty-first Amendment went into effect in less than a year, on December 5, 1933. "[T]he American people have not yet lost the spirit of individualism," Beck rejoiced.[32]

Although Beck's constitutional philosophy commanded wide respect in the 1920s, not all conservatives wanted to reduce federal power to the extent that Beck prescribed in his writings. More responsive to the needs of the postwar business community were the policies espoused by Herbert Hoover as secretary of commerce under Harding and Coolidge. An advocate of what he termed "associational activities," Hoover sought to preserve the profitable collaboration between industry and government that had characterized the war years. He urged businesses to form trade associations and to develop codes of fair practice that would eliminate wasteful competition, increase productivity, and lower the cost of standardized products to consumers. While the Commerce Department actively aided the trade association movement by hosting periodic conferences and providing valuable data on market conditions at home and abroad, economic planning and policy-making remained in private hands. Hoover hoped that federal sponsorship of such corporate self-regulation would benefit all sectors of society, including the workforce. Like the efficiency-minded Progressives of the prewar years, he called for a partnership between capital and labor to be built on profit-sharing and the settlement of disputes through orderly mediation procedures. Publicists who shared these objectives hailed the 1920s as a "New Era" of economic democracy, in which stockholders, workers, and consumers would all share equitably in the profits of assembly-line technology.[33]

Hoover's "New Era" thinking found ready acceptance in business circles. Trade associations flourished; companies introduced baseball teams, group insurance plans, stock options for workers, and other manifestations of welfare capitalism; and the Department of Commerce became one of the largest and most powerful agencies in Washington, despite Hoover's professed abhorrence of bureaucratic statism. The Supreme Court ruled in 1925 that businesses might exchange valuable pricing and other information through trade associations without violating the antitrust laws, and the nation witnessed a new wave of corporate mergers and consolidations that abolished thousands of firms in the name of greater efficiency.[34] Although the Federal Trade Commission and other prewar regulatory bodies continued to function, their powers tended to be circumscribed by unsympathetic administrators and judges.

The most dramatic instance of deregulation occurred in 1923, when the Supreme Court struck down a congressional law that established a minimum wage for women workers in the District of Columbia. Ignoring such Progressive precedents as *Muller v. Oregon,* a majority of five Justices held that the government could not interfere with an individual's right to "liberty of contract." The case—*Adkins v. Children's Hospital*—signaled a return to the formalistic and abstract style of judicial reasoning that had characterized the late nineteenth century, for Justice George Sutherland dismissed the plaintiff's introduction of sociological data and a "Brandeis brief" as irrelevant: "We have been furnished with a large number of printed opinions approving the policy of the minimum wage, and our own reading has disclosed a large number to the contrary. These are all proper enough for the consideration of law-making bodies . . . but they reflect no legitimate light upon the question of [the law's] validity."[35] In other situations the Court consistently protected the property rights of employers against the threat of strikes, boycotts, and other forms of worker militancy.[36]

The values of a business civilization, which thus influenced the constitutional law of the 1920s, affected the rest of American culture as well. At a time when mass production and relatively high wages meant a rising standard of living for most Americans, the reform impulse languished. The constitutional fiction of the Progressive era found no echo in the postwar decade, as popular novelists again celebrated the virtues of rugged individualism and private control of the economy. The most uncompromising defense of a free market ideology occurred in Garet Garrett's novel *The Driver* (1922), which ran as a serial in the *Saturday Evening Post* before its publication in book form by a major commercial publisher.[37]

Henry Galt, Garrett's hero, is an archetypal self-made man who uses his administrative and financial skills to transform a bankrupt railroad into the centerpiece of a powerful business empire. He cares little for profit-making as such and finds his chief satisfaction in creating great enterprises to serve the public's needs:

> Galt's passion was to build. . . . To see a thing in the mind's eyes as a vision in space, to give orders, then in a little while to go and find it there, existing durably in three dimensions,—that was power! . . . He did not begin by saying: "How can the Great Midwestern be made to earn a profit of ten per cent.?" No. He said: "How shall we make the Great Midwestern system the greatest transportation machine in the world?" If that were done the profit would mind itself.[38]

Galt's organizing efforts bring him into conflict with other Wall Street speculators, who plot to destroy him. They inflame public opinion against the Galt Railroad System by claiming that it is a dangerous and evil trust, "oppressive, arrogant, holding power of life and death over helpless communities."[39] For political reasons, the federal government initiates antitrust proceedings against Galt, and a congressional investigating committee summons him to testify about his business methods. The members of the committee, who know nothing of finance, pander shamelessly to the fears of "the multitude" and rely on the services of their counsel, a devious Jewish lawyer who once represented the very corporate interests he now purports to condemn.[40]

Under questioning, Galt admits that his railroad absorbed several competing railroads, but justifies the process in terms of efficiency and improved public service. Describing himself as a "farmer" who fertilizes the country with his money, he extols the productive uses of capital: "I sow and reap, improve the soil and keep adding new machinery and buildings." Public opinion veers sharply in his favor after he outlines a plan for preventing future economic crises through enlightened business practices:

> "It is my idea," said Galt, "that the financial institutions of the country,—I mean the insurance companies and the banks,—instead of

lending themselves out of funds in times of high prosperity ought then to build up great reserves of capital to be loaned out in hard times. . . . Every financial institution that I have anything to do with will be governed by that idea, and the Great Midwestern properties, while I run them, will decrease their capital expenditures as prices rise and increase them as prices fall. When we show them the whole trick and how it pays everybody will do it. We won't have any more depressions. . . . We won't have any more unemployment. In a country like this unemployment is economic lunacy."[41]

Galt's triumphant vindication of his practices and profits reverses the regulatory assumptions that governed Progressive fiction. Muckraking novelists in the prewar years had denounced the irresponsible power wielded by giant corporations, and called for expanded federal control under the antitrust laws. They believed strongly in the reasonableness of the American masses and the integrity of the democratic political process. Garrett, responding to the changed temper of the 1920s, rejected all of these tenets of the Progressive faith. Public opinion in *The Driver* is irrational and easily manipulable by politicians and the media; those in public office are self-serving demagogues who lack the managerial skills needed to run the country; and monopolists like Galt are true social benefactors, to whom the direction of the economy might safely be entrusted.

While Garrett condemns all government interference in the operations of the marketplace, he fails to provide a convincing rationale for his position within the framework established by his story line. At one point he raises the key issue quite specifically: if, in times of severe economic depression, Henry Galt would relieve unemployment by borrowing money and putting men to work on his railroad, why might not the federal government achieve the same objective by borrowing money and putting men to work on public construction projects? Garrett gives no satisfactory answer, beyond his hero's terse comment: "[I]t isn't the government's business."[42] Nor does he explain why bankers and insurance executives in a competitive economy would voluntarily change their credit policies to accommodate Galt's utopian vision. With such unresolved contradictions and an often wooden style, *The Driver* drew mixed reviews from the critics, and Garrett abandoned polemical fiction a few years later to become a widely read conservative commentator on political and economic subjects.[43]

Unlike *The Driver*, which ignored the constitutional rights of workers, Arthur Train's novel *The Needle's Eye* (1924) focused on the legitimacy of union organizing efforts in an era of business domination. John Graham, Train's hero, is a fourth-generation member of a powerful New York banking family. Like the protagonists of many Progressive novels, John feels an obligation to use his wealth in socially responsible ways, and even sympathizes to some extent with the socialist ideas advanced by his sweetheart Rhoda. But he also finds much merit in his father's defense of the status quo: "Civilization is like a big ocean liner, full of the most complicated machinery, so delicate that the slightest disarrangement will throw it all out of kilter. Maybe a better world could have been devised; maybe human nature could have been improved; maybe a more equable industrial system invented; but we're on the ship, we've started on the voyage, and if we stop in mid-ocean and try to rebuild it, alter our machinery or change the crew, we'll never get to port."[44]

When labor violence threatens to engulf the coal mines owned by Graham & Co. in West Virginia, John travels to the scene in a last-minute attempt to avert bloodshed. He learns that "Graham City" has always been a model company town, in which workers have enjoyed subsidized housing, medical services, recreational facilities, and other benefits associated with welfare capitalism at its best. No serious problems arose until outside agitators from the United Mine Workers launched an aggressive campaign to unionize the few remaining nonunion counties in West Virginia. These labor radicals, in John's view, are working toward a revolutionary takeover of the nation's industries: "As I look at it, . . . the United Mine Workers want to turn the coal industry into a monopoly under union control, capable of making its own price to the public and exerting a political leverage so powerful that our government will cease to operate as a democracy, the revolution being wrought not by violence but through the control of government by the basic industries in turn controlled by unions, or 'blocs,' or minorities." While he agrees that workers have a right to unionize and to bargain collectively, he rejects any talk of a closed shop: "A man must be free to work where and as he pleases. That is the spirit of the Constitution."[45]

From the worker's side, of course, the question of rights may lead to quite different conclusions. To Train's credit, he does not trivialize the prolabor argument, which he entrusts to Dr. Erasmus Dominick, the philosophic scientist who accompanies John on his mission to the coalfields. Dominick distinguishes between the "political liberty" of the individual, which the Constitution protects, and "industrial liberty," which unionized workers are now trying to secure from the giant corporations that employ them in the twentieth century. No liberty or property right is inviolable, he insists: "For example, we are taxed without our consent, we are drafted to serve in war, and we are hedged about with all sorts of restrictions and prohibitions at the whim of the majority—simply in order that greater liberty—the greater good for the greater number—may be attained."[46] Picketing and the closed shop may infringe on the traditional property rights claimed by employers, but they are necessary steps toward the creation of a modern industrial government that will better reflect the political power of working-class voters. Without such protection for labor, the Graham mining properties represent a "feudal island in a sea of democracy."[47]

Unpersuaded by Dominick's views, John refuses to sign any union contract that includes a closed shop provision. Violence quickly develops, as striking miners attack a group of loyal workers whose shift has just ended. In the course of the fighting a union gunman kills Dominick and wounds John. Only the eventual arrival of federal troops puts an end to the disturbance, which has assumed the character of a large-scale civil war. There are no winners. The company has suffered severe damage to its property and must suspend operations for a time; the workers have lost their jobs and the attendant benefits they once enjoyed under the company's welfare program; and the antagonistic interests of capital and labor remain unreconciled. In the hands of a Progressive novelist, John would now embrace some mildly socialistic remedy to empower his workers and restore class harmony. Instead, Train's hero reaffirms his faith in the private ownership of property and finds a solution to industrial conflict in improved management policies.

Deploring the evils of absentee ownership and a depersonalized workplace, he calls for the settlement of worker complaints through face-to-face encounters with understanding supervisors on a daily basis: "Get the right sort of men on the job as superintendents and foremen. To the worker the foreman *was* the corporation. You could introduce all the profit-sharing and welfare schemes in the world and they would amount to nothing if your foreman called the men under him by vile names."[48] Such old-fashioned paternalism excludes the possibility of any real bargaining power for workers, and Train makes it clear that he considers the polyglot industrial workforce unfit to exercise such power. As in his wartime fiction, he displays a condescending attitude toward those not of Anglo-Saxon stock, including many of the striking miners: "Terrible men these! . . . Reds, booze-fighters, profaners of Christ, squirting obscenity through their teeth with their tobacco juice; Sabbath breakers, liars, adulterers; . . . men . . . who cling blindly to one another and to the union. Sheep!"[49]

The union organizers in *The Needle's Eye* likewise have their roots in the propaganda novels of World War I. Like the villainous German spies, Wobblies, and pacifists of those earlier works, the UMW representatives are un-American types who preach class warfare and incite ignorant workers to attack constitutionally protected property. Since existing laws and institutions offer sufficient encouragement to peaceful labor protest, however, no further reforms are necessary to offset the influence of individual extremists within the labor movement. Compassionate corporate officials can alleviate any genuine source of worker discontent, and John vows to continue his fight for better working conditions by staying on as a minority director in his reorganized company.

While Train's apologia for an updated "gospel of wealth" received only faint praise from most reviewers,[50] he touched on one of the central preoccupations of New Era culture through his incidental condemnation of postwar materialism. Other writers across the ideological spectrum explored at greater length the rise of a mechanistic consumer society and its effects on traditional American ideals. Novelist Sinclair Lewis satirized small-town boosterism and conformity in his classic *Babbitt* (1922); Elmer Rice's expressionistic play, *The Adding Machine* (1923), depicted the loss of individual character and initiative in an automated world; and poet Edgar Lee Masters, in *Domesday Book* (1920) and *The Fate of the Jury* (1929), condemned the business civilization of the 1920s for creating a "vast mediocrity of materialism":

> There is America the land, but no
> America as people, or as soul.
> For dinner buckets and prosperity
> Are appetites, not soul.[51]

But these criticisms, comparable to those found in many other works, addressed mainly quality-of-life issues. They did not challenge political institutions or call for any fundamental changes in the legal system. The shift away from narratives of social justice and constitutional change appeared most strikingly in the movies. A substantial number of prewar films had dealt with controversial social problems and given audiences varying perspectives on child labor regulation, woman suffrage, prohibition, strikes, and similar subjects.[52] As the major studios consolidated their power, however, smaller competitors, including some worker-owned companies, had to shut down in the face of rising production costs and monopolistic booking practices.

The more standardized commercial films of the 1920s avoided political topics and focused on problems of individual adjustment to the altered mores that accompanied postwar prosperity. In scores of movies with such titles as *Forbidden Fruit, Old Wives for New, The Merry Widow, Husbands for Rent,* and *Our Dancing Daughters,* characters wrestled with the breakdown of traditional norms governing sex and marital relations. Moviemakers preached a new consumer ethic that encouraged accommodation to changing mores, while averting the threat of state or federal censorship by continuing to pay lip service to older legal and moral standards.[53] The accommodationist formula figured as well in a few films of worker discontent, including King Vidor's impressive *The Crowd* (MGM, 1928).

John, Vidor's young hero, is a white-collar employee who dreams of becoming president of the United States but finds upward mobility impossible to achieve in a world of meaningless routine and bureaucratic anonymity. Through a combination of personal weakness and misfortune, he sinks lower and lower in the economic scale until at last he welcomes the tenuous security offered by a demeaning job as a costumed clown, whose signboard advertises a local eatery: "I am happy because I always eat at Schneider's Grill."[54] Significantly, John and his fellow employees do not rebel against their dehumanized working environment or seek relief from unemployment through state intervention. Since the days of the Red Scare, filmmakers had depicted strikes and other militant labor actions as "un-American," if not Bolshevistic, and studio heads, who espoused their own version of welfare capitalism, vigorously opposed all efforts to unionize their studios during the decade.[55]

But New Era conservatism made its most enduring mark on popular culture through the comics section of the daily newspaper. On August 5, 1924, the *New York Daily News,* one of the nation's leading tabloids, introduced the first ideological comic strip, *Little Orphan Annie.* Created by cartoonist Harold Gray, a fervent advocate of "free market capitalism," *Annie* proved an instant hit with adult readers and children alike, and eventually appeared in more than 300 other newspapers. For more than forty years, until his death in 1968, Gray attacked big government, socialists, communists, labor unions, bleeding-heart liberals, income taxes, and other threats to entrepreneurial liberty through his drawings and accompanying dialogue. And in "Daddy" Oliver Warbucks, Annie's patron and protector, he created a durable symbol of rugged individualism who carried the business values of the 1920s into the alien worlds of the New Deal and the Great Society.[56]

As the "prosperity decade" drew to a close, even some on the left acknowledged the positive contributions made by the new industrial order. "Big business in America," commented the veteran muckraker Lincoln Steffens, "is producing what the Socialists held up as their goal; food, shelter, and clothing for all. You will see it during the Hoover administration."[57] But most liberals and radicals found little to applaud in an era characterized by red-baiting, union-busting, deregulation, and attacks on racial and religious minorities.

To be sure, the constitutional record was not entirely one-sided. A handful of Progressive lawmakers continued to press for new federal programs in the 1920s, and Congress occasionally responded. The Sheppard-Towner Act of 1921, for example, allocated federal funds to aid the states in infant and maternity welfare activities. Congressional legislation also created two new regulatory agencies—a Federal Power Commission and a Federal Radio Commission. But these were minor victories compared to the achievements of the prewar years.[58] Progressivism's waning influence may be clearly seen in the unsuccessful campaigns for child labor and antilynching legislation that took place during the "New Era."

Federal regulation of child labor, as we have noted, was a major concern of Albert Beveridge and other prewar reformers. When the Supreme Court struck down the First Child Labor Act in 1918, its narrow 5–4 ruling provoked an immediate public outcry. A majority of influential newspapers condemned the *Hammer v. Dagenhart* decision, which the Boston *Evening Transcript* characterized as "a national charter of injustice" and the Springfield *Republican* termed "a blow at social reform and economic justice which must be deeply deplored."[59] Art Young well captured the mood of popular indignation in a biting cartoon that he prepared for the *Liberator*, the socialist journal that had replaced the *Masses*. Young's drawing shows a corpulent manufacturer in suit and tie addressing a crowd of ragged children before the walls of a prisonlike factory building. The caption reads "The Boss: 'Now, children, all together, three cheers for the Supreme Court!'"[60]

With strong public support, Congress quickly passed another child labor bill that became law on February 24, 1919. The new measure imposed a heavy tax on the profits of factories, mines, and mills that employed child workers. When a test case reached the Supreme Court in

1922, the Justices held that this law, too, was unconstitutional. For an eight-man majority, Chief Justice William Howard Taft argued that the tax in question was really a penalty assessed against local businesses as part of an impermissible scheme of federal regulation. Disregarding several important precedents that had upheld such use of the federal taxing power, Taft cautioned:

> Grant the validity of this law, and all that Congress would need to do hereafter, in seeking to take over to its control any one of the great number of subjects of public interest, jurisdiction of which the states have never parted with, and which are reserved to them by the Tenth Amendment, would be to enact a detailed measure of complete regulation of the subject and enforce it by a so-called tax upon departures from it. To give such magic to the word "tax" would be to break down all constitutional limitation of the power of Congress and completely wipe out the sovereignty of the States.[61]

Although the decision in *Bailey v. Drexel Furniture Company* foreclosed any possibility of regulating child labor through ordinary legislation, it aroused little protest in the press. The Court had upheld "a good political principle at the temporary expense of a good social cause," declared a representative editorial in the St. Louis *Post-Dispatch;* the *New York Times* observed, "[T]he Supreme Court merely declares invalid unsound legislation, and refers the subject of child labor to the states, where it properly belongs."[62] Wisconsin Senator Robert M. LaFollette did attempt to revive the Progressive spirit by proposing a constitutional amendment to curb the Court's review power over congressional legislation, but LaFollette's third-party movement suffered a crushing defeat in the elections of 1924.[63] The crusading zeal that had fueled child labor reform in the prewar years was in short supply in the New Era.

Still, reformers did succeed eventually in winning congressional approval of a Child Labor Amendment. The American Federation of Labor led the amendment drive and coordinated the activities of the National Child Labor Committee, the League of Women Voters, and other major reform groups by creating a Permanent Committee for the Abolition of Child Labor. As a result of intense lobbying efforts, Congress passed the proposed Twentieth Amendment in 1924 by large majorities: 197–69 in the House and 61–23 in the Senate. Buoyed by such success, the reform coalition launched an enthusiastic campaign to secure prompt ratification of the new measure by the states. Proponents argued that only uniform federal standards could prevent the continued exploitation of young workers in some states, and that Congress had jurisdiction over child laborers by virtue of their "national citizenship."[64]

Contrary to the expectations of reformers, however, a powerful and determined opposition developed at the state level. Diverse social groups—from employers and farmers to churchmen and educators—united in response to fears aroused by the amendment's broad language: "The Congress shall have power to limit, regulate, and prohibit the labor of persons under 18 years of age." The National Association of Manufacturers led the opposition forces, which included many state and local Chambers of Commerce. These business organizations made effective use of their own publicity bureaus and supplied newspapers with a steady stream of "educational" articles that denounced federal efforts to usurp parental authority and "sovietize" America's children. The Executive Committee of Southern Cotton Manufacturers went so far as to create a bogus organization—the Southern Farmers' States Rights League—which inserted columns of advertising in small-town newspapers throughout the western states on behalf of a nonexistent agricultural constituency.[65]

Many legitimate farm groups also opposed the amendment because they feared that it might prevent children from performing daily chores on family farms. Similar concerns about family autonomy and government intrusiveness reappeared in the arguments of religious and educational spokesmen. Some leading educators worried that, if child labor laws were rigorously enforced, the resulting increase in the number of school-age children would swamp the school system and invite federal assistance and control. An editorial in the influential Jesuit weekly *America* drew upon all of these anxieties to create a comprehensive vision of overbearing federal power:

> Out of the Federalized clinic, along a Federalized road comes the Federalized child to the Federalized school. The picture is not overdrawn. If we do not awake to the danger at our doors, we shall have a Sovietized United States within another generation. . . . A more pernicious amendment was never offered. Under its plain terms, all that refers to childhood can be controlled, directly or indirectly, by a well-organized political minority.[66]

A number of patriotic and legal organizations also opposed the amendment on more specific constitutional grounds. Such groups as the Sentinels of the Republic, the Constitutional Liberty League, the Women's

Constitutional League, the National Security League, the Sons of the American Revolution, and the Daughters of the American Revolution charged that the proposed amendment violated constitutional norms of limited government and state rights. In December 1924 the *American Bar Association Journal* published as its lead article a major speech recently delivered by Nicholas Murray Butler, president of Columbia University and a revered elder statesman of the Republican Party. Butler warned the group of lawyers that the Child Labor Amendment was symptomatic of a larger danger: a "quiet and orderly revolution . . . that is taking place in the hearts and minds of men."

> The American revolution that is now going forward manifests itself . . . in an impatient willingness to permit government to absorb a steadily increasing control over private life and occupation, and to build up at the national capital, with smaller replicas at the several state capitals, a huge, cumbrous and incompetent bureaucracy to manage at great and burdensome cost activities which the highest public interest and the national tradition require should be let alone. . . . [I]t was clearly settled [at the Founding] that the sphere of government was definite and reasonably precise, while the sphere of liberty was indefinite and large enough to contain all powers not specifically delegated to the national government in the Constitution. . . . Every attempt to make uniform by the force of federal power the conduct and activities of citizens in the several states, is an undermining of the foundations. . . . If it [the new American revolution] is permitted to continue without check, it may readily and within an easily measurable time transform our Federal Republic . . . into an unrecognizable and novel form of despotism in which now a majority, and now various minorities, will wreak their will on all that most intimately concerns the individual, the family, the community and the state.[67]

Around the same time Everett P. Wheeler, chairman of the ABA's Committee on Jurisprudence and Law Reform, outlined several further objections to the amendment and urged his fellow members to "appeal to the many citizens, both men and women, . . . who really desire the welfare of young people, to consider these arguments and to do all in their power to secure the election of a legislature who will vote against the ratification of this amendment, which is a wolf in sheep's clothing."[68]

Under attack from multiple and well-organized constituencies, the ratification movement stalled. By the end of 1925 only four states had ratified the Child Labor Amendment and nineteen had rejected it. Supporters complained that in some key states, such as Massachusetts, major newspapers would not accept their advertisements or print their replies to anti-amendment editorials. (Newspapers generally opposed the amendment because of its potential effect on the hiring of young delivery boys.) In addition, popular trust in the wisdom of the business community was high, and there was widespread acceptance of the argument that little abusive child labor in fact still existed, thanks to enlightened management policies. "For the present," concluded the *New Republic,* "the tide is running irresistibly against any proposed progressive legislation which the business interests now in control of American politics have any sufficient interest in defeating."[69] (Although the requisite number of states never ratified the amendment, Congress included child labor provisions in the Fair Labor Standards Act of 1938, one of the last important New Deal measures. A new Supreme Court unanimously upheld the law as a valid exercise of congressional power over interstate commerce. In his opinion Justice Harlan Fiske Stone specifically overruled *Hammer v. Dagenhart,* which he described as an "aberration" and "a departure from the principles which have prevailed in the interpretation of the commerce clause both before and since the decision.")[70]

Like the struggle for a child labor amendment, African-American efforts to secure a federal antilynching law in the 1920s likewise ended in defeat. As the number of lynchings and race riots increased in 1918 and 1919, the NAACP made the enactment of such legislation a top priority. John R. Shillady, a social worker recently installed as executive secretary of the organization, undertook to compile the first adequate statistical study of lynching in the United States. Shillady sent two researchers to the Library of Congress, with instructions to comb the nation's newspapers for the last thirty years and note the facts surrounding every reported lynching: date, location, name of victim, age, sex, manner of death, and the offense the victim had allegedly committed. This data, supplemented by material previously gathered by the NAACP, formed the basis of a lengthy report, *Thirty Years of Lynching in the United States, 1889–1918,* which the Association published in April 1919.

Some of the conclusions were eye-opening: less than 20 percent of the 3,224 identified lynchings involved accusations of rape, the major justification advanced by southern politicians for tolerating the practice. The largest number of lynchings grew out of murder situations, although some blacks had been lynched for "talking back" to white persons or for "not driving out of the road" to let white drivers pass. Whites as well as blacks figured among lynch victims, and more than fifty black women had been lynched during the thirty years under study. Publication of this data proved indispensable to the campaign for federal antilynching legislation. The NAACP sent copies to libraries throughout the United States and in many foreign countries and prepared an annual supplement thereafter to bring the lynching record up to date.[71]

In a more dramatic bid for immediate public attention, the Association also convened a national conference on lynching that brought together notables from both major political parties, including Attorney General A. Mitchell Palmer, former Supreme Court Justice Charles Evans Hughes, and former Governor Emmett O'Neal of Alabama. The meeting took place in New York's Carnegie Hall in May 1919, with some 2,500 persons in attendance. As its sponsors had hoped, the event received national press coverage and culminated in the passage of resolutions demanding that lynching be made a federal crime. In a follow-up gesture, the NAACP dramatized the story of lynching by placing a full-page advertisement headed "THE SHAME OF AMERICA" in the *New York Times,* the nation's leading newspaper. And the Association hired its first full-time publicity director to oversee the orderly distribution of future news items for maximum political effectiveness.[72]

By 1921 the NAACP was ready to launch an all-out drive in support of an antilynching law that its Legal Committee had helped to draft. The chances for success seemed uniquely favorable. Republicans now controlled the White House and both Houses of Congress; the GOP platform of 1920 had included an antilynching pledge; and President Harding had publicly urged Congress to "wipe the stain of barbaric lynching from the banners of a free and orderly representative democracy."[73] The Dyer antilynching bill, introduced by Missouri Representative Leonidas C. Dyer, a Republican, in April 1921, was a comprehensive measure solidly grounded in the civil rights guarantees of the Fourteenth Amendment. It undertook to protect "citizens of the United States" against lynchings that a state took no action to prevent or punish. Under such circumstances victims were denied the equal protection of the laws, and delinquent officials faced a fine and imprisonment for their failure to act. In addition, the county in which a lynching occurred had to pay damages of $5,000 to $10,000 to a victim's heirs, and individual members of a lynch mob (defined as three or more persons acting without legal authority) could be prosecuted for a capital crime in a federal court.[74]

The task of mobilizing massive public support for the Dyer bill fell particularly to James Weldon Johnson, who had recently replaced Shillady as executive secretary of the NAACP. A noted African-American poet, novelist, orator, and diplomat, Johnson brought imagination and drive to his new position. With the help of his assistant, Walter White, he lobbied tirelessly on Capitol Hill, testified before congressional committees, arranged mass meetings, and kept 250 black newspapers supplied with regular press releases. "For nearly two years, during the periods when Congress was in session," he recalled, "I spent the greater part of my time in Washington. I tramped the corridors of the Capitol and the two office buildings so constantly that toward the end, I could, I think, have been able to find my way about blindfolded. . . . I saw and talked with every man in Congress who was interested in the bill or who, I thought, could be won over to it."[75]

Such persistence eventually paid off. On January 26, 1922, the House passed the Dyer bill by a vote of 231 to 119. An estimated seven hundred African Americans packed the galleries during the floor debate, in which opponents of the bill raised traditional arguments based on state rights and the rape issue, while supporters made effective use of factual data supplied by the NAACP.[76] When the vote was announced, black newspapers around the country hailed the victory in jubilant editorials. Typical was the commentary that appeared in the *City Times* of Galveston, Texas:

> A great work of congress happened last Saturday in the passage of the Dyer anti-lynching bill, which has elevated a new spirit in the whole nation's justice for giving a remedy that will prove beneficial to the obedience of law and order and respect for civilized society. Unborn Americans will give praise of Godly hearts to this republican congress of manly courage that was necessary during these times for our nation's welfare, regardless of section as this country must continue united as one and unseparable. The senate of the United States is in duty bound to the highest principles of American justice as set forth in the government's constitution to protect the lives, property and the pursuit of happiness of its citizens and thusly upon such foundation the senate of the United States, both republican and democratic members, can not do otherwise than to vote for the passage of the Dyer anti-lynching bill.[77]

But Johnson and White knew that the hardest struggle still lay ahead. In addition to a group of hard-core southern Democrats who opposed any federal interference in the south's racial practices, there were even some liberal senators who doubted the Dyer bill's constitutionality. Among the skeptics was William E. Borah, a Republican from Idaho and the influential chairman of the Senate Judiciary Committee, who had built an impressive prewar record as a Progressive reformer. Although Borah sympathized with efforts to abolish lynching, he condemned the Dyer bill for invading the police power of the states, which was constitutionally protected by the Tenth Amendment. Lynching, he reasoned, was a form of murder and properly fell under the jurisdiction of the states. The Dyer bill threatened to destroy local responsibility for law enforcement and to overturn the traditional balance of power between the nation and the states.[78]

In response to such concerns, Johnson appeared before Borah's committee to urge that lynching was a uniquely dangerous crime that the states had proved unable to control:

> The analogy between murder and lynching is not a true one. Lynching is murder, but it is also more than murder. In murder, one or more individuals take life, generally, for some personal reason. In lynching, a mob sets itself up in place of the state and acts in place of due processes of law to mete out death as a punishment to a person accused of crime. It is not only against the act of killing that the federal government seeks to exercise its power through the proposed law, but against the act of the mob in arrogating to itself the functions of the state and substituting its actions for the due processes of law guaranteed by the Constitution to every person accused of crime. In murder, the murderer violates the law of the state. In lynching, the mob arrogates to itself the powers of the state and the functions of the government. The Dyer Anti-Lynching Bill is aimed against lynching not only as murder, but as anarchy—anarchy which the states have proven themselves powerless to cope with.[79]

Other NAACP spokesmen suggested that a state's failure to prevent or punish lynchings deprived African Americans of a republican form of government, and that Congress might therefore legislate under the guarantee clause of the Constitution: "The United States shall guarantee to every state in this Union a Republican Form of Government." Moorfield Storey, the Association's president and a distinguished constitutional lawyer, further warned that failure to pass the Dyer bill might lead in time to civil war.[80]

Meanwhile, as the antilynching measure stalled in the Senate, a wave of new lynchings swept the country. In Texas, where ten persons were killed during a period of three weeks, the Dallas *Morning News,* a white newspaper, published a memorable cartoon in support of federal intervention. Captioned "Looks as tho Some One Needed Help," the drawing pictures an enraged bull ("Lynching Evil") that has just crashed through a rancher's fence. The rancher, a small figure who has managed to get a rope over the beast's horns, is being dragged helplessly through the air as two scrolls (labeled "States Rights" and "States Power") float beside him. Outside the fence a resolute Uncle Sam, armed with a pitchfork and a stout rope, prepares to lasso the rampaging bull, while the rancher calls, "Don't Interfere, Uncle! I Can Hold Him!" The cartoon, drawn by John Francis Knott, attracted national attention when it was reproduced in the June 10, 1922 issue of the popular *Literary Digest*.[81]

Many other newspapers, while deploring mob violence, condemned the Dyer bill on both constitutional and pragmatic grounds. "The bill is a dangerous invasion of the residuary powers of the States," charged the Asheville (N.C.) *Times* in a representative editorial. "It clothes the Federal Government with the authority to sit in judgment upon the police administration of the individual States. It places the United States in the position of a super-government that levies penalties upon the counties of the nation." Collecting such penalties would not be practicable in any event, maintained the New York *World;* the Providence (R.I.) *Journal,* as well as the Nashville *Tennessean,* noted that state law enforcement methods were improving and would soon solve the lynching problem without federal interference.[82]

Under continued pressure from NAACP lobbyists and some senior Republican leaders, the Judiciary Committee at last endorsed the Dyer bill on June 30 by a vote of 8 to 6. But the measure never came before the full Senate for a vote. After repeated scheduling delays, southern Democrats threatened to filibuster indefinitely against the bill and to prevent any other business from being transacted for the rest of the session unless the measure was withdrawn. Republican supporters, for whom antilynching legislation was not a top priority, gave in without a real fight. A party caucus on December 2 voted to abandon the bill, and Senator Henry Cabot Lodge of Massachusetts announced that no further effort would be made to secure its passage during the Sixty-seventh Congress.[83]

The defeat of the Dyer bill was a crushing disappointment for Johnson and the NAACP, since it meant that any future legislative campaign would have to start all over and win the approval of *both* Houses of a new Congress. With its funds seriously depleted, the Association in the late 1920s looked more and more to the courts to vindicate a broad array of black rights through selective litigation. At the same time it kept up its legislative lobbying and achieved some success at the state level with the passage of laws against lynching and other forms of mob violence. A cartoon in the Baltimore *Afro-American* early in 1923 supported the NAACP's policy of continued activism and called for greater aggressiveness in the ongoing struggle for black civil rights. The drawing depicts a stalwart African American challenging a pirate ("White Supremacy") for the possession of a treasure chest labeled "Negro Rights." Beside the chest lies a scroll ("Dyer Bill"). The caption reads: "For Fifty Years I Have Been Pleading for That Which Is Mine—Now I Am Going to Fight for It."[84]

Despite the best efforts of the NAACP and other civil rights organizations, however, Congress never passed an antilynching law. Congressman Dyer reintroduced his measure in every session of Congress during the rest of the 1920s, to no avail; a vigorous campaign in the 1930s likewise failed.[85] Still, reflected James Weldon Johnson, the hard-fought struggle of 1921–1922 had done much to educate politicians and the public about the reality of racial injustice and the need to protect black civil rights. "The Dyer Anti-Lynching Bill did not become a law," Johnson wrote, "but it made of the floors of Congress a forum in which the facts were discussed and brought home to the American people as they had never been before. Agitation for the passage of the measure was, without doubt, one of the prime factors in reducing the number of lynchings in the decade that followed to less than one-third of what it had been in the preceding decade— to one-tenth of what it was in the first decade of the keeping of the record."[86]

But more radical advocates of constitutional change drew other lessons from the temper of the 1920s. To some it seemed that the spread of Constitution worship and a restrictive view of government regulatory power spelled the end of meaningful constitutional reform for the future. "[I]t is clear that the conditions and values which the Constitution was designed to fulfill have changed," argued critic Waldo Frank in 1929.

> Yet to this antiquated makeshift, constructed by shrewd but spiritually callous men, we Americans must swear allegiance! In order to do so, we must be careful not to understand it. And in order to guard our ignorance, we have erected systems of subsidiary censors, to bar our minds and emotions from any contact with the Constitution which would bring it into touch with life at the cost of sanctity. It is

vigorously lied about in our schools, glossed with adjectival sugar in our churches. It is occultly protected by nine pontifical judges—high priests without a god—in whom is solely vested the ticklish business of so interpreting it, that thought about it *by Americans* (but not legislation under it *by Money*) may be wholly estopped. It has become, in other words, no mere instrument for government, but an absolute whose power is so perfect that the notion of government as a creative, evolving exercise of thinking groups has almost died from the land.[87]

Ironically, Frank's gloomy assessment appeared just as the New Era was about to end in economic shambles. Contrary to expectations, the Hoover presidency failed to maintain prosperity, and, as conditions worsened, the media gave voice to increasing public demands for a more active and compassionate federal government. Meanwhile, rumors of an impending revolution of some sort grew ever louder.

5

Symbols of Authority in a Collapsing Economy

Mellon pulled the whistle,
Hoover rang the bell,
Wall Street gave the signal,
And the country went to hell.

— *NEW YORK TIMES* (1932)

The laissez-faire constitutionalism of the 1920s came under sharp attack in the early years of the following decade. After the Wall Street crash of October 1929, the nation entered a period of prolonged and frightening economic depression. As New Era policies failed to reverse the downturn, the public mood soured. Creative writers now took renewed interest in political themes and revived the kind of documentary fiction that had been popular before World War I. Once again, novelists and playwrights put the system on trial in their works and called for major changes to correct the defects of an "obsolete" Constitution.

Herbert Hoover's public image as the "Great Engineer" and a prime architect of New Era prosperity propelled him into the presidency in the election of 1928. "We in America today are nearer to the final triumph over poverty than ever before in the history of any land," he told cheering crowds. "The poor-house is vanishing from among us."[1] When the bottom fell out of the stock market seven months after his inauguration, Hoover continued to make reassuring statements and to insist that relief was a matter for state and local authorities. But he also approved the Agricultural Marketing Act of 1929, which created a Federal Farm Board to loan money to agricultural cooperatives and to stabilize farm prices by purchasing surplus crops in the open market. A year later the Board had loaned almost one-third of its authorized fund of $500 million to regional and national marketing associations, but, in the absence of compulsory production quotas, the program encouraged still larger crop surpluses.[2]

James M. Beck, now a Republican representative from Pennsylvania, joined other conservatives in denouncing the federal plan as unconstitutional and socialistic. Terming the Marketing Act "the greatest legislative folly . . . in the history of America," Beck warned that it would convert "our limited government, with its constant recognition of the value of individual initiative, into a bureaucracy which destroys the individual, of which the Soviet Republic, so called, is the final and greatest expression."[3] Although the Board failed to raise agricultural prices, its efforts paved the way for subsequent federal farm programs under the New Deal.

The marketing experiment illustrates the strengths and limitations of Hoover's approach to economic recovery. Confronted by a depression of unparalleled severity, he acted more vigorously than any previous president in extending federal assistance to ailing businesses and farm organizations while denying relief to destitute individuals. The centerpiece of the Hooverian recovery program was the Reconstruction Finance Corporation (RFC), a federal agency established by Congress in January 1932 to lend public funds to major corporations, such as banks, insurance companies, and railroads, that were on the verge of financial collapse. Modeled on the War Finance Corporation of World War I, the RFC represented the most sweeping federal intervention in the marketplace since the war years. During its first six months, the agency loaned more than $1 billion to some four thousand credit institutions and railroads.[4]

Critics, including New York Congressman Fiorello LaGuardia, characterized the program as "a millionaire's dole . . . a subsidy for broken bankers—a subsidy for bankrupt railroads—a reward for speculation and unscrupulous bond pluggers."[5] In a lighter vein, George S. Kaufman and Morrie Ryskind satirized the illogic behind the legislation in a sketch written for the liberal *Nation:*

> *Mr. K.* Let me get this straight. The Reconstruction Finance
>   Corporation just keeps on lending money?
> *Mr. R.* That's right. On condition that there's no security.
> *Mr. K.* Well, whose money is it? Whose money are they lending?
> *Mr. R.* It's very simple. You see, they take the money that the
>   depositors put into the good banks—
> *Mr. K.* And lend it to the bad banks.
> *Mr. R.* Now you've got it![6]

Hoover and other defenders of the RFC hoped that it would invigorate the commanding heights of the economy, encourage renewed investment, and create new jobs. While the program did prevent some major bank failures, its anticipated trickle-down effects did not occur. Instead of using RFC funds to promote business expansion, most corporations chose merely to shore up their reserves with the money. When the RFC reportedly refused to lend $70 million to the city of Chicago to pay municipal employees and teachers while advancing $90 million to the powerful Central Republic Bank of Chicago, public indignation mounted. And Hoover added to popular resentment by championing a new revenue measure in June 1932 that raised personal and corporate income taxes to their highest levels since World War I.[7]

Despite their growing unpopularity, the president's recovery efforts at least acknowledged that widespread business distress created a national problem and called for federal action. At the same time, he rejected all appeals for federal assistance to the unemployed and needy. Convinced that the depression—a world-wide phenomenon—grew out of foreign banking practices and trade policies, he ignored serious structural defects in the American economy. These ranged from an overproduction of durable goods to a dangerous maldistribution of income that prevented large numbers of Americans from buying assembly-line products, even on credit. Since he continued to insist that American business was "fundamentally sound," Hoover relied on Community Chests and other local organizations to relieve the growing numbers of the hungry and the homeless. Drawing on his World War I experience as Food Administrator, he sought to mobilize public support behind federally orchestrated campaigns for voluntary giving in 1930 and 1931.[8]

Advertising again played a key role in these attempts at mass persuasion, as it had during the war. A representative ad in one mass market publication showed a brawny worker rolling up his sleeves in a fighting stance. The caption below read: "Of Course We Can Do It!" An accompanying text recalled the spirit of unity and sacrifice that had characterized the war years, and appealed anew to "[t]he people who went to France, or bought Liberty Bonds, or went without sugar—Mr. and Mrs. John K. American."

> We're going to share our luck with the folks out of work, aren't we? Remember—there's no National fund they can turn to for relief. It's up to us! . . . But if we all dig deep enough we can keep a roof over every head, food in every pantry, fuel on every fire, and warm clothing on every needy man, woman and child in America.[9]

Sponsored by the President's Organization on Unemployment Relief, the ad concluded with a reminder to give "through your *local* welfare and relief organizations."[10] The emphasis is suggestive. When Hoover drew analogies between the depression and World War I, as he did on several occasions in 1931 and 1932, he was thinking in moral, not political, terms. The Wilsonian model of war socialism seemed to him a dangerous experiment in "centralized despotism" that should never be repeated in peacetime America. "I am convinced," he declared, "that . . . [the federal government] should limit its responsibilities to supplement the states and local communities, and that it should not assume the major role or the entire responsibility, in replacement of local government, which is the very basis of self-government."[11] Any direct federal aid to victims of the depression would, he feared, undermine individual initiative and destroy the traditional balance between state and federal authority.

Many local and state officials expressed similar concerns. When the *Nation* asked several hundred municipal executives early in 1931 for their views on unemployment relief, most insisted that they wanted no help from Washington. And a year later thirty-eight state governors reported that their respective relief programs were still working satisfactorily. Journalists and social workers, however, told a different story; moreover, no reliable statistics on joblessness existed at the time in any of the major industrial nations, including the United States.[12]

Convinced that large numbers of Americans were virtually starving, liberal congressmen introduced several relief measures, beginning in 1930. Although these initiatives failed, they did engender some well-publicized debates over the meaning and scope of the Constitution's general welfare clause. Particularly revealing was an exchange between Republican Senators William E. Borah of Idaho and Simeon D. Fess of Ohio soon after the passage of the RFC legislation. Noting that Fess had supported the RFC as a proper exercise of congressional power to "promote the general welfare of the United States," Borah asked whether "it is not for the general welfare that we prevent men and women and children from dying of starvation." To which Fess retorted, "We are loaning funds to business, but you are trying to give away money to these people *who will never pay it back!*"[13] Fess's response beautifully articulated the narrow view of government responsibility espoused by New Era businessmen. And he made his position even more explicit in a follow-up statement: "The Senator from Idaho is proposing that the government should support the people, when it is the duty of the people, instead, to support the government."[14] From this perspective, which turns John Locke on his head, governments do not exist to serve the popular will; rather, the people must look for direction to those in authority over them.

By July 1932, with national elections fast approaching, Congress finally passed a major relief bill that made federal assistance directly available to those in need. There was no longer any doubt that public and private welfare services were breaking down under the overwhelming demands being placed on them. Although Hoover vetoed the bill, as he had pledged to do, he quickly agreed to a compromise measure that took account of his most serious objections. The Emergency Relief and Construction Act, which he signed on July 21, 1932, authorized the RFC to lend $300 million to the states for unemployment relief and provided an additional $1.5 billion for temporary loans to finance self-liquidating construction projects.[15] In theory, the new legislation signaled a further departure from Hoover's restrictive philosophy of federal power; in fact, the president and his bureaucratic appointees limited the nationalizing potential of the law in drastic ways.

To qualify for federal relief funds, for example, a governor had first to certify "that the resources of the State or Territory, including moneys then available and which can be made available by the State or Territory, its political subdivisions, and private contributions, are inadequate to meet its relief needs." The bookkeeping language encouraged protracted haggling between the RFC and state authorities over the adequacy of state fund-raising efforts. Thus, after two months of acrimonious negotiation, the RFC granted Pennsylvania a minimal loan of $2.5 million—barely enough to provide each unemployed worker with a daily ration of 3 cents.[16] A similarly parsimonious attitude characterized the agency's response to state requests for the support of income-producing public works. As historian Albert U. Romasco has concluded,

> While Congress was busily considering ways of spending money for programs to lift the country out of the depression, Hoover was preoccupied with balancing the budget as an essential prerequisite for economic recovery. . . . The President's distaste for enlarging federal authority, together with his analysis of the depression, accounts for his determined opposition to expanding federal activities which he himself had started. . . . Herbert Hoover's great achievement was that he led the nation in its struggle against depression; the fact that he forestalled others from continuing and widening the experiment was his greatest failure.[17]

As the president's half-hearted recovery efforts failed to restore prosperity, cartoonists mocked the image of the "Great Engineer" that had dazzled the electorate in 1928. A representative cartoon of 1931 featured Hoover as a portly construction boss, whose latest achievement—a ramshackle bridge labeled "Administration Record"—shocks a disbelieving Uncle Sam. "Surely Not the Work of a Great Engineer!" read the accompanying caption.[18] In popular songs and poems the president became a symbol of depression ills and of an unresponsive government. The term "Hoover-ize" had been used in World War I to encourage patriotic Americans to conserve food; now it referred to the denial of aid to hungry families, as in the protest song "Beans, Bacon, and Gravy":

> We have Hooverized on butter,
> For milk we've only water,
> And I haven't seen a steak in many a day;
> As for pies, cakes, and jellies,
> We substitute sow-bellies,
> For which we work the county road each day.[19]

Other derogatory terms entered the language for the first time and associated the president with a variety of welfare problems that his administration had done little to resolve. Freight cars in which the destitute traveled became "Hoover Pullmans"; newspapers used by vagrants for covering were "Hoover blankets"; joblessness was "Hoover time"; and the shanty-towns that sprang up near urban garbage dumps were "Hoovervilles."[20] The president contributed to his negative public image by referring disparagingly to well-fed hoboes and insisting that nobody was "actually starving." A shy and reserved person, he seemed cold and uncaring to many who watched him in movie newsreels or listened to one of his infrequent radio addresses. ("He is the sort of man who, if he had to recite the Twenty-third Psalm, would make it sound like a search warrant under the Volstead Act," quipped H. L. Mencken.)[21]

A parody of that very psalm circulated widely around the country toward the end of Hoover's term. It often appeared in rural or small-town newspapers and offered the most comprehensive cultural indictment of the Hoover program at the grassroots level:

> Hoover is my shepherd; I am in want.
> He maketh me to lie down on park benches; He leadeth me beside still factories.
> He restoreth the bread lines; He leadeth me in the paths of destruction for his Party's sake.
> Yea, though I walk through the Valley of Unemployment, I fear ev-

ery evil; for thou are with me; the Politicians and Profiteers they frighten me.

Thou preparest a reduction in mine salary before me in the presence of mine creditors; Thou anointest mine income with taxes; my expenses runneth over mine income.

Surely unemployment and poverty will follow me all the days of the Republican administration; and I shall dwell in a mortgaged house forever.[22]

Although the president became the most visible symbol of an ineffective and undemocratic government, Congress also came under sharp attack in the mass media by the early 1930s. Cartoonists pictured fat and well-dressed congressmen rejecting pleas for aid from starving farmers and jobless workers. One powerful cartoon of 1931 portrayed Congress as a giant hand holding a stone marked "Politics" over the heads of a multitude of expectant "Unemployed" and "Drought Sufferers." The caption above read "And They Asked for Bread."[23] Other cartoonists attacked congressional self-indulgence and subservience to special interest groups. In a representative example, a determined Uncle Sam wields an ax against a huge cactus labeled "Gov't. Waste," as chips fly off to strike surrounding congressmen. The chips bear such identifying tags as "Reelection Bait," "Appropriations," "Salaries," and "Soft Jobs."[24]

Democratic and Republican politicians shared the blame for the prolonged depression in songs like "Wandering," which described the rootlessness of many frustrated job-seekers:

> I've been wanderin' early and late
> From New York City to the Golden Gate,
> And it looks like I'm never gonna cease my wandering.
>
> . . . .
>
> Ashes to ashes and dust to dust,
> If the Republicans don't get you, the Democrats must,
> And it looks like I'm never going to cease my wandering.[25]

Hollywood joined the chorus of disapproval in 1932 with two films that denounced congressional venality on the eve of national elections. *Washington Masquerade* (MGM), a summer release, promised moviegoers a look at "the shadowy figures of intrigue in the political arena" as well as "inside details of the 'lobbyist' rackets."[26] Lionel Barrymore starred as Jeff Keane, a newly elected senator from Kansas, who has promised to lead a crusade for public power. In Washington, he meets a beautiful and design-ing woman who persuades him to abandon his ideals and accept a bribe from a lobbyist for the power industry. But, at a climactic Senate hearing, Keane repudiates the bargain, confesses his guilt, and makes an impas-sioned plea for government ownership of public utilities:

> The Almighty Hand . . . placed all the ingredients for the creation of power and light at the disposal of mankind. This land belongs to its millions of people! . . . [I]f we, here in Washington, blinded by old formulas, if we haven't learned the lesson that every wind has carried in these last three tragic years, a hundred million people in this coun-try have learned it. They've been forced to learn it! With the tears streaming down their cheeks, and their families famished—in the land where there's more than plenty! It's my solemn belief that a hundred million people are making up their minds that the things that belong to them and to nobody else, have been taken out of their hands and have been given back to them again at heart-breaking and impossible prices![27]

The film ends inconclusively, as Keane collapses and dies of a heart attack brought on by his courageous stand against the corruption of lobbyists and their congressional allies. "[M]en like you," he charges, want to "take this land that Washington gave us and make it your own and laugh at us!"[28] Despite its bursts of populist rhetoric and references to depression conditions, the script merely recycled the conventions earlier established in many Progressive narratives. Writers again found convenient scapegoats for the nation's ills in grafting politicians and reduced complex political problems to a simple conflict between good and evil. The movie's implied message was ultimately reassuring: constitutional government was still alive and well. If voters would only elect more honest politicians like Jeff Keane to represent the interests of "the people," these "days of corruption and depression" would soon end.

Washington Merry-Go-Round (MGM), which reached the nation's movie houses in early November 1932, presented a much darker view of congressional reform. The hero, a freshman congressman named Button Gwinnett Brown, claims direct descent from a signer of the Declaration of Independence. An idealist who hopes to reform the system from within, Brown finds himself outmaneuvered by the "malignant" special interests that control both houses of Congress. "They've made a scrap of paper out of the Declaration of Independence, they've made a joke out of the Constitution," he complains. The master lobbyist, Norton, is an immensely wealthy individual with dictatorial ambitions. Through his influence Brown loses his congressional seat after a bogus electoral recount, and Norton's megalomania even drives him to murder another honest congressman, who was preparing to testify against him. Since official Washington is either too weak or too venal to oppose the powerful lobbyist, Brown rallies a group of World War I veterans for a grassroots crusade. "We're going to have law and order again," he tells Norton. "The people are not going to stop until they get their government back."[29] Brown's resort to extralegal action works, as his men kidnap Norton and force him to confess his misdeeds. Faced with public exposure and disgrace, the lobbyist kills himself, using a gun that his captors have obligingly left behind.

Like many other political films of the 1930s, *Washington Merry-Go-Round* sent mixed messages to its viewers. From one perspective, it simply reaffirmed the need to elect more honest reformers, such as Button Gwinnett Brown, to Congress. The movie's dedication "to those public servants in Washington who . . . are serving their country sincerely and well" supports this view, as do statements that Brown makes at several points in the film.[30] On the other hand, the plot clearly suggests that constitutional procedures and established institutions are no longer adequate to protect the public welfare in a time of grave national crisis. Is it coincidental that Representative Brown traces his ancestry back to a Revolutionary patriot or that he chooses to lead a vigilante force in the name of popular government? By introducing the libertarian symbolism of the Declaration into their narrative, the filmmakers established a precarious tension between reform initiatives and the threat of revolution.

Playwright Maxwell Anderson, who wrote the story from which *Washington Merry-Go-Round*'s scriptwriters worked, also provided the most incisive treatment of congressional corruption in his Broadway comedy, *Both Your Houses*. Conceived as an attack on the discredited Congress of the later Hoover years, the play experienced lengthy production delays and did not open until March 6, 1933, two days after the new administration of Franklin D. Roosevelt had come to power. Despite the awkward timing, Anderson's witty script highlighted an issue of continuing importance: the nature of political representation in a constitutional democracy.

Set in the offices of Simeon Gray, chairman of the House Appropriations Committee, *Both Your Houses* traces the progress of a federal spending bill that allocates millions of dollars for worthless pork-barrel projects. The only member of the committee who opposes this flagrant misuse of public funds is Alan McClean, a newly elected representative from Nevada. A former schoolteacher who ran on a platform of economy in government, McClean is the stereotypical idealist in politics. His leading traits, as summarized by his secretary, immediately identify him as yet another spokesman for "the people": "Serious. Wears mail-order clothes. Reads Thomas Jefferson. He came down to Washington three months ago, and he's spent all his time in the Congressional Library."[31]

When McClean learns that the bill, despite its obvious graft, will likely be passed by both the committee and Congress, he adopts a bold stratagem to ensure its defeat. Before the committee takes its final vote, he proposes to include in the measure all of the pet projects that had previously been rejected. With these additions, what began as a $40 million deficiency bill becomes a monstrous boondoggle with a price tag of $475 million. McClean is confident that the committee will not dare to approve such a transparent fraud on the taxpaying public; but, to his dismay, a majority votes in favor of his bill. The House of Representatives, in turn, passes the measure overwhelmingly, since it promises to distribute an unprecedented amount of patronage.

Appalled at the results of his scheme, McClean decides to resign from Congress and urges his colleagues to do the same: "How long do you think a governing body can go on when it's made itself a laughing stock, the length and breadth of the country, the way this one has?" Echoing the Progressive faith in the power of enlightened public opinion, he plans to expose the inner workings of a system of bribery and special privilege:

> More people are open-minded nowadays than you'd believe. A lot of them aren't so sure we found the final answer a hundred and fifty years ago. Who knows what's the best kind of government? Maybe they all get rotten after a while and have to be replaced . . . It takes about a hundred years to tire this country of trickery—and we're fifty years overdue right now. That's my warning. And I'd feel pretty damn pitiful and lonely saying it to you, if I didn't believe there are a hundred million people who are with me, a hundred million people who are disgusted enough to turn from you to something else. Anything else but this.[32]

Had Anderson ended his play on this note, it would have represented merely a belated expression of the optimistic reformism that had characterized constitutional fiction at the turn of the century. Instead, the playwright undercuts his hero's idealistic appeal to the people by giving the last word to McClean's antagonist, the wily old pol Solomon Fitzmaurice. The most fully realized character in the play, Sol is an amiable cynic who has long succumbed to a system of bribery and favoritism in order to secure continuous reelection. "Everybody wants something," he explains to McClean; "everybody's trying to put something over for his voters, or his friends, or the folks he's working for. So they all get together, and they put all those things in bills, and everybody votes for 'em. All except the opposition. They don't vote for 'em because they don't get anything. . . . [T]he sole business of government is graft, special privilege and corruption—with a by-product of order. They have to keep order or they can't make collections."[33] Under such conditions it is useless to talk of electing "honest" individuals to office, since they must conform to existing practices if they hope to survive politically. And reformist appeals to "public opinion" will likely prove unavailing, since the voters—a far cry from the "virtuous citizenry" envisaged by the Founding Fathers—condone a system that gives them periodic handouts. Thus, when McClean leaves on his crusade to arouse the electorate, Sol reassures his colleagues: "It'll blow over, it'll blow over. As a matter of fact, the natural resources of this country in political apathy and indifference have hardly been touched."[34] While he concedes that the public may "some day" rise up against a corrupt establishment, he has no fear of such an occurrence during his lifetime. To which the only rejoinder is a faint "Maybe" from McClean's secretary.

Anderson's pessimistic and uncertain conclusion reflected the temper of much social criticism in the early 1930s. In particular, *Both Your Houses* might almost be read as a gloss on the constitutional commentary of Walter Lippmann. In a column of May 17, 1932, titled "The Ideal of Representative Government," Lippmann sounded a theme that would form the core of Anderson's play. After noting that the nation had experienced a decade of disillusionment with the workings of elected government, the columnist identified the cause of such disaffection: "The chief complaint against Congress, and it is well founded, is that it does not succeed in representing the national interest, that its members are preoccupied with their own special interest in re-election, and that to this end, in the effort to placate, cajole, and even to bribe their constituents, they will as a general rule sacrifice every other consideration." Although various remedies had been proposed, including longer terms for members of the House, none of them addressed the fundamental issue. The country, Lippmann charged, had lost sight of the true meaning of representative government. Drawing upon the writings of Edmund Burke, he argued that Congress—

like the British Parliament of the eighteenth century—had been intended to function as a national deliberative assembly, whose members should represent the entire nation rather than any local constituency. To the voters of his day, Burke had insisted that a representative "ought not to sacrifice to you, to any man, or to any set of men living . . . his unbiased opinion, his mature judgment, his enlightened conscience."[35] If Americans want good government, Lippmann concluded, they must revive the ideal of disinterested public service and stop treating their elected lawmakers as errand boys.

This appeal for statesmanlike leadership grew out of Lippmann's distrust of the political capacity of the electorate. In an earlier book, *The Phantom Public* (1925), he demolished some of the most cherished myths of Progressive reformers. He particularly attacked the idea that "the people" direct government policy through the exercise of a coherent "public opinion": "The individual man does not have opinions on all public affairs. . . . He does not know what is happening, why it is happening, what ought to happen. I cannot imagine how he could know, and there is not the least reason for thinking, as mystical democrats have thought, that the compounding of individual ignorances in masses of people can produce a continuous directing force in public affairs." Except on those few occasions when their personal interests or specialized knowledge may be involved, voters tend to be as apathetic and dull-witted as Sol Fitzmaurice believed them to be. Since they lack the information needed to comprehend the complex problems facing the modern state, they must leave policy-making to the professional politicians who actually govern. But the legitimating force of majority opinion remains important, especially in times of national emergency: "Public opinion, in this theory, is a reserve of force brought into action during a crisis in public affairs. . . . [T]he ideal of public opinion is to align men during the crisis . . . in such a way as to favor the action of those individuals who may be able to compose the crisis."[36] By 1932 Lippmann expressed cautious optimism that voters would meet the depression challenge by electing wiser and more responsible leaders to office.[37] His prognosis may well have influenced the stance of qualified pessimism adopted by Maxwell Anderson in his play.

Both Your Houses won the Pulitzer Prize as the best play of 1933.[38] The award testified in part to a recent upsurge in the popularity of political satire, as the federal government continued its halfhearted efforts to end the depression. A year earlier another satire, *Of Thee I Sing*, had also received a Pulitzer, the first musical comedy to be so honored. With a script by

George S. Kaufman and Morrie Ryskind, music by George Gershwin, and lyrics by Ira Gershwin, this rollicking production ridiculed all of the institutions of government, from the president to the Supreme Court. The story follows the presidential campaign of John P. Wintergreen, a compliant machine politician who wins election on a platform of "Love" after promising to marry the winner of a national beauty contest. When he later reneges on his promise and marries instead his true love, Mary Turner, he is nearly impeached. But Mary saves the day by announcing that she is pregnant, thus making a sure-fire appeal to the invincible sentimentality of the American public. When she later gives birth to twins, Wintergreen is restored to public favor; the jilted beauty queen consoles herself by marrying Throttlebottom, the inept vice president.

Although the farcical plot avoided any attack on specific politicians or programs, its barbs clearly appealed to popular resentment against an ineffectual and apathetic government. As the Senate prepares to meet in one scene, for example, its members break into song:

> The country thinks it's got depression;
>   Ha! Ha! Ha!
> Just wait until we get in session!
>   Ha! Ha! Ha![39]

And, true to their words, they spend their time discussing trivial matters and pushing personal bills, instead of confronting such critical problems as unemployment. On that subject, one senator observes, "The Committee on Unemployment is gratified to report that due to its unremitting efforts there is now more unemployment in the United States than ever before."[40] Such lines carried an undertone of bitterness that was not lost on radical critics. Alfred Saxe, a director with the Communist Workers' Laboratory Theatre, suggested that the musical might be easily converted to "constructive" revolutionary uses if Marxist mass chants replaced the song-and-dance routines.[41] Broadway audiences, however, preferred the bourgeois version. *Of Thee I Sing* ran for 473 performances after its opening on December 26, 1931, and the published script went through seven printings between April and October of 1932.

Somewhat surprisingly, it was not filmed. Another musical, written for the screen, covered some of the same themes with less success. *The Phantom President* (Paramount, 1932) featured music and lyrics by Richard Rodgers and Lorenz Hart and starred the aging vaudevillian George M. Cohan in his first sound movie. Cohan plays a smooth-talking medicine-show doctor who is hired to impersonate a lackluster political candidate. Through a series of comic misadventures, the real candidate disappears and the charismatic con man replaces him in the campaign. By prescribing a medicine of thirteen herbs that he claims will cure the country of depression, the imposter wins the election and the hand of his double's girlfriend. As in *Of Thee I Sing*, the script lampoons the emptiness of political rhetoric and the gullibility of voters, and depicts elected politicians as self-serving incompetents. The Senate comes in for some especially rough treatment, as the face of a smug senator dissolves at one point into the image of a horse's ass.[42]

Such concentration on the most obvious symbols of governmental inadequacy struck more left-leaning critics as misplaced. They insisted that the real cause of the nation's ills lay elsewhere—in a weakened, but still powerful, capitalism and the oppressive social relations it created with the support of the law. Elmer Rice's play *We, the People*, which opened during the last days of the Hoover administration, made the most ambitious attempt to explain the depression in terms of class domination. The kaleidoscopic plot, which required a cast of fifty, revolved about the increasing hardships experienced by a middle-class family, the Davises. In twenty sharply drawn scenes, the author moves from one family member to another, then cuts away to explore the lives of friends, employers, and related establishment figures. The cinematic technique enables him to construct a comprehensive indictment of an inhumane capitalist order; but it also leads to some confusion at times, as the focus shifts ever farther from the direct concerns of the major characters. In the end, however, Rice brings all of the strands together and shows how a ruthless business elite is responsible for both the misfortunes of the Davis family and the larger ills of the nation.

In many ways, *We, the People* suggests an updated version of those Progressive narratives that pitted "the people" against "the interests" of Big Business and its government allies. Rice gradually introduces the villains of his piece—a circle of representative types, including a banker, an industrialist, a university president, a young diplomat, and a judge whose father owns a powerful publishing and broadcasting empire. Linked by ties of family and social class, these men are not moral monsters. They contribute as individuals to private charities and sit on local relief committees, but they acknowledge no need of government intervention and are implacably committed to the preservation of the status quo. "The interests of business are the interests of the whole country," intones the banker Willard Drew in an echo of New Era thinking.[43] Drew and his colleagues never question the beneficence of laissez-faire principles and continue to pursue a lavish lifestyle as workers and farmers sink deeper into poverty.

The hapless Davis family suffers one misfortune after another at Rice's hands. Father William, a foreman at a large industrial plant, loses in turn his job, his life savings, and his home. When he leads a peaceful march of unemployed workers in a vain attempt to meet with the company president, panicky guards shoot and seriously injure him. Daughter Helen, a schoolteacher, must postpone her wedding plans indefinitely, as she becomes the only remaining breadwinner in the family. Finally, young Allen, a promising college student, has to drop out of the university to join the growing army of unsuccessful job-seekers. Radicalized by his experience, he participates in a protest meeting, which the police try to break up by force. When a policeman is killed in the fighting, other police frame Allen for the murder. After a pro forma trial, the jury finds him guilty and the judge—one of Drew's circle—sentences him to death for his crime "against the authority of the state."

The play reaches a powerful emotional climax in the final scene, which represents a mass meeting called to demand a stay of execution and a new trial for Allen Davis. In an effective bit of staging, the actors sit at the rear of the stage facing the footlights and step forward one by one to make their appeals directly to the theater audience, which becomes for a time the imagined group of spectators at the meeting. As in the rest of his dramas, Rice moves beyond the specific circumstances of Allen's case to address the plight of all Americans crushed by unyielding economic hardship. "It doesn't seem right that people who want to work can't find any work to do and that their homes should be taken away from them," pleads Helen Davis. "Is it too much to ask: just to be allowed to live your own life in peace and quiet? . . . A chance to live, that's all we want, that's all we ask for. That's all Allen wanted."[44] Other speakers appeal to the Declaration of Independence as a charter of fundamental rights and vow to continue Allen's protests against economic and social injustice. But the final speaker, C. Carter Sloane, goes further and proposes a campaign of concerted political action to aid all victims of the depression.

Sloane, a liberal college professor who once taught Allen Davis, traces his ancestry back to the *Mayflower*. One of his forebears signed the Declaration of Independence, from which he quotes extensively. No social system that denies people a "right to live," he maintains, "has a claim to a continuation of its existence." But he quickly backs away from this apparent endorsement of revolution and calls instead for constitutional change.

In a concluding burst of oratory, he anticipates the rhetoric of the impending New Deal:

> In the name of humanity, ladies and gentleman, in the name of common-sense, what is society for, if not to provide for the safety and well-being of the men and women who compose it? "To promote the general welfare and secure the blessings of liberty"—you'll find it there, set forth in the preamble to the Constitution. Does that mean a denial of the rights of assemblage and of free speech? Does that mean millions without employment or the means to provide themselves with food and shelter? We are the people, ladies and gentlemen, we— you and I and every one of us. It is our house: this America. Let us cleanse it and put it in order and make it a decent place for decent people to live in![45]

Despite its occasionally militant language, *We, the People* remained securely within the liberal reform tradition. As journalist William Allen White noted in a congratulatory letter to the author, the play's main points could all be found in the 1912 platform of the Progressive Party.[46] The production received mixed reviews, with most critics complaining of its sprawling structure, stereotyped characters, and preachiness. Some also found fault with the inconclusive ending, although, as Joseph Wood Krutch pointed out in *The Nation*, propaganda plays customarily left audiences with the question, "What are you going to do about it?"[47] For Rice, at least, the audience response to his drama was gratifying. "The opening night was unlike anything I had ever seen in the theatre," he recalled. "The performance was frequently interrupted by mingled expressions of approval and disapproval. At the end there was a demonstration: cheers and bravos, mainly from the balcony; boos and hisses, mainly from the orchestra."[48]

Such emotional demonstrations continued throughout the play's brief run. Each night noisy supporters packed the gallery, where tickets sold for one dollar, while the three-dollar orchestra seats remained virtually empty. Rice, who had invested his own funds in the production, shouldered the nightly losses for three weeks, then announced the play's closing. To his amazement, the cast members refused to quit, offering to work without pay so that performances might continue. Heartened by such loyalty and by a "flood" of supportive mail, Rice managed to keep the production going for another three weeks. Despite its disappointing record of only forty-nine performances, Burns Mantle included it in his compilation of the best plays of the 1932–1933 season. "From whatever angle it is accepted or rejected," he observed, "'We, the People' remains a forcefully written, excessively timely and socially significant drama."[49]

Communist reviewers applauded Rice's economic analysis but condemned his liberal prescription for ending the depression. The only way to restore prosperity, they argued, was to overthrow the capitalist system and replace it with a workers' state on the model of the Soviet Union. Proletarian writers, who included both Party members and sympathetic left-liberals, drew upon the symbolism of the American Revolution and the Declaration of Independence to promote the cause of popular insurrection. In such novels as Mary Heaton Vorse's *Strike!* (1930), Fielding Burke's *Call Home the Heart* (1932), and Myra Page's *Gathering Storm* (1932), the case for a "Soviet America" gained added strength through its association with such familiar imagery.

All three narratives deal in a documentary fashion with the Gastonia, North Carolina, textile strike of 1929. That strike, which grew out of spontaneous worker protests against wage cuts and speedups, attracted national press coverage after a small group of communist organizers arrived to recruit the striking millhands for the militant National Textile Workers Union. Under communist leadership, the strike continued for several months despite a vicious smear campaign by the local newspaper, repeated instances of police harassment and brutality, vigilante terrorism, and the calling out of the state militia. The mill owners and their legal allies eventually broke the strike after twice bringing the leaders to trial on criminal charges. The situation seemed made to order for dramatizing a revolutionary agenda, since the strikers were old-stock mountaineers whose lineage sometimes stretched back to the days of King's Mountain and other Revolutionary battles.

Communist characters in each of the three works appeal to historical memory in explaining the communist movement to backwoods audiences. An organizer in *Call Home the Heart* recalls the conditions of frontier settlement:

When your forefathers made their first trails through this land, they travelled in groups, bound together against forest enemies. . . . When they settled along the rivers, or in the upland valleys, they helped one another to dig wells, to build fences, to hew logs, to build houses and barns. . . . Today we have greater need to band together than our forefathers knew. We are living in a wilderness more bewildering, more threatening than theirs. An industrial wilderness that will subdue mankind, if we workers do not unite in our million-powered strength to conquer it. . . . I need not tell you that the millions and millions of workers bound hand and foot to factories and fields, are no shareholders in the earth and its riches. . . . Our birthrights as members of the human society are gone. Communism will restore these rights. The workers of the earth, wherever they toil, under roof or open sky, in every country of the globe, should and shall own the industries of the world and administer them. This is communism.[50]

On a more militant note, a speaker in *Gathering Storm* assures his listeners that the approaching strike will mark their "Declaration of Independence from mill slavery."[51] In these proletarian novels, the Declaration figures not only as a repository of shared democratic principles, as in *We, the People,* but also as a call to violent action. Unlike earlier socialist authors who prescribed a "legal" revolution, proletarian writers insisted that the Constitution, too, must be smashed, along with the capitalist class whose interests it protected.

Myra Page provides the most detailed forecast of the inevitable revolution and its consequences in *Gathering Storm.* Her protagonist, the communist organizer Tom Crenshaw, outlines the class nature of the struggle: "On the one side, the owning class, on the other the wage-slaves, poor farmers, propertyless, and oppressed." Under Party leadership, millions of "Negro peasants" in the Black Belt will rise up in armed revolt against their white landlords, while elsewhere industrial and transport workers will seize banks, factories, and power plants. "The White House would be emptied. Everywhere Soviets would be forming, laying the basis for the new government of workers and all who toil." In the Black Belt, where "Negro toilers" constituted the majority of the population, they would be encouraged to establish their own "Negro Toilers' Socialist Republic."[52] Page's scenario faithfully followed the current Party line, as reflected in such works as William Z. Foster's *Toward Soviet America* (1932).

Despite their endorsement of worker militancy, however, the three Gastonia novels describe no acts of violence initiated by the millhands. The strikers merely engage in peaceful marches and picketing and hold orderly meetings to discuss strategy. The mill owners and their agents, on the other hand, employ all kinds of violent and illegal methods to break the strike. "At no time and in no State, suh, have the liberties and rights of a sovereign people been so trampled underfoot," complains an old southern lawyer hired to defend the strikers in Vorse's narrative. "What is their crime? . . . They have exercised their constitutional rights and for that the military forces of the country are illegally being used against them. Machine guns, tear gas, bayonets, intimidations, threats, dynamitings."[53] By emphasizing the repeated violations of civil liberties endured by the mill workers and their families, Vorse and the other Gastonia novelists stayed close to the historical record. The Gastonia strikers had in fact been law-abiding and had carried no weapons on their marches. Although their behavior did not conform to the heroic demands of communist ideology, it made for a better story and one with greater appeal for American readers. *Strike!* and *Call Home the Heart* appeared under the imprint of mainstream publishers and received respectful reviews in major newspapers and magazines.[54]

From a propaganda perspective, Whittaker Chambers's short story, "Can You Make Out Their Voices," supplied the working-class insurgency that the Gastonia novels lacked. The plot drew upon a recently reported uprising of 500 drought-stricken and starving Arkansas farmers, who marched on the business section of a nearby town and demanded food at gunpoint. Although communists had played no part in this desperate venture, Chambers invented a heroic communist farmer, Jim Wardell, and placed him at the center of his tale. A hardworking and generous man, Wardell wins the support of his suspicious neighbors by sharing his own dwindling food supply with them. When asked to define communism, he avoids political theorizing to focus instead on immediate group needs: "Well, just now it means I want free food for every farmer that can't pay for it, free milk for the babies, free rent, and if we can't get free food, I'm going and taking it."[55] When the federal government fails to offer more than token relief through the Red Cross, the beleaguered farmers put aside their respect for private property and join Wardell in seizing the food supply held for sale by the town's storekeepers.

The expedition goes off successfully and without bloodshed, but Wardell warns that the authorities will now send in troops to punish the perpetrators. With a small cadre of his most trusted supporters, he prepares to resist the repressive forces of the state. In the meantime, he sends his two young sons to the East for safety, entrusting them with a message for the Party members they are to contact: "Tell the comrades . . . we're organizing. Tell them that already there are many of us. Tell them we've got the dirt farmers here in motion."[56] As the boys wave goodbye from a windy hillock and promise to return in the spring, their anxious mother asks, "Could you make out both their voices?"

Chambers's story appeared in the March 1931 issue of *New Masses,* the Party's literary magazine, and became an instant "revolutionary classic." "It had a success far beyond anything that it pretended to be," Chambers recalled in his autobiography:

> The New York *World-Telegram* spotted it at once and wrote a piece about it. International Publishers, the official Communist publishing house, issued it as a pamphlet. Lincoln Steffens hailed it in an effusion that can be read in his collected letters. Hallie Flanagan, then head of Vassar's Experimental Theater, turned it into a play. In a few months, the little story had been translated even into Chinese and Japanese and was being played in workers' theaters all over the world.[57]

Ironically, the dramatized version of Chambers's story, which may have reached the largest audience, replaced his revolutionary message with a call for liberal action that resembled Elmer Rice's reformist plea in *We, the People.*

For this development Hallie Flanagan and her coauthor, Mary Ellen Clifford, were responsible. Flanagan, who had been looking for a way to arouse theater audiences to the plight of the nation's farmers, found in Chambers's tale the human interest materials she needed. But she opened up the narrative in important ways, both by adding new characters and by introducing much factual data in the form of charts, graphs, and statistics. In the end, the play—retitled *Can You Hear Their Voices?*—looked beyond the troubles of a few Arkansas farmers to document the general failure of congressional relief policy in the face of mounting unemployment and poverty. As a reviewer for the *New York Times* reported, the production consisted of a "series of black and white vignettes . . . capped by small blackouts and interwoven argumentatively with the stark facts of Congress's inaction thrown at you from printed slides on a huge white screen."[58]

Flanagan and Clifford positioned their characters in a class-conscious fashion at opposite sides of the stage. One group includes Congressman Bagehot and his Washington friends; the other, Wardell and his impoverished neighbors. Scenes of growing desperation and militancy among the farmers are juxtaposed with episodes from the comfortable life of the fatuous congressman. Bagehot, who condemns all proposals for federal farm relief, willingly spends a quarter of a million dollars on a coming-out party for his daughter. But the playwrights reject Chambers's commitment to class warfare and introduce a mediating character who suggests the possibility of a peaceful resolution of the farm crisis.

Harriet, Bagehot's daughter, is a college-educated liberal who sympathizes with the farmers and criticizes her father for his indifference to their suffering. In one scene, after drinking too much champagne at her coming-out party, she publicly attacks her own privileged class and warns: "Well, if we want the country to go Communist, carrying on stampedes like this one . . . is the quickest and surest way to do it."[59] To picture communism as a remedy of last resort is a far cry from Chambers's insistence that it offers the *only* solution to the economic crisis. And implicit in Harriet's outburst is a call for timely federal assistance to avert more radical alternatives. The reformist thrust of the play appears most clearly in its conclusion. After Wardell takes leave of his sons, the following message flashes on the large screen that has served as a backdrop to the evening's action: "These boys are symbols of thousands of our people who are turning somewhere for leaders. Will it be to the educated minority? CAN YOU HEAR THEIR VOICES?"[60]

Despite—or because of—its ambivalence, the drama received almost universal acclaim after its first performance in May 1931. The *New York Times* termed it "smashing propaganda"; *New Masses* hailed it as "the best play of revolutionary interest produced in this country." In a short time it was being performed by little theaters, college drama departments, and farm and worker groups around the nation. Theaters in Greece, China, Hungary, Finland, Denmark, France, Russia, Spain, and Australia also requested copies of the published script for use in their own productions. "Like an American forerunner in another field, it was a shot heard 'round the world,'" wrote the communist critic Ben Blake.[61]

In the months following the play's premiere, incidents of sporadic violence in the nation's farm areas increased. By the fall of 1932 some farmers in a dozen midwestern states were using armed force to prevent further mortgage foreclosures and evictions; others were blocking highways to prevent the delivery of milk and other farm products to city markets until prices rose. There was much talk of a new Declaration of Independence and a new American Revolution. (During the Sioux City, Iowa, milk strike, Route 20 was renamed "Bunker Hill 20.") Despite such inflammatory rhetoric, the farmers' demonstrations did not seek to overthrow existing institutions but to make them more responsive to the urgent needs of the farm population. "Demonstrations . . . are the most primitive form of advertising," noted the radical journalist Mary Heaton Vorse.

"Demonstrations about injustice or hunger or oppression advertise to the rulers the suffering of a people. . . . As soon as the farmers demonstrated things began to happen. Several states granted moratoriums, several of the largest insurance companies which were mortgage holders granted moratoriums as well."[62]

Grassroots farm protest reached the national level in December 1932, when 250 farmers from twenty-six states marched on Washington to attend a Farmers' National Emergency Relief Conference called by militant rank-and-file farm groups in the Midwest. "I have never heard speeches which were more to the point, or which seemed the result of more mature deliberation," wrote Vorse, who covered the proceedings for *The New Republic*. "The farmers were generally conservative in political and social points of view; they had been driven by the relentless sweep of events into a militant position. . . . They say from the platform and to each other, 'We are making our Declaration of Independence as that other glorious declaration was made in Philadelphia, in 1776.'"[63] After discussing the plight of small farm owners, tenant farmers, and sharecroppers throughout the country, they adopted a program for legislative action and presented it to Congress.

Their proposals included an appropriation of $500 million for immediate cash relief, to be administered by local committees of farmers; federal regulation of food processors and other middlemen to ensure that farmers received higher prices for their crops; a moratorium on taxes and other farm indebtedness; and no more evictions. Sympathetic congressmen introduced these proposals in the House and Senate, and the president also received a copy. Rightly anticipating that their demands would ultimately be rejected, the farmers warned of further rank-and-file militancy, as they pledged to "protect our fellow farmers from suffering, and their families from social disintegration by our united action, if our duly elected national representatives and Senators fail as did the local county and State authorities."[64]

The respectful hearing given to the farmers by Washington authorities contrasted sharply with the treatment of nonfarm groups of the unemployed and the poor, who also converged on the nation's capital during 1932. The rout of the Bonus Army, in particular, showed how far the Hoover administration would go in suppressing those whom it considered serious threats to the established order. A group of needy veterans of World War I, the so-called "Bonus Expeditionary Force," came to Washington in late May to press for the immediate payment of a military bonus not legally due to them until 1945. When favorable legislation failed to pass the Senate on June 17, about 5,000 of the 20,000 ex-servicemen returned home. The rest stayed on, occupying some abandoned buildings near the Capitol on Pennsylvania Avenue or joining the main encampment on some marshy flats across the Anacostia River in southeast Washington. They remained quiet and well behaved, sang patriotic songs, and hoped for some further action from Congress or the president. As the weeks went by, however, their continued presence provoked increasing uneasiness on all sides.

The president, who refused to meet with BEF leaders, isolated himself in the White House behind heightened security. The front gates were chained shut, for the first time since the war; swarms of Secret Service agents patrolled the lawn; and hastily erected barricades denied access to all traffic for one block around the Executive Mansion. Finally, on August 28, an incident occurred that gave Hoover and his Secretary of War, Patrick J. Hurley, a pretext for federal intervention. When the D.C. police attempted to evict the veterans from the buildings they occupied on Pennsylvania Avenue, some brief fighting broke out and the District Commissioners appealed to the president for assistance. In response, Hoover ordered local United States Army units under General Douglas MacArthur to drive the ex-servicemen out of downtown Washington. The mission was easily accomplished, but MacArthur went further and launched a night attack on the veterans' main encampment on Anacostia Flats, in direct violation of his orders. Using tear gas and bayonets, his troops descended on the unarmed Bonus Marchers and their families, drove them screaming from their makeshift quarters, and set fire to the camp to prevent their return. More than one hundred casualties resulted, including an infant who died from the effects of the gas.[65]

In an impromptu midnight press conference, MacArthur characterized the BEF as an insurrectionary mob that would have seized control of the government without the president's timely action. Hoover echoed this argument in his own public statements and charged that most of the Bonus Marchers had not been bona fide veterans, but communists and criminals. "A challenge to the authority of the United States Government has been met, swiftly and firmly," he declared. "After months of patient indulgence, the Government met overt lawlessness as it always must be met if the cherished processes of self-government are to be preserved. We cannot tolerate the abuse of Constitutional rights by those who would destroy all government, no matter who they may be. Government cannot be coerced by mob rule."[66] Most major newspapers fell into line behind the administration, and few even bothered to reprint the results of a recent exhaustive survey undertaken by the Veterans Administration. According to VA records, 94 percent of the Bonus Marchers had served in the Army or Navy, 67 percent had seen overseas duty, and 20 percent had been disabled.[67] Knowledge of their military service may have made little difference, in any event, to the millions of Americans who saw the issue, in administration terms, as a symbolic struggle between law and anarchy.

For the Bonus Marchers and other critics of the Hoover administration, of course, the episode involved a very different set of symbols. It represented a clash between a government of wealth and privilege and a group of ordinary Americans, whose peaceful petitions had been answered by official violence. Malcolm Cowley interviewed many of the veterans during their headlong flight from Washington and concluded that they scarcely qualified as revolutionary material. "No, if any revolution results from the flight of the Bonus Army," Cowley wrote, "it will come from a different source, from the government itself. The army in time of peace, at the national capital, has been used against unarmed citizens—and this, with all it threatens for the future, is a revolution in itself."[68] From this perspective, MacArthur's rout of the Bonus Army was undisguised class warfare, carried on by a government that had lost confidence in its own legitimacy.

A new protest song, which appeared soon after the expulsion of the BEF, combined censure of a privileged ruling class with continued pleas for relief. The anonymous production may better reflect the feelings of the average disgruntled veteran toward Hoover, MacArthur, and other government officials than any other surviving source. Its biting verses, which parody the self-serving statements of the president and his secretary of war, offer their own distinctive images of Washington officialdom after three years of depression:

> "Only two courses were open,
> As anyone can see:
> To vindicate law and order
> Or yield to anarchy."
> Granted! the Chiefs of Government
> Cannot tolerate mobs—
> But isn't it strange you never thought
> Of giving the workless jobs?

"Only two courses were open"—
When men who had fought for you
Starved in the streets of our cities,
Finding no work to do—
When in the richest of the countries
Babies wept unfed—
Strange it never occurred to you
To give the hungry bread!

"Only two courses were open"—
To the Higher Racketeers
Who look on human suffering
With lofty well-fed sneers.
And thus will your names be noted
By history's merciless pen:
"They knew how to rise to Power,
But not how to act like Men!"[69]

Such protest literature recalled the Progressive tendency to blame individuals for the failures of the system. But the Progressive era also encompassed a vigorous utopian tradition, which resurfaced in the early 1930s in a variety of ambitious proposals for reshaping constitutional structures and values.

6

Imagining a New Constitutional Order

> For ten years the American people have been sunk first in the
> political lethargy of war-weariness and then in the stupor of the great
> inflation. They are coming out of it. There has been more thought
> and more feeling about public affairs in the last year than in the ten
> which preceded it.
>
> —WALTER LIPPMANN (1931)

As disturbances of all kinds flared up around the country in 1931 and
1932—from hunger marches, rent strikes, and taxpayer revolts to farm
holidays and foreclosure riots—suggestions for political and constitutional
change again filled the pages of newspapers and magazines. "The heads of
young men formerly addicted to belles lettres now buzzed with schemes
for changing or saving our society," recalled Matthew Josephson. "George
Soule said he could have spent the whole year just examining the letters
that came to *The New Republic* outlining different plans."[1] Not since the
heady days of Progressive reform had constitutional criticism aroused such
widespread interest. Even conservative congressmen doubted that the existing Constitution, with its archaic checks and balances, would prove adequate to the demands of the depression crisis. "I do not often envy other
people their governments," declared Republican Senator David A. Reed
of Pennsylvania in May 1932; "but I say that if this country ever needed a
Mussolini, it needs one now."[2]

A revival of pamphlet literature encouraged political discussion among
those with little cash to spare, and supplemented the reduced offerings
of a depressed book publishing industry. "The pamphlet was frozen out
by prosperity and the custom of the bookseller's trade," explained critic
Lewis Mumford; but "booksellers [of the early 1930s], confronted with
no sales, are now not averse to little ones, and the pamphlet has come back
again."[3] Mumford had special words of praise for the "pioneering" work
of the John Day Company, whose pamphlets averaged thirty-five pages
and sold for only 25 cents. Day's titles included such timely critiques of

124

the established order as Charles Beard's *The Myth of Rugged Individualism*, Henry Hazlitt's *Instead of Dictatorship*, Louis M. Hacker's *The Farmer Is Doomed*, Walter Lippmann's *A New Social Order*, Osgood Nichols and Comstock Glaser's *Work Camps for America*, and Archibald MacLeish's poem, *Frescoes for Mr. Rockefeller's City*, with its mocking profiles of the financial and industrial "Empire Builders" of the past.[4]

Utopian visions of a revitalized government, which had almost ceased to exist in the 1920s, reappeared with increasing frequency as the 1932 elections approached. The *Nation* contributed to this trend by inviting eight prominent individuals from varied backgrounds to offer their prescriptions for ending the depression. The resulting series of essays, titled "If I Were Dictator," ran in weekly installments from November 18, 1931, to January 20, 1932. Although each author approached the subject from a distinctly personal perspective, most drew upon the constitutional legacy of Progressivism and World War I in formulating their forward-looking programs.

Economist Stuart Chase launched the series with a comprehensive view of a new order in the making. Chase envisaged a purely administrative state, directed by enlightened engineers and other expert social planners. To provide immediate relief for the unemployed and destitute, he proposed a massive public works program that would put more than a million persons back to work at once: "Highways, waterways, public buildings, power-site development, flood control, afforestation, slum clearance, construction of great recreational centers—these will be among the chief projects."[5] For those who might still remain without work, direct federal relief payments would be available, and no family would be permitted to fall below a prescribed minimum standard of living. The federal government would also establish a network of employment exchanges and vocational clinics to rationalize the job market for the future, along with a complete system of unemployment insurance and old-age pensions.

While acknowledging that these initiatives would be hugely expensive, Chase identified several new sources of potential federal revenue. Some major savings might be achieved, he noted, by abolishing the army and navy, leaving only a "magnificent air force" to defend the nation until such time as "Europe ceases to simmer." In addition, heavy taxes should be imposed on those in higher income brackets, as the Wilson government had done in World War I, and new "supertaxes" should be levied on large inheritances. If all of these measures failed to balance the budget, the country had nothing to fear from a substantial deficit: "The United States borrowed some $15 billion for destructive purposes in 1917 and 1918 and soon afterwards embarked on a great prosperity joy ride with surplus governmental revenues which were positively embarrassing. We can borrow up to $5 billion for constructive enterprises and necessary human relief without a qualm."[6]

To devise a long-range recovery program, Chase suggested a national planning board of one hundred experts, to be drawn from the ranks of leading scientists, academics, financiers, and statesmen. This group would be responsible for coordinating all basic industries, including huge mechanized farms, into state trusts. While the federal government would exercise a general supervisory control over these trusts, each component industry would be permitted to operate in large part as an independent unit. Intelligent planning for the future production needs of the nation would be facilitated by a federal incorporation law affecting all companies capitalized at $1 million or more. Through the detailed reports required of such federal corporations, Chase's experts would be able to construct a "glorious system of industrial statistics, leading to wise measures of coordination, guidance, and control."[7] Once the new machinery had begun to function smoothly, Chase would end his imagined dictatorship and turn over the management of the state to a permanent board of engineers.

There was no room for democratic politics in this scheme. Although Chase presupposed at the outset that public opinion supported the creation of his dictatorship, he made no provision for protecting the rights of future dissenters. In fact, concern for civil rights or civil liberties of any kind is conspicuously absent from his utopia. The benevolent social planners, it appears, must be protected from any misguided efforts to obstruct their work. It will be necessary, Chase declares, to maintain a "stout and efficient federal police corps . . . for future reference in domestic reforms." And his solution to the crime problem is a chilling exercise in cost-benefit analysis:

The flower of the ex-army, the ex-navy, and the ex-marine corps will be picked to declare immediate war on the gangster, to invest every great city, and by any means, military or civil, to drive him to immediate capitulation or death. . . . Of the gunmen who escape alive, the youths I shall put in special schools and strive to recondition their habits; the veterans I can waste no further time upon. Their reconditioning is too expensive a matter. Hopeless cases will be placed on a large, roomy, uninhabited island, together with all the surplus stocks of government munitions, especially bombs and firearms, and bidden to go to it in one last grand fusillade.[8]

Chase's fellow contributors all agreed on the importance of national planning but differed over the extent of such planning and whether it should be carried out by public or private agencies. Glenn Frank, a university president and syndicated editorial writer, looked to enlightened business leaders to restructure the economy by creating and managing an "integrated national organization in each distinctive field of economic enterprise." In a return to the New Era thinking of the 1920s, Frank argued that visionary industrial statesmen were best qualified to restore the nation to prosperity by developing a "practical" program for the wider distribution of national income through policies of higher wages, shorter working hours, and lower prices. The key to recovery did not lie in restricting production, he insisted, but in expanding the purchasing power of consumers: "We need neither a Stalin nor a Mussolini if enough of our *big-business* men are really *big* business men, and if they will think socially and act nationally respecting this central problem of the wider distribution of buying power, which, while imperative in the interest of social justice and social stability, is at the same time both the best insurance policy for capitalism and the best business policy for capitalists."[9] Should business leaders fail to embrace the concept of limited wealth redistribution, Frank proposed to bring them into line by threatening to impose punitive income taxes on them and their companies. Unlike Chase, he did not envisage the need for any further exercise of government power. The business civilization of the 1920s had already established the preconditions for an "ideal society" in the United States, he maintained, and the entrepreneurs who had solved the problem of mass production could be relied on to provide as well for the mass distribution of machine-made goods.

No other commentator shared Frank's trust in the self-governing capabilities of a now discredited business elite. Two English publicists, impressed by the worldwide nature of the depression, called not merely for government planning but for the creation of a new world order to maintain peace and ensure the equitable distribution of the world's goods. "The planning must be world-wide," asserted G. Lowes Dickinson. "The first thing a world order would do would be to adjust production to consumption; and nothing but a world order could do it." Dickinson urged the United States and Great Britain to take the lead in pressing for disarmament and free trade as first steps toward the construction of a viable world government: "If they can cooperate, if they can so use their popular institutions that capital itself will cooperate in its own transformation, and if meantime they can maintain the peace of the world, they may inaugurate the new order before its collapse into chaos."[10]

In a similar vein, Harold Laski looked to the creation of a peaceful world order as part of a larger policy of democratizing human relationships. A socialist in politics, Laski favored public control of the "essential sources of wealth—finance, power, coal, transport, iron and steel" and the equalization of income for men and women. He also advocated sweeping changes in existing educational systems, which catered to the privileged few and denied the majority any meaningful access to the "cultural heritage of the race": "The creative use of leisure, which, in an age dominated by the machine, is for most the period of significance, is unattainable by men whom education has not trained to the use of the mind in speculative matters. An unequal society does not permit this training to be widespread; partly because it wants, as nearly as may be, a monopoly of knowledge for the class already in possession, and partly because a society in which men and women were educated, that is, trained to the use of mind as a skeptical instrument, would not long continue to endure the consequences of inequality."[11]

The remaining four contributors paid greater attention to political details and constitutional procedures in their utopian projections. Lewis Mumford described a future society—the "Green Republic"—whose managers are held accountable to the occupational groups they represent: "Today the citizen does not vote through his political party; he votes through his corporation—through his city, his university, his factory, his consumers' cooperative, his professional association; he has as many votes as he has interests and functions."[12] In Mumford's utopia old-style political demagogues have been replaced by able administrators, whose task is to harmonize the disparate needs of organized corporate bodies. Land, capital, and credit have all been socialized, and the system guarantees every individual a minimum level of subsistence. But the planning process no longer seeks to maximize production or to serve only market needs, as under capitalism: "Our problem in America, unlike that of our comrades in Soviet Russia, is to reduce the tempo of industrialism. We must turn society from its feverish preoccupation with money-making inventions, goods, profits, salesmanship, symbolic representations of wealth to the deliberate promotion of the more humane functions of life."[13] Such an agenda requires government sponsorship of the arts, decentralized factories and workplaces, new regional cities of livable size, small progressive schools, and a reliance on local corporations as vehicles for the expression of grassroots political opinion. In short, Mumford urged, "[W]e must recover the human scale." Unlike Stuart Chase, he distrusted engineers and other specialists schooled only in "hard facts"; they might be tempted to carry the organizing principle too far, he thought. Humanistic college administrators would make better social planners, since they were more likely to recognize that "the real use of organization is to leave large tracts of life in freedom and peace."[14]

Morris L. Ernst, lawyer and civil libertarian, pledged that his recommendations would conform to constitutional guidelines, including those mandated by "the nine venerable men who sit in the United States Supreme Court as ultimate-veto dictators."[15] In an essay retitled "If I Were a (Constitutional) Dictator," Ernst called for immediate constitutional conventions on both the state and federal levels, so that the people might reconsider basic provisions, such as "our present wasteful theory of checks and balances." To keep the law abreast of changing social conditions, he proposed that constitutional conventions be held automatically every ten years, and that all statutes similarly terminate at the end of each decade, unless previously reenacted.

Having established a basis for legitimate government action through constitutional revision, Ernst outlined a broad welfare state agenda. In addition to high income and inheritance taxes, his proposals included government ownership of transportation and communication facilities and natural resources; regulation of milk, bread, coal, and other necessities of life as "public utilities"; the pooling of repossessed farmholdings to create a gigantic farm corporation for the cooperative development of the farming industry; extensive public works and slum clearance programs; health, unemployment, and old-age insurance; the encouragement of large trusts in every field of American business under the regulatory supervision of an enlarged and powerful Federal Trade Commission; an end to all forms of state censorship; and the enforcement of the constitutionally guaranteed civil rights of African Americans.

A similar emphasis on civil rights and constitutional revision appeared in the thinking of Oswald Garrison Villard, a liberal publisher and the grandson of abolitionist William Lloyd Garrison. Villard urged the need for "vital alterations" in the Constitution to permit government ownership and operation of major industries and to achieve the other welfare state objectives advocated by Morris Ernst. He also called for new state constitutions that would abolish bicameral legislatures and replace them with a single chamber of some twenty-four members, "more in the nature of a governor's council." These one-house legislatures would be elected on a non-partisan basis, and all patronage positions would henceforth be subject to rigorous civil service rules. The plan recalled some Progressive proposals for more efficient administrative government, as did Villard's design for restructuring municipal institutions: "So with our municipalities, I should eliminate politics and make the office of mayor a scientific job to be held by professional mayors freed from all political control, precisely as is the case today in Germany, instituting local referendums that the people might vote upon policies."[16] Like Ernst, he favored an end to government censorship and suggested that literary "censors and snoopers" should be exiled to the Virgin Islands.

The last contributor to the series, Kansas newspaper editor William Allen White, drew even more heavily than Villard upon the Progressive reform tradition. Confessing at the outset that he did not consider the existing political system "half bad," White proposed to mobilize popular support for his constitutional initiatives by commandeering the services of powerful lobbying groups—"all those happy little soviets in American life that form public opinion and hold Congress in leash."[17] With the aid of this "invisible government," he would convene a small conference of capable politicians, such as Al Smith and Calvin Coolidge. These practical statesmen would be charged with developing programs to guarantee every American job and wage security, a minimum standard of living, and comprehensive health, accident, and old-age insurance. The entire process might take as long as two decades, and grassroots input would be secured through a favorite Progressive device: the referendum. Specifically, White called for a "constitutional amendment which shall provide that when half of the States, through a majority of each house in their legislatures with the governor concurring, shall demand a national referendum upon any given subject, whether of [a] statute or a constitutional enactment, then the Congress shall submit the proposition to a direct vote of the people of the States." If a future constitutional proposal should be approved by a majority of voters in two-thirds of the states, it would become a new amendment to the Constitution. Under such a liberalized procedure, White argued, "no minority, no section, no class could ever rule this country against the wishes and the will of a majority of the people."[18]

Other publicists moved beyond magazine and newspaper articles to offer book-length prescriptions for constitutional change. "[T]he abysmal year 1932 became for many of us a time of hope," Matthew Josephson remembered.

> Was it only utopian hope? Virtually all the social inventions that had come into use in other societies in the name of human welfare or progress had been denounced in former times because they were based on intelligent calculations of the probable or the possible. Many people were now aware of the inherent contradictions within the society that were pressing with intolerable force against the bonds of the old order; that in these days the busy workers of our cities were being turned into idle and hungry louts while our once patriotic farmers became increasingly rebels and lawbreakers; and now they were confident that our people would soon say as with one voice that they could no longer live in a world where such things can be.[19]

In keeping with this optimistic mood, six representative works from 1932 and early 1933 described alternative societies in which constitutional changes laid the foundation for a utopian future.

William Kay Wallace provided the most sustained critique of the existing Constitution in *Our Obsolete Constitution* (1932). A diplomat turned historian and political analyst, Wallace charged that a preindustrial, eighteenth-century plan of government could no longer serve the needs of a modern industrial society. Framed by men who believed in a mystical natural law and who feared the oppressive power of the state, the Constitution sought to protect the basic political rights of the individual against all governmental encroachments. It controlled ordinary legislation as a form of higher law and derived its authority from the sovereign people. With the rise of a mature industrial system, however, economic factors have replaced political principles "as the determinants of social life," and the Constitution has become increasingly anachronistic.

"Our Constitution has to be rewritten," Wallace contended. "It must take cognizance of the new mentality that has grown up among us. . . . It should accept new economic values, in place of worn-out political shibboleths. . . . We do not need to-day a Declaration of Independence that sets forth in high-sounding phrases platitudes about political liberty and equality, the rights of man and the sovereignty of the people. What men and women of to-day are interested in is *economic liberty and social welfare*. It is with these that our new Constitution must be concerned."[20]

The industrial process itself furnished a model for constitutional reorganization. Successful corporations have maintained good relations with their employees and the consuming public, engaged in long-range planning, and achieved greater efficiency through scientific management techniques and cost-saving mergers. As lobbying organizations, moreover, they have wielded great political power, albeit in an extralegal and irresponsible way. "Our Government has already passed under group control," Wallace remarked in an insightful passage. "Yet these groups that have grown up in the state and are the corner stone of our economic structure have no public status, no recognition as part of the essential fabric of the state. The result is corruption and chaos."[21]

He proposed to bring all productive enterprises directly into the governing structure by stripping the state of its pretended sovereignty and reducing it to the level of a simple corporation like any other, "chief among equals—*primus inter pares*": "Under our new Constitution, the state will include many corporations, all of which will perform public functions." The new system of "Scientific Capitalism" will be based on ascertainable economic facts rather than such political fictions as "natural law" and "popular sovereignty." Individual rights will no longer exist, since the state will deal only with corporate groups: "In the new society our first allegiance will be to the corporation which directly affords us the economic liberty and security which we crave." Government will become primarily administrative—an efficient business operation—with the Constitution serving as "a guide in procedure, more in the nature of a body of rules for conducting public affairs than claiming to be a source of authority, a sacred writ."[22]

Although Wallace did not attempt to draft a model constitution for his readers, he did outline some key provisions in a concluding chapter. The new instrument of government, he affirmed, must recognize that all citizens have certain inalienable economic rights, including:

1. The right to the full fruits of one's labor.
2. The right to economic security.
3. The right to education.
4. The right to leisure.[23]

To protect these rights, the state must guarantee social security to its citizens through comprehensive programs of public insurance and job training. Since traditional politics will play no role in the new order, the structure of government must be downsized and reconstituted along efficient business lines. Instead of the current forty-eight states, Wallace recommended a system of nine regional units, each of which would elect four to six representatives to form a "Board of Directors of the United States." The board would select one of its members as president; it would also exercise legislative functions and appoint federal judges and other national officers from the ranks of the civil service. All corporations that serve a "preponderantly social need," such as public utilities, transportation facilities, banks, and insurance companies, will be brought under public ownership, and a system of national economic planning will replace the competitive business practices of the past. In a faint echo of Edward Bellamy's *Looking Backward,* Wallace predicted that all citizens of his projected state "will come to be looked upon as stockholders of the national industrial and commercial enterprises and . . . beneficiaries under a highly developed scheme of insurance that will insure their social welfare."[24]

A national constitutional convention should be called at once to frame the new instrument of government, he urged. Such a gathering of delegates representing "all of the diverse elements of our social life" would command popular respect and win the support of a majority of voters in state ratification campaigns. "[T]he only alternative," he warned, "is an armed revolution, at a not distant date."[25] Although Wallace thus promised to install his version of the welfare state through peaceful constitutional revision, certain aspects of his plan raise troubling questions. What about minority rights? In a system that has replaced political conflict with administrative management, will there be any room for nonconformity? Wallace assured his readers that his code of economic rights would supplement their existing political rights, but he provided no mechanism for the enforcement of those political rights. He seems to have assumed that group negotiation would resolve all problems, especially since the state has been reduced to the level of a mere corporation like any other. But in matters of social planning, the state remains "the supreme economic arbiter," and some of its "coordinating" powers appear highly threatening to individual liberty: "The state must be able to conscript if need be, and at all events control, the services of all of its citizens, in peace as well as in war."[26] Despite its benign objectives, then, Wallace's model of corporate government demanded some heavy sacrifices of individual freedom in return for its guarantee of social security.

James Cooper Lawrence imagined a very different constitutional system in *The Year of Regeneration: An Improbable Fiction* (1932). Dean of a large midwestern university and a former corporation president, Lawrence drew upon his experience as a member of the President's Emergency Committee for Unemployment of 1930–1931 in constructing his utopia.

The narrative, set fifty years in the future, purports to explain, through recently discovered documents, how one man saved the country from impending collapse in 1932. The hero of the tale is "the Master," who founds a secret patriotic society, the Sons of Liberty, to rescue the nation from a "calamitous sense of drift." With the aid of a powerful truth drug, the Master and his associates effect a bloodless coup by persuading the president, the vice president, the cabinet, and half of Congress to resign their offices. Thereupon the rump Congress names an interim president— the Master's choice—and proceeds to enact a sweeping program of government reorganization.

At the heart of this program lies a determination to reduce the size and power of government and restore individual initiative and self-sufficiency. Congress takes immediate steps to consolidate departments and dismiss unnecessary government employees. A Reorganization Act suspends for one year all federal regulatory and service functions and provides that no federal money may be spent during that time on any project that does not directly benefit "*all* of the people." To deal with the unemployment problem, Congress enacts a comprehensive Civil Draft bill modeled in part on the Selective Service legislation of World War I. Pursuant to the new law, all persons between the ages of sixteen and seventy must report to a local board for job classification and must carry a registration card with them at all times.

The potential workforce falls into several broad categories, ranging from self-employed professionals to a "subnormal" class of criminals and mental defectives. While the system seems to involve an extraordinary degree of regimentation, Lawrence insists that it avoids the excesses of both Soviet state planning and capitalist "vocational anarchy." Under the civil draft, an individual is free to choose any fulfilling occupation, but one's initial "self-appraisal" must be confirmed or rejected by a panel of neighbors in light of mental and physical tests and current data on national labor needs. If a person fails to receive a coveted job assignment, he or she may secure a reclassification hearing at a later date. The process ostensibly preserves individual initiative, while acknowledging society's interest in preventing the costly misuse of human resources.

Lawrence's most original proposals relate to those in Class III: "Citizens enlisted in the Industrial and Agricultural Reserve." Noting that the market economy of the 1920s had produced large numbers of marginal farmers and laid-off workers, he argues that these groups may become self-supporting if they break their dependence on market forces by joining a "homestead center." Such centers—subsistence farming and manufacturing villages—serve only the needs of their local inhabitants; they have no contact with the larger economy. Yet they do not reflect any nostalgia for a simpler way of life or any effort to recreate the utopian communes of the nineteenth century. Modern homesteaders will enjoy all the benefits of technology, including electricity, up-to-date sanitation facilities, labor-saving appliances, and access to the latest techniques of scientific farming. In addition, by cultivating their land successfully for ten years, they will receive free title to their subsistence tract, a house, and shares in village enterprises.

The object of the program, explains the Master, is individual self-sufficiency: "to make one-eighth of our population (Class III) independent of the other seven-eighths and to free that one-eighth from exploitation as part of a system of production and distribution dependent upon the fluctuations of the market place."[27] Homesteaders will not constitute a permanent "peasant" class, since they will be free, like other citizens, to apply for reclassification. To pay for the construction of the homestead villages, the states have merely to divert tax funds formerly used to maintain their criminal and dependent classes—a function now taken over exclusively by the federal government.

Like the homestead program, federal crime-fighting combines costly innovation with fiscal conservatism. Gangsters and other "social liabilities" in Class V find themselves permanently removed from productive society and shipped to federal "cantonments" in several southern states. Such persons do not have to be convicted of a specific crime to incur such lifetime banishment; for example, mere failure to register for the draft constitutes prima facie evidence of one's parasitic nature and places on civil draft evaders the burden of proving that they are useful members of the community. Individuals assigned to the "Class V" category enjoy no constitutional rights, except the right to engage in whatever self-supporting and useful activities the cantonments may afford. Males and females are strictly segregated to prevent any increase in the number of misfits, and, in a related move, the federal government bans all further immigration from abroad. The Master's rationale for this repressive policy draws heavily on the xenophobic attitudes of the 1920s:

If we are to survive and to achieve an existence as a homogeneous healthy people, there can be no place for maudlin sentimentality seeking to preserve the "right" of the unfit to pollute and break down the fit. It is time for what is left of a healthy body-politic to assert its own right to self-protection. In legislating for social liabilities, our first thought must be to insure maximum protection and a minimum burden for social assets. Then enlightened programs for the social liabilities can be carried out behind barriers forever separating them from that part of the world which, in return for support and constructive care, should reasonably insist upon permanent protection for itself.[28]

All expenditures for the building and operation of the cantonments are offset by corresponding reductions in other federal programs. The all-out assault on organized crime thus moves forward with no increase in taxes and with the prospect of additional funding from the forfeited estates of deceased criminals and incompetents.

While the Civil Draft bill mandates an expanded role for the federal government in crime control, a companion measure—the Economic Readjustment Act—removes all federal supervision of the economy. "The production and the distribution of consumer goods and services are neither necessary nor desirable functions of our government," declares the Master. "As an alternative to promoters' and productionists' anarchy, existing 'regulation' makes government undertake to do for consumers things which consumers can do much better for themselves through another agency."[29] The new law encourages citizens to combine their purchasing power by forming a Consumers' National Buying Corporation to obtain goods and services at reasonable cost. Businesses are likewise permitted to pool their resources; the antitrust laws are repealed; and a single "managing corporation" emerges in each industrial and commercial field to negotiate on equal terms with the consumers' group. The system, Lawrence argues, eliminates the old Progressive conflict between "the people" and "the interests," since consumers ("the people") now have an important voice in the shaping of corporate policies. In practice, however, all important consumer decisions will be "guided" by disinterested experts— "men who really knew standards, costs, and values"[30]—within the national consumer organization. Stripped of its democratic rhetoric, the proposed economic restructuring merely replaces government regulators with private businessmen in an updated version of New Era ideology.

To institutionalize the Master's vision of "simplified" government in a more permanent form, Congress issues a call for a new Constitutional Convention, to meet in Philadelphia at the end of May 1932. The names of the delegates—"150 carefully chosen leaders of the nation"—are not revealed to the public, and the group is secretly diverted to a chartered ocean liner in New York harbor on the eve of the first session. Under destroyer escort the ship sails to an undisclosed point in mid-ocean, providing the delegates with an atmosphere of total seclusion in which to conduct their deliberations. The result is a document that radically changes the nature of American government.

Under the new Constitution, the federal government may exercise only a handful of expressly conferred powers: to preserve the public peace; to conduct foreign policy and wage war on rare occasions; to maintain the postal service; to establish courts of justice; and to impose such taxes as may be needed to carry out those specified functions. In addition, a balanced budget provision prevents Congress from increasing expenditures during a twenty-year period without making corresponding reductions in the existing federal budget. Such a drastic curtailment of federal power recalls the "night watchman" model of government that prevailed through much of the nineteenth century.

Downsizing and simplification affect the institutional structure of the federal government in equally striking ways. The framers of the new Constitution abandon checks and balances between the executive and legislative branches and reduce Congress to a one-house body of 170 members. Besides three representatives from each state, the national legislature now includes in its sessions the president, the vice president, sixteen other executive officers, and eight members-at-large, who are chosen by party caucus from the top leaders of the two major parties. General elections occur every six years, and the president may not seek a second term. To enable a newly elected president to implement his program, voters in each state select congressional candidates on a group basis; the winner of the presidential contest receives two of the three representatives from every state that he carries. As Lawrence explains, "Under this provision Congress and the executive arm of the government were definitely merged into a single action group, with responsibility for action resting upon the President and his two-thirds majority in Congress. Upon the remaining one-third of the members, there rested the duty of criticizing, challenging, and bringing into the clear light of day motives and methods in connection with all of the acts of the majority party."[31] While this cumbersome machinery seeks to avoid the gridlock that had developed during Hoover's administration, it energizes a government that has already been stripped of most powers by other constitutional provisions.

To enforce such restraints on federal action, the Constitution continues to rely on the judicial branch, which it leaves unchanged. In addition, it creates an important new review agency, the "Tribunes of the People." These three officers, chosen by state electors immediately following each presidential election, hold their positions for a single six-year term and receive the same compensation as the president. Their duty is "to defend and to uphold the rights of the people of the United States against personal, corporate, or state infringement." In carrying out this mandate, they may at any time by unanimous vote suspend for one year any congressional law or executive order that they judge to be "not in the interest of the people of the United States."[32]

The Convention completes its work in July; voters ratify the Constitution in a November election; and the new system goes into effect in March 1933. During the same transition period the forty-eight states overhaul their own constitutions and follow the federal model by providing that new laws may be enacted at only one regular session of their legislatures every six years: "The character of American state legislative bodies therefore changed with the character of the federal Congress, and these bodies became small groups devoted primarily to the formulation and criticism of governmental policies, to the carrying out of those policies, to the making of necessary governmental appropriations, and only incidentally and occasionally to the making of laws."[33]

In contrast to Lawrence's call for less government, Duval McCutchen argued for a dramatic expansion of the welfare state in *America Made Young: A Plan for a More Perfect Society*. "Almost all of the Constitution is written on one idea and one alone: quantity to the lives of the subjects," asserted McCutchen. "Only with the institution of the 18th Amendment, whether it is good or bad or whether it accurately expresses the intention of the people or not, did the people of the United States recognize, however vaguely they did recognize it, that a Government has a duty to . . . regulate the quality of people's lives in the interest of society."[34] His protagonist, the visionary Quint Garnickel, proposes to end the depression by means of a new amendment—the Twentieth Amendment—which will comprise a "Constitution of Quality" for the American people.

Like some Progressive novelists of a generation earlier, McCutchen includes the full sixteen-page text of Article XX in the body of his work. The new amendment creates a system of educational governance that parallels the political structure established in the original Constitution. The central institution in McCutchen's utopia is the University of the United States, an arm of the federal government that offers three years of subsidized training to any high school graduate who wishes it. (In fact, educational

subsidies for the children of needy parents begin with elementary school.)
The state pays young people to stay in school at all levels, since it regards
the educational process as an essential training ground for altruistic and
enlightened citizens.[35]

At the university, students pursue a program heavily weighted toward
sociology, political science, and philosophy. They spend much of their
time doing factual research and preparing monographs on important
social issues. The professors in turn criticize and coordinate these monographs and eventually transform them into legislative policy recommendations, which voters approve or reject in popular referenda. As a government research institute, the university somewhat resembles a Legislative
Reference Library, of the sort pioneered by Wisconsin in the Progressive
era. But its agenda extends far beyond the solution of specific social problems. Through its Social Council, staffed by the most brilliant members of
the faculty, it aims at nothing less than the elaboration of an authoritative
system of moral values to guide the emerging new order. "Government, in
itself, ought to be almost a religion to its citizens," Garnickel maintains.
"One of the pressing needs of the day is an up-to-date, authoritative, and
intellectual viewpoint, a viewpoint such as religion once gave. The whole
World badly needs a social philosophy that includes the advanced learning
of the day while not clashing with the astuteness of the modern mind: this
intellectual social and cosmic philosophy is needed as a correlative factor
to lend the sense of direction to the people of the Earth that they so badly
yearn for."[36]

In more mundane terms, modern government must provide all citizens
with an equal opportunity for advancement and must further guarantee a
comfortable livelihood to those who promise to become worthy members
of society. The determination of a person's merit rests with the Judiciary
Department of the university. All graduating students must take a final ex-
amination, which assesses both their academic knowledge and their personal qualities. If they pass, they receive a certificate of merit, and their
judges (who double as a personnel board) attempt to place them in a suit-
able job with a private business or industry. Should no opening be currently available, a graduate may continue to do subsidized research at the
university or enter a postgraduate program elsewhere at state expense.
Such an extensive welfare system presupposes a radical redistribution of
the nation's wealth, which the government manages by nationalizing all
banks and insurance companies and taking complete control of the economy.

Reviewers paid little attention to McCutchen's book,[37] for understandable reasons. Apart from its heavy-handed style, it offers no credible political analysis of the sort found in the works of Wallace and Lawrence. In fact, McCutchen makes no real effort to relate the complex workings of his amendment to the rest of the Constitution, beyond noting that the president of the university will also serve as secretary of education in the cabinet of the president of the United States. *America Made Young* thus remains a fantasy of social planning by a nonpartisan intellectual and scientific elite, rather than by members of the business community.

And this utopia has its dark side as well. Although every healthy woman will receive a payment from the state to insure her economic independence, all undesirables—the physically and mentally defective and criminals—will be weeded out and exiled to isolated colonies for the remainder of their lives. In time, McCutchen suggests, the university community will absorb the larger "good society," and the Twentieth Amendment will swallow up the older Constitution. Despite its blatant weaknesses, his book does raise some important questions concerning the role of government in a postindustrial society.

A more traditional model of an emerging welfare state appears in Charles Elton Blanchard's *A New Day Dawns: A Brief History of the Altruistic Era (1930 to 2162 A.D.)*. Blanchard, a physician and socialist, uses a fictitious government historian of the future to describe the "great change" that transformed American society in the middle years of the twentieth century. This narrative device, familiar to readers of Bellamy's *Looking Backward,* enables him to contrast the oppressive conditions under capitalism with the benefits of a collectivist order. The transition to a fully socialized economy occurs gradually through the political process, as a coalition of Feminists and National-Progressives summons a "National Congress" to frame a modern Constitution in 1950.

The delegates, who represent "the many phases of our industrial, commercial and social activities" rather than geographic areas, devise a constitutional system that builds on the Progressive reform legacy. A one-house Congress of 500 members operates through committees that reflect the interests of major industrial and social service groups. Old-style political parties have no place in this "industrial democracy," which relies on centralized and coordinated planning. A popularly elected president holds office for a single five-year term, assisted by a cabinet of ten department heads, four of whom oversee social welfare programs. Federal judges, too, are subject to popular election for a term of years and may no longer strike down "any action of Congress" on constitutional grounds. All public officials may be removed from office by a majority vote of the electorate, and controversial congressional measures may acquire instant constitutional status through a popular referendum. "We should be able to change the constitution from year to year," explains the first woman president in 1963. "Any law passed by Congress and approved by a referendum vote of the people should automatically amend the constitution and repeal any existing statutes it contradicts. The Supreme Court will be no longer needed to thwart the will of the people expressed through Congress."[38]

Despite its democratic features, however, Blanchard's utopia relies ultimately on rule by experts. Eugenic considerations dominate his account of the "New Day," and the true heroes of his narrative are the dedicated professionals of the National Health Service, a major executive department. Every law must serve the cause of "race welfare," from literacy tests for voting to the elimination of the "unfit," a broadly defined category: "Laws were passed authorizing the health officials to sterilize all persons of both sexes not proper subjects for parenthood. If now and then a baby came into the world which from any cause could not possibly make a success of life, the law permitted its removal by humane and painless methods."[39] Eventually the Health Service regulates every aspect of "sex hygiene" and the reproductive process. Through its control of drug manufacturing and distribution, it eliminates infectious diseases; through its licensing requirements for marriage and procreation, it monitors the national birthrate; and by perfecting a method of artificial insemination, it enables women to beget genetically superior children by utilizing the sperm of carefully selected male "seeders." The popularity of this "injection method" among black women solves America's race problem in time, as they continue to "give birth to whiter and whiter-skinned babies":

> [A]t this writing, in 2160, the black race has really disappeared and in its place we have a dark-skinned people, yet with but few specimens showing any of the old negroid features. Our colored people today are fine physical and mental developments. Many of the females are beautiful, and both sexes have given us individuals of special talent in all departments of our life. We have not absorbed the black race, but into it have injected enough white blood to hasten its evolution and prepared it to take a worthy place in our Collective life.[40]

With its trappings of noblesse oblige, Blanchard's world of "applied eugenics" proves as odiously racist as Thomas Dixon's idealized version of the southern caste system a generation earlier.[41] To enjoy the benefits of life in the New Day, one must conform at all times to the will of the majority, as guided by a benevolent bureaucratic elite. Even voting becomes a communal obligation, which the state rigorously enforces. Any qualified voter who fails to cast a ballot in an election is liable to criminal prosecution and the loss of citizenship. While Blanchard's utopia guarantees full equality to its female citizens, the loss of constitutional protections for the individual heavily outweighs such advances.[42]

Constitutional changes precede and justify the utopian systems described by Wallace, Lawrence, McCutchen, and Blanchard. In Frederick Palmer's *So a Leader Came,* on the other hand, it takes an extraconstitutional dictatorship to launch the new order. Palmer, dean of American war correspondents, established his literary reputation in the Progressive years, and his novel owes much to Colonel House's prewar utopia, *Philip Dru, Administrator.* Like Dru, Constant ("Connie") Spenser is an impossibly heroic figure who lives only to serve his nation and his fellow man. The son of a brilliant scientist, Connie distinguishes himself on the battlefields of World War I and earns a national reputation for his leadership qualities. A close student of government, he deplores the evils of machine politics and calls for radical constitutional revision to restore a responsible party system.

"What would Washington or Jefferson say to the spectacle of our two national conventions?" he asks in an impromptu debate with a fatuous senator.

> There is no authority for them, and all the political system of which they are the supreme expression in the Constitution. At the Conventions our rulers make their secret bargains for politic's sake. The convention is the last word in standardization in an age which requires suppleness. Its public appeal is that of the old town meeting idea. Delegates from all the country gather. They cheer the platform chosen by a little group of insiders—our priests of Isis, our conventionalized machine rulers.
>
> . . . And the people are left to choose between two indefinite platforms, two indefinite candidates. So the two political parties arrange our affairs. They have so mechanized politics that we must be ruled by one or the other. Thus we submit to fate, without much interest as to which it is, as the Colonists submitted to the royal governors.[43]

With its accompanying denunciation of an "invisible government" of financial and industrial oligarchs, Connie's complaint might have been lifted bodily from the pages of any Progressive reform novel. But Palmer does add one new ingredient to the standard picture: powerful criminal gangs, who have their own reasons for supporting a corrupt and ineffective two-party system.

To revive principled democratic leadership, Connie proposes a system based on European parliamentary models. Under the new institutional structure, the president will lose all political power; he will serve merely as a nonpartisan head of state, whose ceremonial duties will include calling Congress into special session in times of emergency. Real executive power will vest in an elected Premier, a seasoned politician with a proven record of public service, "instead of being the hit-and-miss choice of a national party convention." As head of the majority party in Congress, the Premier will be under constant public scrutiny to carry out his party's announced program. His cabinet appointees will sit in Congress, chair major congressional committees, and take part in legislative debates on pending measures. Such an arrangement will minimize interbranch friction and encourage Congress to act as a truly national body: "Congress would be occupied with nation building instead of home fence building."[44]

Connie outlines his program in a book—*Soon or Never!*—that stimulates popular interest in the Constitution and quickly becomes a best-seller. In the aftermath of his well-publicized debate, his supporters—the "Minute Men of the Restoration"—set to work organizing a Constitution Party in communities around the country. (Their slogan: "Are you for restoring or continuing to betray the spirit and intent of the Constitution?")[45] Although the old party machines manage to keep Connie's name off the ballot for the forthcoming presidential election, his followers nevertheless flock to the polls and give him an overwhelming (if unofficial) electoral victory.

When Congress ignores this result and refuses to approve an amendment incorporating the central features of his plan, Connie marches on Washington with a large force of unarmed "Constis," representing a cross-section of "honest" Americans from all social classes. Units of the army and national guard, dispatched to turn back the marchers, join them instead and ensure the success of this bloodless revolution. In Washington, Connie proclaims a temporary dictatorship until his new constitutional system can be firmly established. Congress adjourns; the Supreme Court Justices resign en masse; and Connie becomes "Premier of the Provisional Government of the United States."

For the next four years he governs by executive decrees, which do little to reshape American institutions, apart from the structure of the federal government. "I am for private enterprise in banking and in industry for the same reason that I am for direct, responsible, open government," he explains.

> Let me simplify my meaning. A man who owns a car, a horse, a cow, an acre of ground, a shop, pays close attention to that property which is under his hand. . . . But when he owns stocks of a value as great as his shop, or car, or acre of ground, his property is remote. He takes no active interest in management. . . .
>
> If he owns a small portion of a steel plant or a biscuit factory then he ought to study steel and biscuits. Frequent and full reports of the corporations should be at his disposal. There should be as active and resolute a public opinion turned on the management of each corporation as upon that of national and local government. The choice of directors of a corporation should be under as strict scrutiny by industrial stockholders as that of Congressmen by the citizen stockholders. Once the stockholders of our industries and the stockholders of the nation show really intelligent self-interest, individualism will have proved itself worthy of the situation and master of it. We shall have better leaders, and a restoration of true spirit in private and public affairs.[46]

The only economic innovation that Connie favors is the creation of a central bank to help stabilize private financial markets.

Since organized crime has become a national problem, however, he does approve the establishment of a new national police under the secretary of the interior. And he orders all citizens to register on a certain day and receive an identity card from the state. Those who cannot prove that they are lawfully employed are segregated and forced to work under government supervision. The crime-control initiative represents the most significant expansion of federal power in the new order, which otherwise resembles a streamlined model of laissez-faire. Committed to the revival of "responsible individualism" as a solution to the depression crisis, Connie rejects all forms of public relief.

Once his ideas are embodied in a new Constitution, he steps down as Premier to permit the normal political process to resume. On the day when his successor is being inaugurated, he and a bodyguard are attacked by a crazed gunman (harboring "an ancient gangster grudge") as they walk the quiet streets of Washington. Mortally wounded, Connie sacrifices his life for his vision of constitutional renewal.

Implicit in Palmer's narrative is the idea that, in times of extreme emergency, the sovereign people may exercise their power directly and approve a course of action that violates constitutional norms. Connie establishes his dictatorship in response to an overwhelming popular mandate. His march therefore represents a legitimate expression of the public will, not a lawless demonstration of force, argues a liberal Supreme Court Justice:

> Force, in the form of the Roman legions, supported the Justinian code. It gave us Magna Charta. Under Washington it made the Declaration of Independence the treasure of a nation's archives when, if Washington had failed, the Declaration would have been a curiosity put up for sale to collectors at auctions. . . . Physical force becomes master when moral force will no longer support law. Public opinion, when it is backed by physical force, must prevail. . . . And physical force, backed by public opinion, is there before us in the streets—a police force speaking for a decision made by unarmed civilians whom armed men would not resist.[47]

By the time Palmer's novel appeared in the fall of 1932, newspapers and magazines were discussing real-life proposals for strong executive leadership grounded in popular consent. Typical was Ralph Adams Cram's essay "How Shall We Govern?" in the July 13th issue of *The Commonweal*, a Catholic weekly review. Cram, a conservative social critic, dismissed constitutional quibbles at the outset: "Under the implied powers of the President, as these exist in the American Constitution, he, in times of critical danger to the republic, may assume and does assume something approaching dictatorial power. I suggest that in the present crisis in world affairs, . . . the danger that confronts us is equal to that which develops in time of civil war, and that therefore it is the duty of the President of the United States to act outside the law."[48] In keeping with this expansive theory of presidential power, Cram urged President Hoover to proclaim a state of national emergency, dissolve Congress, and invite the governors of the several states to join him and his cabinet in the formation of a provisional government. Until the November elections this "Council of State" should govern by decree, taking any actions that promised to restore public confidence and establish "a just and equitable system of government." In November voters would select a new Congress, as well as a president and vice president. If the new electorate rejected the president's program by voting his opponents into office, he would be expected to ratify the popular will by surrendering to the courts for possible disciplinary action. While a *Commonweal* editorial disavowed this "bold plan," the writer nevertheless agreed "that the inadequacy of the type of men who have seized political and economic power has been shockingly exposed, and that some form of dictatorial reaction against such a situation is more than likely."[49]

Fantasies of a presidential dictatorship culminated in *Gabriel over the White House,* the most remarkable utopian novel of the early 1930s and the only one to reach a mass audience through its movie adaptation. Published anonymously in January 1933, the work attracted instant public attention both in the United States and in England, where it was released under the title *Reinhard.* The author's identity soon became known; he was an Englishman, Thomas Frederic Tweed, an underwriter for Lloyds of London and a trusted political adviser to David Lloyd George and others in Britain's Liberal Party.[50] Tweed's novel impressed readers on both sides of the Atlantic. As Herbert Horwill reported from London, "All the reviewers pay tribute to its boldness of conception and its brilliance of execution. . . . One of our weeklies says it is 'so far the big literary sensation of the year,' and certainly it has made a stir in both literary and political circles."[51] And American reviewers likewise responded positively. "The narrative treats with rare common sense a multitude of contemporary affairs," wrote a critic in the *New York Times,* "and though the author masters them with a rather dubious ease, his handling of them seldom transcends the conceivable."[52] The book, written in the course of a leisurely summer trip aboard a Mediterranean freighter, could not have been better timed. Democratic President-elect Franklin D. Roosevelt had recently promised the American people a "new deal"; his fictional counterpart establishes a "New Order"—a comprehensive program of constitutional reconstruction—that successfully ends the economic crisis.

Tweed's story opens in the late 1930s, when the worldwide depression has grown even worse. Judson ("Jud") Hammond, president of the United States, lies in a coma following a near-fatal car accident. Hammond is a machine politician—a genial, flag-waving, rather shallow individual of the Warren Harding type—who fully subscribes to the tenets of his National Party: a sacrosanct Constitution, limited federal power, an isolationist foreign policy. When he regains consciousness, however, he is a changed person. To Hartley Beekman, his secretary and the narrator of the tale, he seems no longer human—a cadaverous, unsmiling figure with deepset eyes "like live cinders, burning, unwinking, mesmeric."[53] In short order, the president displays uncharacteristic leadership qualities, as he overrides his cabinet of party hacks and pushes through Congress several measures designed to lay the foundations for a centralized and authoritarian state. At his urging, Congress enlarges the membership of the Supreme Court from nine to fifteen Justices; empowers the president to appoint a personal representative at each state capital to supervise the expenditure of federal relief funds; and consents to the creation of a Department of Education, which quickly becomes an official propaganda agency for Hammond and his program.

In describing the operations of the new department, Tweed makes his most original contribution to the utopian fiction of the day. Hammond names a young advertising executive as secretary of education, and the two take immediate steps to win popular support for the president's plans. Since television has now been perfected, Hammond uses the new medium to carry his message to the entire population. Before the first of his scheduled talks, agents from the Department of Education set up giant television screens in public parks around the country; hire empty movie theaters and open them to the public; and commandeer auditoriums in all schools receiving federal aid. In front of the television cameras, Hammond's features soften, and he projects an image of warmth and paternal concern. The experiment is an unqualified success:

> Crowds in the parks stood spellbound and breathless for a solid hour as they beheld their President ten times larger than life talking in heart-to-heart fashion to them from the White House. Even the bookcases and mantel in the Lincoln Study were plainly visible as a background. Countless citizens got the impression that they had been individually invited into the White House to receive from the President a private report on the state of the nation.[54]

Through frequent television appearances, Hammond quickly becomes a folk hero. He denounces the greed and shortsightedness of big financiers and industrialists, attacks legislators for their uncaring response to mass suffering, and assures the unemployed that they are not responsible for their plight. The government has a duty to provide for the welfare of every citizen, he thunders, and he pledges to take whatever action may be needed to lead the nation back to prosperity:

> I believe in the Constitution of the United States in the terms in which it was first drawn up by those noble men who sat and laboured

in Philadelphia more than a century and a half ago. I intend that the Constitution shall be maintained in that spirit, but I refuse to believe that either Washington or Lincoln or Wilson or any of those who in this office I now hold helped to create and build up this Nation would permit a mere document, no matter how sacred, to bind the hands and shackle the rights of their own people, struggling mightily with grievous adversity in another age and under completely changed conditions.[55]

True to his word, Hammond goes before a joint session of Congress to demand a resolution of national emergency vesting extraordinary power in the president. Threatened with martial law as the only alternative, Congress passes the measure and adjourns sine die. The president then assumes full control of the government, assisted by a new cabinet made up of experienced corporation executives.

To revive the economy, Hammond institutes a Keynesian program designed to boost the purchasing power of consumers.[56] He takes the country off the gold standard, orders the gradual withdrawal of gold and gold bonds from circulation, and authorizes the Treasury to print a new series of paper money unsecured by gold. (An already packed Supreme Court dutifully approves these inflationary measures.) At the same time, the president puts the unemployed to work on various federal projects. When an army of 20,000 members of the National Unemployed Citizens' League marches on Washington, Hammond permits them to occupy a public park and directs the War Department to supply them with food and medical supplies. He further announces the immediate creation of a National Reconstruction Corps, in which unemployed men may enlist for three years at army pay to work at dam construction and other public improvements. The jobs program will be scaled back as private industry recovers from the depression slump and seeks to hire more workers.

On other fronts the president takes equally straightforward and decisive action. To combat widespread violations of the prohibition laws, he abolishes the Eighteenth Amendment by executive order and places the manufacture and sale of alcoholic beverages under exclusive federal control. To eliminate gangsters and other criminals, he federalizes the police forces of the nation and sets up a Department of Public Safety to supervise their operations. The new national police must conform to high professional standards, free of any hint of the political corruption that often characterized local police units in the past. "[W]hat causes me the most concern is the contempt in which the law is regarded by large sections of the people," Hammond confides to an associate. "By using illegal methods to punish law-breakers, you don't increase respect for the law. All you do is to condone illegality."[57]

Despite such rhetoric, the president's war on crime employs methods that often ignore both due process and constitutional rights. Although the Second Amendment prohibits the federal government from infringing "the right of the people to keep and bear Arms," Hammond orders all citizens to surrender their weapons to the state, on pain of heavy penalties. The government seizes every ammunition plant in the country, shuts down most of them, and limits future production to the needs of the military and the police. Hammond further creates a mobile elite force—the Green Jackets—to enforce the weapons ban against known gangsters.

Modeled on the Canadian Northwest Mounted Police, the Green Jackets are a motorcycle unit of expert sharpshooters whose mission is to raid the homes and business headquarters of mobsters in search of contraband arms. (These searches are carried out under the authority of lawful warrants, since "[i]t was one of the most cast-iron rules both of the Federalized police and of the Green Jackets that there should be no extra-legal processes employed to obtain evidence or convictions.")[58] On the other hand, anyone who forcibly resists such a search is arrested, imprisoned in a "special concentration camp" on Ellis Island, and brought to trial before a military court of three judges. In this summary proceeding, one's prior criminal record may be used in evidence against him, and conviction means death by a firing squad.

As his domestic policies prove successful, Hammond turns to international reconstruction. "The United States must set itself to the task of getting the wheels of international trade turning again by breaking down economic nationalism which is the curse of this and every other country," he tells his secretary of state.[59] His first step is to engineer the creation of a Pan-American Customs Union, a great free trade zone encompassing the United States, Canada, Mexico, and the nations of Central and South America. Other countries soon begin to emulate this model and respond favorably as well to Hammond's call for a World Council of all nations to replace the moribund League of Nations. At a plenary session of the new organization in London, the American president unveils some startling proposals for world peace and economic stability. Noting that the increased use of air power and advanced technology in a future war might well destroy civilization, he urges the Council to "outlaw the national armies, navies and air forces of every State, including the manufacture, storage and distribution of munitions other than those required for domestic police purposes."[60] Under this plan only the World Council might maintain a limited military force, to be used exclusively for international peacekeeping duties.

To regulate the global economy, Hammond advocates an International Central Bank, which will control the world's gold supply and prevent dangerous fluctuations in the general level of world prices. As a major contribution to worldwide recovery, he further agrees to transfer virtually all of America's extensive gold reserves to the Bank and to cancel any war debts that foreign nations may still owe to the United States. Although some delegates adamantly oppose these initiatives, public opinion soon forces them to yield. The people of every country have heard Hammond's pleas for international cooperation and brotherhood, since the Council's proceedings have been broadcast by radio at his insistence. Confronted by an outpouring of popular support for the president's program, every nation signs the London Covenant, with its disarmament and trade provisions, and the British government cedes a sparsely populated peninsula of Northern Ireland as the site of a future "International City," the permanent home of the World Council and the Central Bank.

At this point most utopian writers would end their story. Hammond has established a model system of government at home and abroad, and the masses of the world acclaim him as an inspired leader. (Perhaps even divinely inspired. Beekman notices that the president sometimes fails to recognize one of his own draft speeches, and that he often seems to be listening to some unseen presence. Pendela Malloy, Beekman's assistant, comes to believe that this invisible counselor may be the Angel Gabriel, whom God has sent "to do for Hammond what He did for Daniel . . . to bring the messages of God to man.")[61] Whatever the source of Hammond's achievements, they do not bring the tale to a triumphant conclusion. Instead, Tweed complicates the narrative in some intriguing and uncharacteristic ways that take it out of the genre conventions of the time.

To begin with, many Americans actively protest Hammond's continuing dictatorship. By the third year of presidential rule, an organized opposition party—the Liberal League—begins to develop. Composed of old-style politicians and local bosses, disgruntled manufacturers who favor protective tariffs, libertarians wary of executive tyranny, and financiers angered by the internationalization of gold, the League demands the restoration of the old Constitution. Like the Antifederalists of the eighteenth century, its members champion state rights, which have been completely abolished under the president's regime. Pressed by the need for federal funds, every state has agreed to control from Washington, which includes the imposition of a uniform governing mechanism: "The Legislature was adjourned *sine die* as Congress had been, and authority was vested in a Council appointed by the Governor, subject to the President's approval. In some States the practical power of the President's special fiscal agent surpassed that of even the Governor and his Council."[62] This consolidation of federal power—of which Martin Van Buren only dreamed in *The Partisan Leader*—gives the Liberty Leaguers their most potent slogan: that Pennsylvania or Virginia or Oregon "never will be a slave State."[63]

Aware of the growing unrest around the country, Hammond takes steps to constitutionalize his program. At his direction the Justice Department prepares sixteen amendments that incorporate his radical reforms and greatly increase presidential power at the expense of Congress. Henceforth Congress will sit only at the president's call; a system of proportional representation will go into effect; and the president will be eligible to serve only a single term of six years. Once the amendments are ready, Hammond announces a national election—the first in more than three years. Voters will choose both a president and a Congress obligated to submit the proposed amendments to a popular ratifying convention in every state. The Liberty Leaguers and the pesident's supporters assume that he will be a candidate in the approaching contest, which will serve as a referendum on his policies.

Before the voting can take place, however, Hammond suffers another severe head injury in the course of an abortive attempt on his life. On regaining consciousness, he can remember nothing that has happened since the automobile crash. As he learns of the establishment of the "New Order," he is horrified at what he now considers "acts of treason against the democracy of the United States. . . . Liberty has been destroyed and the Constitution I swore to uphold has been practically scrapped."[64] Conscience-stricken, he plans a televised speech to announce his withdrawal from the race and to apologize to the American people for his criminal acts. To prevent such a disaster on the eve of the election, his advisers arrange to have transmission cut off as the president begins his talk. When Hammond realizes what has happened, his angry response triggers a fatal heart attack. "It . . . is . . . better . . . so,"[65] murmurs one of the group, as he restrains Beekman from trying to offer assistance.

While most utopian fiction describes societies that are homogeneous and smoothly functioning, Tweed's novel ends on a note of uncertainty and ambivalence. With Hammond out of the picture, the election may well result in the abandonment or drastic modification of his New Order. In addition, the president's second thoughts about his program invite readers to take a more critical look at the substance of his policies and the methods he has used to carry them out. The constitutional discourse, in short, remains open-ended, and the new system falls far short of providing a perfect model of government.

No such doubts arise in the movie version of *Gabriel*, which subverts Tweed's internationalism and turns the story into a strident flag-waving polemic. Filmed at William Randolph Hearst's Cosmopolitan studio on the MGM lot, the screenplay strives for maximum timeliness by setting the plot in the present. Hammond now speaks to the American people by radio, and the parallels between his initial policies and those of the Hoover administration are sharply drawn. The first twenty minutes of the film deal with events prior to the auto crash, a period barely mentioned in the book. One highlight is the president's first press conference, at which Hammond responds to reporters' questions in typical Hooverian fashion. Unemployment and racketeering are local problems, he declares, and the federal government has no authority to resolve them. When pressed to discuss specific measures for combating the depression, he falls back on platitudes: "America will weather this depression as she has weathered other depressions. . . . Through the spirit of Valley Forge—the spirit of Gettysburg— and the spirit of the Argonne. The American people have risen before— and they will rise again."[66] ("Prosperity is just around the corner," mutters a cynical newsman, echoing Hoover's most famous bromide.)

The arrival of the angel Gabriel leaves nothing to the viewer's imagination. As Hammond lies unconscious from his head injury, a light breeze flutters the curtains of his bedroom window, portentous music sounds in the background, and a light from above shines down on him. He awakens, as in the novel, a changed man, who now proclaims: "As President of the United States my first duty is to the people!"[67] The screenplay remains generally faithful to the book in depicting Hammond's peaceful takeover of the government and his dealings with the unemployed. But it takes drastic liberties with Tweed's plot in its treatment of two other major themes: crime and foreign policy.

Unlike the novel, which at least nods in the direction of civil liberties on occasion, the movie revels in official lawlessness. The gangster menace is personified in racketeer Nick Diamond, whom the president invites to the White House for a personal confrontation. Warning the mobster that he will tolerate no more bootlegging, Hammond announces that the federal government is taking control of the nation's liquor supply. Unimpressed, Diamond sends a carload of thugs to attack the presidential mansion. (As in the typical gangster film of the day, the gang drives up to the front entrance in a large black sedan and opens fire with machine guns.) In response, Beekman takes command of a special force of army tanks and demolishes the mob's fortified headquarters. Diamond and his men are captured and face an immediate court-martial, over which Beekman presides.

"You're the last of the racketeers, Diamond," he tells the fallen leader as he orders his execution by firing squad. "And why? Because we have a man in the White House who has enabled us to cut red tape and legal procedures and get back to first principles. An eye for an eye, Nick Diamond; a tooth for a tooth, a life for a life."[68] There is no hint here of training a professional and law-abiding national police, as in the novel; Hammond sanctions the ruthless elimination of all public enemies by whatever means may be necessary. (The reference to the Mosaic Code suggests that Gabriel, too, may approve this application of Old Testament justice.)

In foreign affairs, Hammond displays a comparable strain of unbending righteousness. Determined that the "crafty" Europeans shall pay their war debts, he convenes an International Debt Conference aboard the presidential yacht. With a battery of microphones before him, he berates the assembled delegates for repudiating their just obligations and adding to the tax burden of the American people. The United States will no longer permit foreign nations to restrict the size of its navy by international agreement, he announces: "We must be able to command peace" by building the strongest navy in the world. Then, in a dramatic demonstration of military destructiveness, he orders a naval air squadron to sink two unmanned battleships before the eyes of the startled diplomats. "The next war will be a terrible story of the failure of antiquated machinery and antiquated methods," he warns. "Armies and navies will be destroyed from the air, and as these airplanes destroy armies and navies, they will destroy cities, they will destroy populations. . . . The next war will depopulate the earth."

To avert such a catastrophe, he appeals for immediate and universal disarmament, pointing out that the huge sums currently allocated for military purposes will then be available for more constructive uses, including the payment of war debts:

> People of the world, I speak to you. Shall we save this world? . . . Shall the United States of America build such a Navy to force peace? Or will the other nations agree to eliminate their armaments, balance

their budgets, restore honor among nations? The United States would be glad to fall in line with such a movement, but only after the other nations have proven their good faith by convincing action. The very fate of our civilization rests here and now where it belongs—in the hands of the people of the world.

Inspired by Hammond's millennial vision, the public clamors for disarmament, and the movie reaches a climax with the formal signing of the "Washington Covenant" at the White House. As the president completes his signature—using the same quill pen with which Lincoln signed the Emancipation Proclamation—he suffers a heart attack and collapses. Carried to an upstairs room, he dies in the presence of his loyal secretary Pendie Malloy (who in this version is also his mistress). Fluttering curtains again denote the passage of the departing Gabriel, as a crowd of silent mourners gathers before the White House fence.

The contrast between Tweed's internationalism and the movie's endorsement of a "Pax Americana" could hardly be more striking. For this altered perspective William Randolph Hearst was largely responsible. A pacifist as well as a defender of national sovereignty, the millionaire publisher made personal changes in the screenplay until it conformed to his program for ending the depression.[69] The film's authoritarianism, which struck some reviewers as fascistic, owed much to Hearst's youthful flirtation with Progressive liberalism. Certainly Hammond's bullying response to the foreign debt crisis recalls Theodore Roosevelt's "big stick" diplomacy, while the "New Order" resembles Philip Dru's "legal revolution" in many respects. But Hearst's scenario makes no effort to reconcile constitutionalism with temporary dictatorship, as Colonel House, Palmer, and Tweed had done. The movie's Hammond gives no indication of a willingness to relinquish his power, and only divine intervention, in the form of his death, saves the nation from a continuing despotism.

The screenplay seeks to avoid this troubling conclusion by suggesting that the president is merely carrying on a tradition of strong executive leadership that stretches back to the Founding. When a congressional opponent charges that Hammond is subverting "the government of our fathers," he replies: "I believe in democracy as Washington, Jefferson and Lincoln believed in democracy, and if what I plan to do in the name of the people makes me a dictator, then it is a dictatorship based on Jefferson's definition of democracy—a 'government for the greatest good of the greatest number.'"[70] The shadow of Abraham Lincoln, in particular, hovers over much of the film, as the camera frequently highlights a bust of the "Great Emancipator" in the Oval Office. On the eve of his constitutional coup, Hammond receives unexpected moral support from a ghostly chorus that suddenly materializes beneath his windows to offer a midnight rendition of "The Battle Hymn of the Republic." The same music recurs from time to time on the soundtrack, along with snatches of "John Brown's Body"; Walter Huston, in the role of Hammond, even manages to look a bit Lincolnesque by the end of the film. Unfortunately for the credibility of the analogy, the historical Lincoln never tried to govern without Congress, much less establish a dictatorship, even in the midst of a bloody civil war.

For audiences today, accustomed to a steady diet of sensational fare, *Gabriel* still remains a startling film. But the original screenplay and first print must have been still more provocative. When James Wingate of the Hays Office got a look at the initial story line, he immediately notified his superior Will Hays:

> As a matter of policy, I wonder if it would not be advisable for you to sound a note of warning to some of the responsible heads of the industry about making a type of picture portraying large groups of distressed, dissatisfied or unemployed people going en masse in an anti-government attitude of mind to the national capital to make their protest felt?
>
> These are trying times. Industry, business and government are being keenly criticised and . . . it is not beyond possibility that [such a] custom may lead to the radicals and communists . . . doing the same thing, thus helping to lessen the confidence of people in their form of government and perhaps attempt to change the same through radical and unconstitutional methods.[71]

As the head of Hollywood's self-censorship agency, Hays authorized Wingate to demand numerous changes in the script to bring it into compliance with the industry's Production Code of 1930. The suggested revisions included the avoidance of all use of the word "revolution"; a more subdued depiction of organized popular protest; and a cosmetic effort to lend some constitutional legitimacy to Hammond's dictatorship:

> Scene I-1: In the headlines stating that the President has assumed dictatorship, we think it might be well to follow this with some such statement as 'Country-Wide Constitutional Referendum Supports

President In This Action' thereby indicating that this extraordinary situation has been reached through constitutional means.[72]

Unless changes were made, Wingate warned, the Hays Office would not approve the picture's release, since it might encourage revolutionary violence and lead to federal censorship legislation.

Louis B. Mayer of MGM gladly agreed to successive revisions of both the screenplay and the initial version of the film. A diehard Republican who had supported Hoover's presidential campaign, Mayer thought the movie dangerously radical when he previewed it for the first time. "Put that picture in its can, take it back to the studio, and lock it up!" he reportedly sputtered.[73] Nevertheless, he promised Wingate that he "would do all he could to see that it was re-edited in such a way as to avoid giving offense."[74] After several scenes were reshot, the Hays Office professed itself satisfied. "I am delighted that you have made it into such an excellent picture," Wingate wrote in a congratulatory note.[75] Released in early April 1933, Gabriel became one of the top six box-office attractions of that month. It even found an eventual place on the New York Times's list of "Fifty Red Ribbon Films" representing "noteworthy examples of cinematic entertainment made in 1933."[76]

While some reviewers denounced the movie as an exercise in fascist brainwashing, most critics found nothing sinister in its authoritarian outlook. Mordaunt Hall of the New York Times provided a detailed summary of the plot and concluded: "It is a curious, somewhat fantastic and often melodramatic story, but nevertheless one which at this time is very interesting."[77] Other commentators were less restrained in their praise. "Don't miss this one!" advised the Chicago Tribune, while the Hollywood Reporter expressed the hope that the movie would "put an end to the great problems that confront our nation today by showing . . . how a President of the United States handled the situation and the marvelous results he attained."[78]

Even those who disagreed with some of Hearst's remedies conceded the movie's importance in opening up, "for good or evil, a new channel of influencing the mass emotions and judgment of a people." As Richard Dana Skinner observed in The Comonweal:

If it served no other purpose, the new film, "Gabriel over the White House," would establish once and for all the superiority of the screen over the stage as a vehicle for outright propaganda. For this picture is propaganda of the baldest sort. It could not support certain views and ideas more directly if it were an underscored Hearst editorial. Yet it is good "theatre" in spite of this. It hangs together, moves swiftly, has plenty of dramatic and melodramatic contrast, and has more than enough emotional interest. No stage play dealing with the same materials and the same ideas could possibly succeed.[79]

FDR screened the film several times at the White House. In a congratulatory note to Hearst, the new president declared, "[H]ow pleased I am with the changes you made," and added that the movie "should do much to help."[80] Across the country *Gabriel* drew mixed reactions from local audiences. A theater manager reported that moviegoers in Greenville, Michigan, showed little interest in the film, although he considered it "one of the best pictures we ever played."[81] On the other hand, critic Bruce Bliven detected something ominous in the response of a boisterous New York audience, which "cheers loudly both the promise of jobs for the unemployed and the threat of a big navy. It is as enthusiastic over the abandonment of democracy as it is over reverential mouthings about Lincoln."[82] Such casual acceptance of presidential rule should not have surprised Bliven, however, since the public had responded in much the same way to the authoritarian rhetoric of Roosevelt's inaugural address several weeks earlier.

7

Inauguration Day, 1933

Plodding feet
Tramp—tramp
The Grand Old Party's
Breaking camp.
Blare of Bugles
Din—din—
The New Deal is
Moving in.
    —ROBERT E. SHERWOOD (1933)

As the nation prepared to inaugurate its thirty-second president, the mood in Washington was apprehensive. "Solemn days this capital has seen before, but never in our time have the people been as twitchy and jerky as they were the last day of Mr. Hoover's unhappy Presidency," reported columnist Westbrook Pegler. "Generalities are necessary to describe the mental state of a whole townful of citizens, and if you will permit me one generality I will choose to say that Washington was suffering from the jumps."[1] Other observers agreed. Arthur Krock of the *New York Times* compared the city to "a beleaguered capital in wartime," and Edmund Wilson, covering the inaugural for the *New Republic,* noted "The people seem dreary, even apathetic."[2] Bank holidays had been declared in all but two of the forty-eight states, and many visitors learned to their dismay that the hotels would no longer honor out-of-town checks or cash money orders. Still, they managed to purchase fifty thousand grandstand tickets for the inaugural parade at prices that ranged from $2 to $7, as well as ten thousand tickets to the inaugural ball at $5 apiece.[3]

The weather did little to lift their spirits. Inauguration day—Saturday, March 4, 1933—was raw and blustery, with dark clouds that threatened rain or snow. Shortly before noon the president and the president-elect entered an open car for the ceremonial journey from the White House to the Capitol. Silent and unsmiling, the two leaders passed through crowds of spectators in blankets and overcoats who lined both sides of Pennsylvania Avenue. Security was unusually tight, since an attempt on Roosevelt's life had been made only two weeks earlier during a public appearance in

158

Miami. General MacArthur, charged with preserving order along the parade route, called out large numbers of troops and installed machine-gun nests at strategic points around the Capitol. Local police were also much in evidence, their numbers augmented by a special detachment of 100 young parade cops from New York City. (The Manhattan contingent might well have been needed at home, where a hunger march went on simultaneously as a grim counterpoint to the inaugural festivities.)[4]

At the Capitol all was confusion. Roosevelt, his legs permanently crippled from poliomyelitis, was wheeled through a pushing crowd of congressional staffers and sightseers into the Military Affairs Committee Room. There he waited until word came that his running mate, John Nance Garner, had taken the vice-presidential oath in the Senate chamber. The United States Marine Band then struck up "Hail to the Chief," and Herbert Hoover moved from the rotunda to the inaugural platform that had been constructed above the steps on the east front of the Capitol. A few minutes later Roosevelt appeared, walking stiffly down the red-carpeted aisle on the arm of his son James.

"I watched with interest his approach to the platform," commented an English visitor.

> Very slowly, painfully slowly, he shuffled down an interminable gangway, leaning on the shoulder of his young son and on a stick, dragging one limb after another until he reached the inclined ramp which, for his benefit, had been substituted for the four steps that led to the platform. It ought to have been rather embarrassing, but I remember that I was unconscious of any feeling of embarrassment. There was something in the poise of the head on the broad shoulders which made one forget the nearly helpless limbs beneath. There was an expression on the face of relaxed good will, of unconcern, of utter unselfconsciousness, which made it impossible for the onlooker to be aware of a disability of which the victim himself was so supremely unaware.[5]

Despite the chill wind, Roosevelt wore neither topcoat nor hat for the swearing-in ceremony. With one hand on the family Bible, he repeated in a strong voice the words of the presidential oath solemnly administered by Chief Justice Charles Evans Hughes. At 1:08 P.M. his term of office officially began. Ignoring the applause that followed, he turned to the podium with a stern air and began his inaugural message. The audience of 100,000 persons gathered on the Capitol grounds grew quiet.

The address, one of the greatest ever delivered by an American president, drew upon familiar Progressive themes and stereotypes but added some radical rhetoric hitherto found mainly in works of fiction. Roosevelt began by promising candor and bold leadership in a time of severe economic crisis. "This great Nation will endure as it has endured, will revive and will prosper," he affirmed. "So, first of all, let me assert my firm belief that the only thing we have to fear is fear itself—nameless, unreasoning, unjustified terror which paralyzes needed efforts to convert retreat into advance. In every dark hour of our national life a leadership of frankness and vigor has met with that understanding and support of the people themselves which is essential to victory."[6] The military imagery—"retreat into advance," "support . . . essential to victory"—was carefully chosen and would recur through the rest of the speech.[7]

After a brief recital of the nation's current problems, from urban unemployment and bankrupt governments to business failures and farm distress, Roosevelt traced the cause of the economic malaise to the Progressive era's favorite scapegoats: Wall Street bankers and Big Businessmen. These false leaders, he charged, had subverted the traditional values of the American people by encouraging speculation and the single-minded pursuit of material gain. But their self-seeking policies had failed, and public opinion now rejected them and their pretensions to leadership: "The money changers have fled from their high seats in the temple of our civilization. We may now restore that temple to the ancient truths."[8]

At this point a burst of applause interrupted the address for the first time. The display of popular resentment against New Era ideologues made newspaper headlines across the country, and most editorial comments were positive. The Salt Lake City *Deseret News,* a Republican paper, called the president's attack on the money changers the high point of his speech, and the Dayton *News,* a Democratic paper, concurred: "This means the abandonment of the pivot on which American power has turned for twelve years past. Those were years of dependence upon a hierarchy of favorite interest. We gave them power; they were to return us to prosperity. What we see now is the prosperity we got. Now for the laying of a broader base. Thus Roosevelt in the spirit of Lincoln calls the country to a right about face."

Only a few observers disapproved of the president's scapegoating technique. "By his direct assault against the established order in finance," complained the independent Portland *Oregonian,* "he dashes the hopes of thousands of financial institutions already sorely prest that his address would include something reassuring to public confidence and public credit. If this is the new deal, the best one can say of it is that while it may offer betterment for the future, it offers little for the present and the emergency of the present."[9] Despite his belligerent rhetoric, the president posed no credible threat to the existing financial order, as the "money changers" themselves well understood. Like his Progressive predecessors, he carefully refrained from attacking the capitalist system itself and instead directed popular anger toward individual (and unnamed) malefactors. Radical journalists thus denounced him for failing to challenge establishment values in any meaningful way, or, as Edmund Wilson put it, for continuing to indulge in "[t]he old unctuousness, the old pulpit vagueness."[10]

Indeed, when Roosevelt came to define "the old and precious moral values" that his administration intended to restore, he fell back on a handful of hoary platitudes. The New Deal, he declared, would insist on an ethic of social responsibility in business and politics, along with a revival of the pioneer tradition of self-help and hard work: "The joy and moral stimulation of work no longer must be forgotten in the mad chase of evanescent profits. These dark days will be worth all they cost us if they teach us that our true destiny is not to be ministered unto but to minister to ourselves and to our fellow men."[11] To prevent a recurrence of the speculative mania that had helped to bring on the depression, he called for strict government regulation of banking and investment as well as "an adequate but sound currency." Other announced policy goals included aid to farmers and small homeowners; a drastic reduction in the cost of government; the unification of relief activities; federal supervision of all public utilities, pursuant to a national plan; and a balanced budget. More ominous, to some critics, was the president's proposal that the federal government recruit the unemployed for service in a great national workforce, which might be used for major construction and environmental projects.

"If I read the temper of our people correctly," Roosevelt explained,

we now realize as we have never realized before our interdependence on each other; that we cannot merely take but we must give as well; that if we are to go forward, we must move as a trained and loyal army willing to sacrifice for the good of a common discipline, because without such discipline no progress is made, no leadership becomes effective. We are, I know, ready and willing to submit our lives and property to such discipline, because it makes possible a leadership which aims at a larger good. This I propose to offer, pledging that the larger purposes will bind upon us all as a sacred obligation with a unity of duty hitherto evoked only in time of armed strife.[12]

The military metaphors and accompanying hints of mass regimentation served to introduce the final section of the speech, in which the president offered a bold vision of executive power unhampered by constitutional restraints.

Any departure from prescribed constitutional norms would not be lightly taken, he assured his listeners. "Action . . . is feasible under the form of government we have inherited from our ancestors. Our Constitution is so simple and practical that it is possible always to meet extraordinary needs by changes in emphasis and arrangement without loss of essential form." As in previous crises, the normal balance of power between Congress and the president should be "wholly adequate" to respond to the nation's pressing problems. And Roosevelt promised to seek congressional cooperation in the immediate passage of remedial legislation. Should Congress delay action on his proposals, however, and fail to come up promptly with a package of alternative measures,

> I shall not evade the clear course of duty that will then confront me. I shall ask the Congress for the one remaining instrument to meet the crisis—broad Executive power to wage a war against the emergency, as great as the power that would be given to me if we were in fact invaded by a foreign foe. . . . The people of the United States have not failed. In their need they have registered a mandate that they want direct, vigorous action. They have asked for discipline and direction under leadership. They have made me the present instrument of their wishes. In the spirit of the gift I take it.[13]

Although no peacetime president had ever laid claim to such sweeping prerogatives, Americans familiar with the policy debates carried on in newspapers and magazines during the past year could not have been too surprised by Roosevelt's words. And readers of recent utopian novels would certainly have recalled comparable manifestos issued by such heroic fictional statesmen as Philip Dru, Connie Spenser, and Jud Hammond.

The threat of presidential rule evoked the most enthusiastic applause of the day. It was "a little terrifying," the First Lady confessed to a reporter several hours later. "The crowds were so tremendous, and you felt that they would do anything—if only some one would tell them what to do."[14] In addition to the immediate Washington audience, an estimated 50 million Americans heard the president's message on radio, and four short-wave transmitters along the East Coast carried his words to foreign listeners around the globe. Editors from Universal Films and Pathé News further selected the dramatic highlights of the speech for inclusion in the newsreels they supplied to the nation's movie houses.

Public reaction, both official and popular, was highly favorable. Democratic and Republican congressmen alike praised the president's courage and professed a willingness to support his recovery initiatives. "Under ordinary circumstances Congress would resist a request for such broad power," noted Democratic Representative Hugo Black of Alabama; "but the critical situation requires instant action and a delegation of power to meet requirements should be granted by Congress." Republican Representative Lloyd Thurston of Iowa agreed that the times called for "unusual remedies": "The entire Congress will undoubtedly respond to a legislative program to meet the present situation." Even the occasional critic, such as Republican Representative John Charles Schafer of Wisconsin, did not attack the message for its authoritarian thrust but concentrated instead on more conventional issues. "Where does he stand?" Schafer queried, referring to the contradictory aspects of the president's program. "His speech cuts both ways—reduce taxes and spend money; sound currency, but at the same time lots of it."[15]

Such negative considerations troubled few of the nation's editorial writers, who responded enthusiastically to the prospect of presidential rule. "If legislators omit useless debate, well and good," commented the Dallas *News,* a Democratic paper; "if not, Congress will be expected to adjourn after delegating to the President extraordinary powers." The Denver *Post,* an independent sheet, went even further, suggesting that giving the president "dictatorial powers at the very beginning will save much time." Although the Republican Boston *Transcript* found Roosevelt's bid for dictatorial authority troubling, it nevertheless acknowledged that "such is the desperate temper of the people that it is welcome."[16]

Foreign observers expressed similar approval of the inaugural message. The leading journals in London and Paris commended the president for his courageous stance and expressed the hope that his administration's foreign policy would help to restore confidence in the world economy.[17] Roosevelt's military metaphors struck a particularly responsive chord in Italy and Germany, where government spokesmen found in his calls for unity and discipline a reflection of their own authoritarian ideology. According to Benito Mussolini's *Il Popolo d'Italia,* "President Roosevelt's words are clear and need no comment to make even the deaf hear that not only Europe but the whole world feels the need of executive authority capable of acting with full powers of cutting short the purposeless chatter of legislative assemblies. This method of government may well be defined as fascist."[18] And Adolf Hitler, recently installed as chancellor of Germany, sent a congratulatory message in which he noted that Roosevelt's "moral demands" for a loyal and disciplined citizen army were "also the quintessence of the German State philosophy which finds its expression in the slogan 'The Public Weal Transcends the Interests of the Individual.'"[19]

For Americans, of course, the president's words did not suggest an impending fascist coup. Rather, they signaled a return to the vigorous leadership style of Roosevelt's Republican namesake, Theodore Roosevelt. In the aftermath of the inauguration, a cartoonist for the Los Angeles *Times* neatly captured popular expectations in a drawing that showed an ebullient FDR taking down a huge nail-studded club—T. R.'s "Big Stick"— from a shelf in the hall closet. The caption read: "It's Been in the Family for a Long Time!"[20] Some commentators even argued that the president threatened an executive takeover mainly to push a potentially obstructive Congress into cooperating with his program. "[T]he fact that he has announced his readiness to make this move may relieve Mr. Roosevelt of the necessity of making it," observed the Kansas City *Journal-Post,* a Republican organ.[21] One thing at least seemed clear. The public temper demanded some sort of prompt action, in contrast to the lethargy that had characterized the Hoover administration. (And Roosevelt acknowledged the demand by repeating the word "action" four times in the course of his fifteen-minute address.) "If he burned down the Capitol," quipped humorist Will Rogers, "we would cheer and say, 'Well, we at least got a fire started somehow.'"[22]

Evidence of grassroots support for the president and his message was instant and overwhelming. During the week following the inauguration 450,000 letters poured into the White House from well-wishers across the nation. A sampling of representative comments suggests the profound impact that Roosevelt's rich voice and confident delivery made on his radio listeners. "Your human feeling for all of us in your address is just wonderful," wrote one correspondent. "People are looking to you almost as they look to God," declared another.[23] A California resident was even moved to scribble a homespun poem, titled "Our New President," on a postcard:

> Tears rose in hardened eyes—from mine they flowed—
> When Franklin Roosevelt's inaugural vow

Broadcast its purpose, with the help of God,
To lift our Country from Depression's slough.
There was a note of action in his voice
That put a prick in Unemployment's ear,
And made our Nation's flagging soul rejoice
With a new hope that a new deal was near.[24]

The inaugural message further became an immediate source of New Deal propaganda in the movies, thanks to the Democratic sympathies of Jack and Harry Warner. At the time of the inauguration the Warner Brothers studio was shooting a topical film, *Breadline,* about the struggles of an ex-serviceman in postwar America. The script called for the death of the selfless hero, Tom Holmes, and a reference to his Christ-like qualities. On March 8, however, executive producer Darryl Zanuck ordered a new and more upbeat ending. In the revised version Tom and his friend Roger, along with other unemployed "forgotten men," have just been driven out of another town by the local police. Destitute and starving, they nevertheless discover fresh hope in the promise of the New Deal:

Roger: What do you think of all this? The country can't go on this way. It's—it's the end of America.
Tom: No. It's maybe the end of us, but it's not the end of America. In a few years it'll be bigger and stronger than ever.
Roger: You know, you're the last guy in the world I'd ever expect to find was an optimist.
Tom: That's not optimism—just common horse sense. Did you read President Roosevelt's inaugural address?
Roger: You're right. You know, it takes more than one sock in the jaw to lick a hundred and twenty million people.[25]

Zanuck explained the need for the new dialogue in an accompanying letter: "The reason I use the Inaugural speech at the finish is that everyone throughout the world is talking about FDR's speech. It was a bombshell and is being compared to great speeches like Lincoln's Gettysburg Address and it seems to me much more constructive for Tom to be talking about what somebody else said than to be talking about what he thinks."[26] Although the movie—released in July under the title *Heroes for Sale*—did not achieve great box-office success, it signaled a willingness by Warner Brothers to inject New Deal ideology into other films of the decade.

Meanwhile, the nation looked on as New Deal programs began to take shape with dizzying speed. "Strange things are moving across this American world of ours," observed the old Progressive William Allen White in April 1933. "The Constitution is straining and cracking. But, after all, the Constitution was made for the people, and not the people for the Constitution. We are toying gayly with billions as we once played cautiously with millions. We are legerdemaining a huge national debt which is to be paid Heaven knows when or how. It is bewildering—this new deal—the new world. How much is false, how much is true, how much is an illusion of grandeur, a vast make-believe, only time will tell."[27]

Afterword

The Constitution's impact on popular culture is a subject to which scholars have paid little heed. Although students of the Supreme Court have long used newspaper editorials (and an occasional editorial cartoon) to assess public reaction to controversial judicial opinions, there has been no effort to explore the broader appeal that constitutional idealism has always made to the American imagination. Even Michael Kammen's magisterial work, *A Machine That Would Go of Itself* (1987), stops short of such an inquiry. In surveying the rise of a constitutional culture stretching back to the Founding, Kammen barely mentions the kind of materials—poems, plays, novels, magazine articles, movies—on which this study rests. Yet such materials, I would argue, make up an important body of constitutional discourse that deserves rediscovery and analysis.

Since the days of the Philadelphia Convention, the Constitution has meant far more to Americans than a simple plan of government. Framed at a time of political and economic crisis, it assumed almost immediately an iconic status. The parades and other rituals that celebrated the progress of ratification brought together members of all social classes in a display of national unity and support for a new constitutional order. Overnight a cult of the Constitution—a kind of civic religion—developed, as publicists hailed the framers for bringing about fundamental changes in the structure of government through a "peaceful revolution." Successive generations of Americans from the Founding to the present have absorbed that message through the media. They have been taught that revolutionary violence is both unnecessary and illegitimate under a system of republican government based on popular consent. In such a system, the argument runs, even radical changes may be achieved through the ballot box and through orderly constitutional procedures. I have sought in this study to demonstrate how this article of constitutional faith was reaffirmed and

167

communicated to the general public during the first three decades of the twentieth century.

The process was complex, but characterized by some recurring themes. Controversies over the reach of federal power and the protection of individual rights have fueled movements for major constitutional change from the Founding to the present. The ratification debates between Federalists and Antifederalists identified these core issues for the first time. Federalists advocated the use of broad federal power to promote the general welfare, while Antifederalists championed a jurisprudence of state rights to prevent the growth of an oppressive central government. The media of the time—newspapers, magazines, poems, plays, an occasional editorial cartoon—contributed to constitutional discourse by popularizing these issues for the general public. A pattern was thus established that still continues. The media do not generally originate proposals for constitutional change at the national level; their function is rather to interpret important issues in terms that will be meaningful for their respective audiences. In this way they help to shape public opinion and perhaps influence voter behavior.

The one instance in which constitutional discourse and official policy conspicuously failed to avert revolutionary violence occurred in 1861. The Civil War, which had been preceded by three decades of argument and compromise, proved to be the bloodiest conflict in American history. Despite the best efforts of publicists and politicians, the moral evil of slavery could no longer be reconciled with constitutional guarantees of republican government. Although the trio of Reconstruction amendments greatly enlarged federal power in theory, little was done to implement their provisions during the turbulent years of the late nineteenth century. Only with the rise of Progressivism after 1900 did a modern era of major constitutional development take shape at the national level, as four new amendments were added to the Constitution.

The reform movements of the early twentieth century provoked constitutional commentary in newspaper editorials, in articles published in elite and muckraking magazines, in utopian fiction, and in some stage plays and early movies. Issues of federal economic regulation were debated both in Congress and in the pages of muckraking novels; African-American writers, such as Charles Chesnutt and Sutton Griggs, used civil rights fiction to challenge the racist arguments of Thomas Dixon and other advocates of white supremacy; and the leaders of the major woman suffrage organizations turned to moviemaking to counteract the harmful gender stereotypes that appeared in early movie comedies as well as in congressional debates. Contemporary observers continued to use the rhetoric of "peaceful revolution" to describe the nature of Progressive reform efforts. Conservatives warned that proposed reforms would overturn the constitutional system established by the Founders, while Progressives urged that timely changes were necessary to prevent a violent uprising by workers and minorities victimized by the workings of a largely unregulated economy.

The emergency legislation of World War I, which expanded the power of the federal government in unprecedented ways, passed with little time for debate in Congress or the media. Once Wilson's war socialism went into effect, however, commentary filled the pages of magazines and newspapers and appeared as well in wartime novels, films, and cartoons. Wilsonian propagandists depicted conscription as merely another Progressive measure that was creating a genuine people's army. The African-American press, on the other hand, documented the racial discrimination and extralegal violence that in fact accompanied the training of black soldiers. The Chicago *Defender,* in particular, served as a clearinghouse of information on violations of black civil rights, and reported many incidents that white mainstream journals ignored.

Such alternative publishing and distribution outlets have existed throughout American history, and their function as carriers of constitutional discourse forms an important subtheme of this study. Members of racial and ethnic minorities and other marginalized groups found their grievances articulated in these publications, along with proposed strategies for bringing about constitutional change. African-American newspapers thus supported the NAACP's wartime call for a massive silent parade down Fifth Avenue to protest lynching, racial discrimination in the military forces, and the wholesale denial of black civil rights. The event received national press coverage and encouraged the NAACP to launch an intensive lobbying campaign on behalf of a federal antilynching law in the early 1920s. At that time, black editors around the country enthusiastically endorsed the Dyer bill and urged their readers with some success to engage in letter-writing campaigns to win over wavering congressmen.

In a similar way, socialists and Wobblies relied on their own presses and distribution networks to disseminate their wartime critique of government policy. Through courtroom speeches, defense bulletins, rallies, leaflets, and party newspapers, they attacked the Espionage and Sedition Acts for violating the rights of free speech and free press guaranteed by the First Amendment. Although their arguments failed to sway juries, they did contribute to a written record of civil rights abuses on which future generations of civil libertarians might profitably draw. This in itself was no mean achievement at a time when the federal government was attempting to suppress all "disloyal" publications and when popular wartime novelists were portraying all dissenters—and especially Wobblies—as dangerous traitors who deserved only summary justice.

The postwar decade witnessed the revival of the kind of Constitution worship that had characterized much of the nineteenth century as well as the introduction of a new medium of mass communication: commercial radio. By the middle of the 1920s "Constitution Day" orators were able to broadcast their speeches to nationwide audiences. Those speeches praised the wisdom of the Founders and urged a return to the principles of limited government and state rights. Such a conservative jurisprudential philosophy found practical expression in the ultimately successful movement to repeal the Prohibition Amendment and turn control of the liquor problem back to the states. The conservative constitutionalism espoused by a dominant business civilization likewise had much to do with the failed effort to ratify a Child Labor Amendment. Publicists for the National Association of Manufacturers and other business groups made skillful use of the media to arouse public fears of an oppressive federal bureaucracy and a "sovietized" family life should the proposed amendment be adopted.

With the onset of the Great Depression, however, the limitations of a laissez-faire approach to constitutionalism quickly became apparent. During the Hoover presidency cartoonists, political columnists, and creative writers attacked the government's half-hearted relief measures and called for more vigorous action to aid those impoverished by the continued economic downturn. While congressmen argued over the scope of the Constitution's general welfare clause, organized groups of farmers, unemployed ex-servicemen, and the destitute staged mass protest demonstrations before city halls, state legislatures, and Congress. Although their rhetoric was sometimes revolutionary, their programmatic demands placed them squarely within the familiar ranks of constitutional reformers.

As the presidential election of 1932 approached, proposals for a wholly new Constitution began to appear in journals and books. Commentators now repudiated the Constitution worship of the 1920s and argued that the depression crisis had demonstrated that the existing system was "obsolete." Utopian fiction, which had all but disappeared since the war, enjoyed renewed popularity, as writers outlined variant models of a powerful future welfare state. Congressmen and journalists, as well as novelists, called for strong executive leadership—even a temporary presidential dictatorship—to restore the country to economic prosperity. Franklin D. Roosevelt responded to such appeals in his first inaugural address, in which he pledged to use his power as commander-in-chief to combat the depression emergency, should Congress fail to act promptly on his legislative proposals. Thus began a new era of "peaceful revolution."

After reading this study, a critic might complain that it adds little to the standard picture of constitutional development provided by such traditional sources as congressional debates and court decisions. I would argue, however, that novels, plays, cartoons, and movies add an important imaginative dimension to constitutional discourse. Such unconventional sources help us to achieve a deeper understanding of the fears and expectations aroused in ordinary Americans by the prospect of major constitutional change. Unlike official policy statements, which speak in formal and abstract terms, these cultural materials illumine the emotional and irrational factors that also enter into constitutional decisionmaking. *The Partisan Leader* gives one a deeper sense of what the doctrines of state rights and secession *meant* to antebellum southerners, for example, than does an address by John C. Calhoun. Similarly, arguments over the enforcement of black civil rights in the *Civil Rights Cases* and *Plessy v. Ferguson* take on new meaning when dramatized in the novels of Charles Chesnutt, Sutton Griggs, and Thomas Dixon. And the slow progress of the woman suffrage movement becomes more understandable in light of the gender stereotypes presented to mass audiences in the suffrage films of the early twentieth century.

I have not discussed every major constitutional development during these years, of course. Nor have I looked into every source of potentially valuable cultural commentary, including the foreign-language press. Still, the varied materials I have examined amply demonstrate that constitutional values are deeply entrenched in the popular imagination. Americans may not understand the mechanics of their constitutional system, but they do share a strong rights-consciousness and a faith in the constitutional process as a peaceful remedy for even the most divisive political controversies. Revolutionary groups, such as the Wobblies and the communists, have never been able to attract a significant national following. Indeed, we have almost banished the idea of a violent revolution from our national discourse. We speak instead of the "Roosevelt revolution" of the 1930s, the "civil rights revolution" of the 1950s and 1960s, the "Reagan revolution" of the 1980s, and the abortive "Republican revolution" of 1994. The legacy of the genuine American Revolution of the eighteenth century has been largely eclipsed by the rise of a powerful constitutional tradition. To this development the popular media have contributed in no small way.

Notes

Preface

1. The best of these studies include Arthur A. Ekirch, Jr., *Ideologies and Utopias: The Impact of the New Deal on American Thought* (Chicago: Quadrangle Books, 1969); Richard H. Pells, *Radical Visions and American Dreams: Culture and Social Thought in the Depression Years* (New York: Harper & Row, 1973); David P. Peeler, *Hope among Us Yet: Social Criticism and Social Solace in Depression America* (Athens: University of Georgia Press, 1987); and Barbara Melosh, *Engendering Culture: Manhood and Womanhood in New Deal Public Art and Theater* (Washington, D.C.: Smithsonian Institution Press, 1991).

1. The Founders' Constitution and Republican Culture

1. On the limits of popular understanding of the Constitution, see Michael Kammen, *A Machine That Would Go of Itself: The Constitution in American Culture* (New York: Alfred A. Knopf, 1986). Kammen's pathbreaking study barely touches on the kinds of cultural materials that are central to this work.
2. For an intriguing analysis of liberty pole ceremonies and other popular modes of colonial resistance, see Peter Shaw, *American Patriots and the Rituals of Revolution* (Cambridge, Mass.: Harvard University Press, 1981).
3. On the importance of wartime constitution-making, see Andrew C. McLaughlin, *Foundations of American Constitutionalism* (1932; reprint, Greenwich, Conn.: Fawcett Publications, Inc., 1961), pp. 86–103.
4. Thomas Paine, *Common Sense* (1776), reprinted in Bruce Kuklick, ed., *Thomas Paine: Political Writings* (Cambridge: Cambridge University Press, 1989), p. 28. For an excellent discussion of the unifying function of law in republican America, see Robert A. Ferguson, *Law and Letters in American Culture* (Cambridge, Mass.: Harvard University Press, 1984), pp. 11–33.
5. Philip Freneau, "On Mr. Paine's Rights of Man," reprinted in Harry Hayden Clark, ed., *Poems of Freneau* (New York: Hafner Publishing Co., 1968),

p. 125. Henry Steele Commager provides a good appraisal of republican ideology in *The Empire of Reason* (New York: Oxford University Press, 1982), pp. 198–235.

6. The best history of Shays's Rebellion is David P. Szatmary's *Shays' Rebellion: The Making of an Agrarian Insurrection* (Amherst: University of Massachusetts Press, 1980). For the anti-Shaysite bias of one New England newspaper, see Paul Marsella, "Propaganda Trends in the *Essex Journal* and *New Hampshire Packet*, 1787–1788," *Essex Institute Historical Collections* 114, no. 3 (July 1978): 164–175.

7. *Works of Fisher Ames* (Boston: T. B. Wait & Co., 1809), pp. 3, 5.

8. "A New Song," *Massachusetts Centinel*, July 11, 1787, quoted in Louie M. Miner, *Our Rude Forefathers: American Political Verse, 1783–1788* (Cedar Rapids, Iowa: Torch Press, 1937), p. 152.

9. On the objectives of those who framed the Articles, see Merrill Jensen, *The Articles of Confederation* (Madison: University of Wisconsin Press, 1940).

10. Jeremy Belknap, *The Foresters, An American Tale* (reprint, Gainesville, Fla.: Scholars' Facsimiles & Reprints, 1969), pp. 173–174, 176–178.

11. Quoted in Carl Brent Swisher, *American Constitutional Development* (2d ed., Cambridge, Mass.: Houghton Mifflin, 1954), p. 30. See also Merrill Jensen, *The New Nation: A History of the United States during the Confederation, 1781–1789* (New York: Random House, 1950), pp. 399–428.

12. Royall Tyler, *The Contrast*, reprinted in Richard Moody, ed., *Dramas from the American Theatre, 1762–1909* (Cleveland: World Publishing, 1966), p. 49.

13. David Humphreys, Joel Barlow, John Trumbull, and Lemuel Hopkins, *The Anarchiad: A New England Poem* (New Haven: Thomas H. Pease, 1861), p. 63. This edition, edited by Luther G. Riggs, claims to be the first published in book form. According to one knowledgeable critic, "*The Anarchiad* provoked hot debate in the taverns and coffeehouses, elicited counter-satire in the public prints, and was widely copied." See James Woodress, *A Yankee's Odyssey: The Life of Joel Barlow* (Philadelphia: J. B. Lippincott Co., 1958), p. 83.

14. On the work of the Philadelphia Convention and its significance, see Forrest McDonald, *Novus Ordo Seclorum: The Intellectual Origins of the Constitution* (Lawrence: University Press of Kansas, 1985), pp. 185–293. See also Bruce Ackerman, *We the People: Foundations* (Cambridge, Mass.: Harvard University Press, Belknap Press, 1991).

15. *The Federalist*, nos. 37–39, 51, in Garry Wills, ed., *The Federalist Papers* (New York: Bantam Books, 1982), pp. 175–182, 189–195, 261–265.

16. *The Federalist*, no. 9, in Wills, *Federalist Papers*, pp. 37–42. The analogy between federalism and Newtonian physics became a popular theme in early American oratory. See, for example, William Crafts, *An Oration Delivered in St. Michael's Church, before the Inhabitants of Charleston, on the Fourth of July, 1812*, in *A Selection in Prose and Poetry, from the Miscellaneous Writings of the Late William Crafts* (Charleston: C. C. Sebring and J. S. Burges, 1828), p. 35: "You can remain free and prosperous, only while you cling to the original prin-

ciples of your government, and scrupulously preserve the regularity, the order, the separate and independent action of a system, which approaches nearer than any human institution to the harmony and beauty of the universe. An union of confederated states, into one nation, sufficiently independent for the regulation of their peculiar interests, and sufficiently connected for the preservation of their common rights, each pursuing its own course, all governed by the same general laws, and revolving round the same centre, is not an inapt emblem of the Sun, enlightening by his beams, and restraining by his attraction the orbs that surround him."

17. "On the New Constitution," *State Gazette of South Carolina,* January 28, 1788, quoted in Miner, *Our Rude Forefathers,* p. 204.

18. John D. Lewis, ed., *Anti-Federalists versus Federalists* (Scranton: Chandler Publishing Co., 1967), provides a convenient collection of representative Antifederalist publications. See especially Samuel Bryan, *Letters of Centinel,* pp. 139–151.

19. For a detailed account of the ratification process, see Steven R. Boyd, *The Politics of Opposition: Antifederalists and the Acceptance of the Constitution* (Millwood, N.Y.: KTO Press, 1979). On the importance of the newspaper debate, see John K. Alexander, *The Selling of the Constitutional Convention: A History of News Coverage* (Madison: Madison House Publishers, 1990), and Robert A. Rutland, *The First Great Newspaper Debate: The Constitutional Crisis of 1787–88* (Worcester, Mass.: American Antiquarian Society, 1987).

20. Francis Hopkinson, *Account of the Grand Festival Procession in Philadelphia, July 4, 1788, to Which Are Added Mr. Wilson's Oration, and a Letter on the Subject of the Procession* (1788), quoted in Catherine L. Albanese, *Sons of the Fathers: The Civil Religion of the American Revolution* (Philadelphia: Temple University Press, 1976), p. 213.

21. Ibid., p. 212.

22. Simeon Baldwin, *An Oration Pronounced before the Citizens of New Haven, July 4, 1788,* quoted in Frank I. Schechter, "The Early History of the Tradition of the Constitution," *American Political Science Review* 9 (November 1915): 726.

23. For a good analysis of these commentaries, see Elizabeth K. Bauer, *Commentaries on the Constitution, 1790–1860* (New York: Columbia University Press, 1952).

24. On Story's work and its influence, see R. Kent Newmyer, *Supreme Court Justice Joseph Story: Statesman of the Old Republic* (Chapel Hill: University of North Carolina Press, 1985), pp. 181–195.

25. Frederick Grimké, *Considerations upon the Nature and Tendency of Free Institutions* (2d ed., New York: H. W. Derby & Co., 1856), p. 485. For Calhoun's constitutional argument, see Ross M. Lence, ed., *Union and Liberty: The Political Philosophy of John C. Calhoun* (Indianapolis: Liberty Fund, 1992); Richard N. Current, *John C. Calhoun* (New York: Washington Square Press, 1963).

26. Quoted in Michael Les Benedict, ed., *Sources in American Constitutional His-*

tory (Lexington, Mass.: D. C. Heath and Co., 1996), p. 85. William W. Freehling provides an admirable survey of the nullification controversy in *Prelude to Civil War: The Nullification Controversy in South Carolina, 1816–1836* (New York: Harper & Row, 1965).

27. Quoted in Benedict, *Sources in American Constitutional History,* p. 86. See also Alfred H. Kelly, Winfred A. Harbison, and Herman Belz, *The American Constitution: Its Origins and Development* (6th ed., New York: W. W. Norton, 1983), pp. 216–219.

28. See generally Harold M. Hyman and William M. Wiecek, *Equal Justice under Law: American Constitutional Development, 1835–1875* (New York: Harper & Row, 1982).

29. A reprint of the cartoon appears in Tony Freyer, "Federal Authority and State Resistance: A Dilemma of American Federalism," *This Constitution: A Bicentennial Chronicle* (Summer 1986): 11–17, at p. 15.

30. Elnathan Elmwood, Esq. [Asa Greene], *A Yankee among the Nullifiers: An Autobiography* (New York: Wm. Stodart, 1833), pp. 17–22.

31. Ibid., pp. 118–120.

32. Ibid., p. 121.

33. The Jackson lithograph is reprinted in Kammen, *A Machine That Would Go of Itself,* following p. 262.

34. *Memoirs of a Nullifier: written by himself. By a Native of the South* (Columbia, S.C.: Telescope Office, 1832), pp. 84, 98.

35. Nathaniel Beverley Tucker, *The Partisan Leader: A Tale of the Future* (reprint, Chapel Hill: University of North Carolina Press, 1971), p. 42. On Tucker's career and influence, see Robert J. Brugger, *Beverley Tucker: Heart over Head in the Old South* (Baltimore: Johns Hopkins University Press, 1978).

36. Tucker, *The Partisan Leader,* p. 156.

37. Ibid., pp. 108, 170.

38. Ibid., p. 243.

39. Ibid., p. 205.

40. Ibid., p. 386. *The Partisan Leader* was a commercial failure when it first appeared, due in part to a mismanaged distribution effort by Tucker's publisher, Duff Green. During the Civil War, however, the work went through several reprintings and attracted a substantial readership. A New York publisher brought out the novel in 1861 with a title page that promised "A Key to the Disunion Conspiracy," while a Richmond firm advertised its edition in 1862 as "A Novel, and an Apocalypse of the Origins and Struggles of the Southern Confederacy." Conspiracy theorists on both sides could find ample support for their views in Tucker's melodramatic tale. See J. V. Ridgely, *Nineteenth-Century Southern Literature* (Lexington: University Press of Kentucky, 1980), p. 44.

41. For an excellent analysis of the Civil War's impact on the Constitution, see Harold M. Hyman, *A More Perfect Union: The Impact of the Civil War and Reconstruction on the Constitution* (New York: Alfred A. Knopf, 1973).

42. Herman Melville, "The Conflict of Convictions" (1860–1861), in Hennig Cohen, ed., *The Battle-Pieces of Herman Melville* (New York: Thomas Yoseloff, 1964), p. 40.

2. Modern Constitutionalism and Progressive Reform

1. The classic account of the muckraking movement is Louis Filler's *Crusaders for American Liberalism* (2d ed., Yellow Springs, Ohio: Antioch Press, 1950). See also David Mark Chalmers, *The Social and Political Ideas of the Muckrakers* (New York: Citadel Press, 1964), and Peter Conn, *The Divided Mind: Ideology and Imagination in America, 1898–1917* (Cambridge: Cambridge University Press, 1983).
2. On the "scientific" nature of American law in the late nineteenth century, see Duncan Kennedy, "Toward an Historical Understanding of Legal Consciousness: The Case of Classical Legal Thought in America, 1850–1940," *Research in Law and Sociology* 3 (1980): 3; Grant Gilmore, *The Ages of American Law* (New Haven: Yale University Press, 1977), pp. 41–67; and Morton J. Horwitz, *The Transformation of American Law, 1870–1960* (New York: Oxford University Press, 1992), pp. 3–31.
3. Roscoe Pound, "The Need of a Sociological Jurisprudence," *The Green Bag* 19 (October 1907): 611–612.
4. 208 U.S. 412 (1908).
5. For an excellent survey of changing legal culture in the early twentieth century, see John W. Johnson, *American Legal Culture, 1908–1940* (Westport, Conn.: Greenwood Press, 1981).
6. Quoted in Michael Kammen, *A Machine That Would Go of Itself: The Constitution in American Culture* (New York: Alfred A. Knopf, 1986), p. 154.
7. Allan L. Benson, *Our Dishonest Constitution* (New York: B. W. Huebsch, 1914); Gilbert E. Roe, *Our Judicial Oligarchy* (New York: B. W. Huebsch, 1912); David Graham Phillips, *The Treason of the Senate* (1906; reprint, New York: Monthly Review Press, 1953). See also Charles Edward Merriam, *American Political Ideas* (New York: Macmillan, 1920), pp. 212–227, and Maxwell H. Bloomfield, *Alarms and Diversions: The American Mind through American Magazines, 1900–1914* (The Hague: Mouton & Co., 1967), pp. 103–130.
8. Oscar Ameringer, *Life and Deeds of Uncle Sam*, with introduction by Paul Buhle (1909; reprint, Chicago: Charles H. Kerr Publishing Co., 1985), p. 26.
9. Ibid., p. v.
10. In a study of 109 utopias published between 1888 and 1917, Charles J. Rooney, Jr., notes that "Bellamy's phenomenal success served as the immediate stimulus for 95 percent" of them. See Rooney, *Dreams and Visions: A Study of American Utopias, 1865–1917* (Westport, Conn.: Greenwood Press, 1985), p. 9.
11. Edward Bellamy, *Looking Backward* (1888; reprint, New York: New American Library, 1960), p. 73.

12. Ibid., p. 144.

13. Edward Bellamy, *Equality* (New York: D. Appleton and Co., 1897), p. 353.

14. Ibid., p. 356.

15. Ibid., p. 375.

16. Ibid., p. 332.

17. Ibid., p. 273.

18. Ibid., p. 275.

19. For a more extensive analysis of Bellamy's treatment of women and blacks, see Sylvia Strauss, "Gender, Class, and Race in Utopia," in Daphne Patai, ed., *Looking Backward, 1988–1888: Essays on Edward Bellamy* (Amherst: University of Massachusetts Press, 1988), pp. 68–90. In the same volume, see also Franklin Rosemont, "Bellamy's Radicalism Reclaimed," pp. 147–209.

20. On the international impact of *Looking Backward,* see Sylvia E. Bowman, ed., *Edward Bellamy Abroad: An American Prophet's Influence* (New York: Twayne Publishers, 1962). See also Frank Luther Mott, *Golden Multitudes: The Story of Best Sellers in the United States* (New York: Macmillan, 1947), pp. 168–170, 310.

21. *Budd v. New York,* 143 U.S. 517, 551 (1892).

22. *If You Don't Weaken: The Autobiography of Oscar Ameringer* (1940; reprint, Norman: University of Oklahoma Press, 1983), p. 182.

23. The most important exception is Jack London's *The Iron Heel* (1908), which describes a prolonged period of class warfare and the eventual triumph of socialism.

24. For a good appraisal of Progressivism, see John Whiteclay Chambers II, *The Tyranny of Change* (New York: St. Martin's Press, 1980).

25. Samuel Merwin, *The Citadel: A Romance of Unrest* (New York: Century Co., 1912), p. 10.

26. Ibid., p. 193.

27. Ibid., p. 329.

28. [Edward Mandell House], *Philip Dru: Administrator, A Story of Tomorrow, 1920–1935* (New York: B. W. Huebsch, 1912), pp. 57–58 (emphasis in original text).

29. On the popularity of Napoleon in turn-of-the-century America, see Theodore P. Greene, *America's Heroes: The Changing Models of Success in American Magazines* (New York: Oxford University Press, 1979), pp. 118–121. Magazine biographers often drew analogies between Napoleon's leadership qualities and those displayed by American "captains of industry" in the 1890s.

30. *Philip Dru,* p. 183.

31. In reviewing *Dru* for the *New York Times,* Walter Lippmann commented, "If [the author] is really an example of the far-seeing public man, then, in all sincerity, I say, God help this sunny land." Lippmann, "America's Future," *New York Times,* December 8, 1912, p. 754.

32. *Philip Dru,* p. 297.

33. Other constitutional fiction includes Frederick Upham Adams, *President John*

Smith: The Story of a Peaceful Revolution (Chicago: Charles H. Kerr & Co., 1897); Henry O. Morris, *Waiting for the Signal* (Chicago: Schulte Publishing Co., 1897); William Stanley Child (pseud.), *The Legal Revolution of 1902. By a Law-abiding Revolutionist* (Chicago: Charles H. Kerr & Co., 1898); Zebina Forbush, *The Co-opolitan: A Story of the Co-operative Commonwealth of Idaho* (Chicago: Charles H. Kerr & Co., 1898); Sidney C. Tapp, *The Struggle* (New York: A. Wessels Co., 1906); Isaac N. Stevens, *The Liberators: A Story of Future American Politics* (New York: B. W. Dodge & Co., 1908); and Alfred O. Crozier, *The Magnet: A Romance of the Battles of the Modern Giants* (New York: Funk & Wagnalls Co., 1908). See also Upton Sinclair's non-fiction utopia, *The Industrial Republic* (New York: Doubleday, Page & Co., 1907).

34. 109 U.S. 3 (1883). For a recent brief appraisal of the decision and its effects, see Michael Les Benedict, *The Blessings of Liberty* (Lexington, Mass.: D. C. Heath and Co., 1996), pp. 217–218.

35. 163 U.S. 537 (1896). On the impact of the *Plessy* case, see Benedict, *Blessings of Liberty*, pp. 218–220.

36. Thomas Dixon, Jr., *The Leopard's Spots: A Romance of the White Man's Burden* (New York: Doubleday, Page & Co., 1902), pp. 411–412.

37. Ibid., pp. 435, 438, 440.

38. For a more detailed account of the disfranchisement effort in Alabama, see John H. Wallace Jr.'s novel *The Senator from Alabama* (New York: Neale Publishing Co., 1904); for conditions in Mississippi, see Emerson Hough, *The Law of the Land* (Indianapolis: Bobbs-Merrill Co., 1904).

39. Dixon, *Leopard's Spots*, p. 242. On the popularity of Dixon's novel, see Maxwell Bloomfield, "Dixon's *The Leopard's Spots:* A Study in Popular Racism," *American Quarterly* 16 (Fall 1964): 387–401, and Raymond Allen Cook, *Fire in the Flint: The Amazing Careers of Thomas Dixon* (Winston-Salem, N.C.: John F. Blair, 1968).

40. Charles W. Chesnutt, *The Marrow of Tradition* (Boston: Houghton, Mifflin and Co., 1901), p. 192.

41. Ibid., p. 283.

42. Sutton E. Griggs, *Imperium in Imperio* (1899; reprint, New York: Arno Press, 1969), p. 181.

43. Ibid., p. 195.

44. Ibid., p. 275.

45. On Chesnutt's relation to the early NAACP, see Helen M. Chesnutt, *Charles Waddell Chesnutt: Pioneer of the Color Line* (Chapel Hill: University of North Carolina Press, 1952), pp. 231–240. In 1917 Chesnutt played a major part in the successful effort by African Americans to ban the showing of *The Birth of a Nation* in Cleveland. That brilliant, but flagrantly racist, film was based on another of Dixon's novels, *The Clansman* (1905). Chesnutt later supported the NAACP's promising, but ultimately unsuccessful, campaign to secure the passage of a federal antilynching law in 1921 and 1922. See Frances Richardson

Keller, *An American Crusade: The Life of Charles Waddell Chesnutt* (Provo: Brigham Young University Press, 1978).

46. Hugh M. Gloster, "The Negro in American Fiction," *Phylon* (4th quarter, 1943): 337.

47. For an insightful analysis of Griggs's work and civil rights activism, see Bernard W. Bell, *The Afro-American Novel and Its Tradition* (Amherst: University of Massachusetts Press, 1987), pp. 60–63.

48. Prosuffrage novels include Gertrude Atherton, *Julia France and Her Times* (New York: Macmillan, 1912); Mary Johnston, *Hagar* (Boston: Houghton Mifflin, 1913); Frank M. Boyce, Jr., *Governor Jane: A Story of "the New Woman"* (Niverville, N.Y.: M. S. Boyce, 1913); Elia W. Peattie, *The Precipice* (1914; reprint, Urbana: University of Illinois Press, 1989); and Margaret Deland, *The Rising Tide* (New York: A. L. Burt Co., 1916). The suffrage issue figured in such Broadway plays as Bayard Veiller's *The Fight* (1913), Arline Van Ness Hines's *Her Honor, the Mayor* (1918), and David Carb's *Immodest Violet* (1920). Suffrage groups regularly employed pageants and plays in their state campaigns. Particularly popular was a comedy, *How the Vote Was Won*, which the movement's newspaper termed "one of the finest arguments for suffrage ever written." See Kay Sloan, *The Loud Silents: Origins of the Social Problem Film* (Urbana: University of Illinois Press, 1988), p. 109. For a representative sampling of prosuffrage cartoons drawn by women, see Alice Sheppard, *Cartooning for Suffrage* (Albuquerque: University of New Mexico Press, 1994).

49. Sloan, *The Loud Silents*, p. 107.

50. Kevin Brownlow's *Behind the Mask of Innocence* (Berkeley: University of California Press, 1990) contains a brief account of this film on pages 232 and 233.

51. For a good analysis of the movie, see Sloan, *The Loud Silents*, p. 105.

52. Quoted in Brownlow, *Behind the Mask*, p. 226.

53. On the film and its distribution, see Sloan, *The Loud Silents*, pp. 112–113, and Brownlow, *Behind the Mask*, pp. 227–228.

54. Sloan, *The Loud Silents*, p. 122.

55. Ibid., pp. 111, 113–116.

56. Ibid., pp. 117–121.

57. Quoted in Carl Brent Swisher, *American Constitutional Development* (2d ed., Cambridge, Mass.: Houghton Mifflin, 1954), p. 698.

58. Ibid. Clark made his remarks on May 21, 1919, the day the House of Representatives overwhelmingly approved the suffrage amendment. The Senate did not vote favorably until June 4.

59. Quoted in Stanley Coben, *Rebellion against Victorianism* (New York: Oxford University Press, 1991), p. 97. For a fine overview of the suffrage movement, see Eleanor Flexner, *Century of Struggle: The Woman's Rights Movement in the United States* (Cambridge, Mass.: Harvard University Press, 1959).

60. I have taken the amendment figures from John R. Vile, *Encyclopedia of Constitutional Amendments, Proposed Amendments, and Amending Issues, 1789–*

1995 (Santa Barbara, Calif.: ABC-CLIO, Inc., 1996). See Appendix D, "Most Popular Amending Proposals by Year & Key Events," pp. 370–371. On the history of the income tax movement, see David E. Kyvig, *Explicit and Authentic Acts: Amending the U.S. Constitution, 1776–1995* (Lawrence: University Press of Kansas, 1996), pp. 194–208.

61. Frederick Upham Adams et al., "Are Great Fortunes Great Dangers?" *Cosmopolitan* 40 (February 1906): 392–400. Panelists included Charles W. Eliot, John Wanamaker, Edward Atkinson, Dr. E. Benjamin Andrews, Ernest Crosby, Henry Clews, David Starr Jordan, Washington Gladden, Jack London, and Oliver Wendell Holmes, Jr.

62. See, for example, Wayne MacVeagh, "The Graduated Taxation of Incomes and Inheritances," *North American Review* 182 (June 1906): 824–828; W. H. Mallock, "Great Fortunes and the Community," *North American Review* 183 (September 1906): 349–364; Philip S. Post, Jr., "The Problem of Enormous Fortunes," *Outlook* 85 (January 5, 1907): 21–25; and Philip S. Post, "The Income Tax," *Outlook* 85 (March 2, 1907): 503–508.

63. "An Appeal to our Millionaires by X," *North American Review* 182 (June 1906): 807–814.

64. See in general Paul Von Blum, *The Critical Vision: A History of Social and Political Art in the U.S.* (Boston: South End Press, 1982), pp. 23–36. One powerful illustration of impending class warfare enjoyed particular celebrity and was widely reprinted in books and magazines. The work of artist William Balfour Ker, it was titled "From the Depths." Political cartoonist Art Young describes it well: "It shows the terror of revelers in a palace of pleasure as a fist is thrust up through the floor by one of the toilers below whose labor enables the revelers to exist. This has often been reprinted, and has been the subject of many editorials and sermons." See Art Young, *Art Young: His Life and Times* (New York: Sheridan House, 1939), p. 266.

65. See, for example, Elihu Root, *The Citizen's Part in Government* (New York: Charles Scribner's Sons, 1907), and Brooks Adams, *The Theory of Social Revolutions* (New York: Macmillan, 1913).

66. See entry on "Progressive Era" in Vile, *Encyclopedia of Constitutional Amendments,* pp. 248–249.

67. Kyvig, *Explicit and Authentic Acts,* pp. 208–215.

68. On Phillips and his influence, see the excellent introduction by George E. Mowry and Judson A. Grenier to their edition of David Graham Phillips, *The Treason of the Senate* (Chicago: Quadrangle Books, 1964). See also Filler, *Crusaders for American Liberalism,* pp. 245–259.

69. On the implications of the amendment, see the entry "Seventeenth Amendment" in Vile, *Encyclopedia of Constitutional Amendments,* pp. 271–274.

70. See Filler, *Crusaders for American Liberalism,* pp. 142–170, 260–273; John Braeman, *Albert J. Beveridge: American Nationalist* (Chicago: University of Chicago Press, 1971), pp. 112–121.

71. Charles F. Amidon, "The Constitution and the Corporation," *Outlook* 87

(September 7, 1907): 25–26. See also "Senator Knox on the New Federalism," *Outlook* 88 (February 22, 1908): 377–379, and Peter S. Grosscup, "Is There Common Ground on Which Thoughtful Men Can Meet on the Trust Question?" *North American Review* 195 (March 1912): 293–309.

72. See, for example, William V. Rowe, "National Tendencies and the Constitution," *North American Review* 175 (May 1907): 147–176. In the same issue Rowe's views were criticized in "The Editor's Diary," pp. 231–236.

73. See Henry Litchfield West, "Shall the Constitution Be Amended?" *Forum* 42 (November 1909): 391–399; Edward L. Andrews, "A National Constitutional Convention," *Forum* 45 (April 1911): 385–412; and Albert Fink, "Trust Regulation: The Solution," *North American Review* 197 (March 1913): 350–361.

74. "The Editor's Diary," *North American Review* 185 (May 1907): 231–236. See also George Harvey, "Social Justice and Socialism," *North American Review* 196 (July 1912): 1–8, and Henry Cabot Lodge, "The Constitution and Its Makers," *North American Review* 196 (July 1912): 20–51.

75. Henry Wade Rogers, "The Constitution and the New Federalism," *North American Review* 188 (September 1908): 321–335.

76. David Jayne Hill, "Taking Soundings," *North American Review* 199 (May 1914): 673–683. See also Hill, "The Crisis in Constitutionalism," *North American Review* 198 (December 1913): 769–778.

77. Elihu Root, "Experiments in Government and the Essentials of the Constitution — I," *North American Review* 198 (July 1913): 8.

78. Representative articles include John S. Sheppard, Jr., "Concerning the Decline of the Principle of Representation in Popular Government," *Forum* 43 (June 1910): 642–650; Hon. Robert W. Bonynge, "Political Innovations," *Forum* 45 (June 1911): 645–660; "Editorial Notes," *Forum* 46 (December 1911): 759–760; William D. Guthrie, "Constitutional Morality," *North American Review* 196 (August 1912): 154–173; and George Kennan, "The Direct Rule of the People," *North American Review* 198 (August 1913): 145–160.

79. On the decline of muckraking, see Filler, *Crusaders for American Liberalism,* pp. 341–378. For business influence on regulatory policy, see Gabriel Kolko, *The Triumph of Conservatism* (New York: Free Press of Glencoe, 1963).

80. Walter E. Weyl, *The New Democracy* (rev. ed., New York: Macmillan, 1914), p. 166. Weyl was a major figure in Progressive journalism and a cofounder, with Herbert Croly and Walter Lippmann, of *The New Republic.* See Charles Forcey, *The Crossroads of Liberalism* (New York: Oxford University Press, 1961), and David Seideman, *The New Republic: A Voice of Modern Liberalism* (New York: Praeger, 1986).

81. Anne W. Lane and Louise H. Wall, eds., *The Letters of Franklin K. Lane* (Boston: Houghton Mifflin, 1922), p. 297. Wilson may have been introduced to *Philip Dru* by the author himself. As House noted in a diary entry of September 28, 1914: "During one of our talks I was interested in hearing him outline some such form of government as I gave in Philip Dru. Some day

when he is my guest in New York, it is my purpose to read from Philip Dru the constitution I wrote both for the nation and the states and see how far we differ. I have a feeling that we largely agree, although when I wrote Philip Dru I had never met the President nor read any of his books. As far as I can see, his thoughts and mine have run parallel for a long while, almost from youth." See Arthur S. Link, ed., *The Papers of Woodrow Wilson*, vol. 13 (Princeton: Princeton University Press, 1970), p. 95. I am indebted to Theodore Brown, Jr., for calling House's statement to my attention. There is no evidence that the colonel ever carried out his plan; his penchant for self-aggrandizement makes him an unreliable witness in any case.

3. The Selling of War Socialism

1. William E. Leuchtenburg, *The Perils of Prosperity, 1914–32* (Chicago: University of Chicago Press, 1958), p. 40.
2. For a good discussion of the constitutional issues raised by federal wartime power, see Alfred H. Kelly, Winfred A. Harbison, and Herman Belz, *The American Constitution: Its Origins and Development* (6th ed., New York: W. W. Norton, 1983), pp. 445–453.
3. 55 *Congressional Record* 4459, quoted in Carl Brent Swisher, *American Constitutional Development* (2d ed., Cambridge, Mass.: Houghton Mifflin, 1954), p. 631.
4. 55 *Congressional Record* 4460, quoted in Swisher, ibid.
5. Quoted in Saul K. Padover, ed., *Wilson's Ideals* (Washington, D.C.: American Council on Public Affairs, 1942), p. 90.
6. On the establishment and objectives of the CPI, see David M. Kennedy, *Over Here: The First World War and American Society* (New York: Oxford University Press, 1980), pp. 59–61. See also John Tebbel and Sarah Miles Watts, *The Press and the Presidency* (New York: Oxford University Press, 1985), pp. 382–385, and George Creel, *Rebel at Large* (New York: G. P. Putman's Sons, 1947), pp. 156–161.
7. Quoted in Mark Sullivan, *Our Times, 1900–1925*, vol. 5 (New York: Charles Scribner's Sons, 1933), p. 425.
8. Ibid., pp. 430–433; James R. Mock and Cedric Larson, *Words That Won the War: The Story of the Committee on Public Information, 1917–1919* (Princeton: Princeton University Press, 1939), pp. 113–126. David Kennedy sees some parallel between the CPI's "Four-Minute Singing" and the "Two-Minutes Hate" exercise practiced by the citizens of Oceania in George Orwell's *1984*. See *Over Here*, p. 62.
9. Quoted in Sullivan, *Our Times*, pp. 295–296.
10. Ibid., p. 298.
11. Ibid.
12. Kennedy, *Over Here*, pp. 152–154; Herbert Croly, *The Promise of American Life* (New York: Macmillan, 1909).

13. Kennedy, pp. 164–166.

14. For an excellent discussion of the Rebellion and its background, see James R. Green, *Grass-roots Socialism: Radical Movements in the Southwest, 1895–1943* (Baton Rouge: Louisiana State University Press, 1978), pp. 354–368.

15. Quoted in Garin Burbank, *When Farmers Voted Red: The Gospel of Socialism in the Oklahoma Countryside, 1910–1924* (Westport, Conn.: Greenwood Press, 1976), p. 151. Burbank provides another first-rate analysis of the Rebellion, which he sees as more influenced by local concerns than by socialist ideology. See also Oscar Ameringer's perceptive account of his contacts with the rebels in his autobiography, *If You Don't Weaken* (1940; reprint, Norman: University of Oklahoma Press, 1983), pp. 347–356. For a sympathetic fictional account of the Rebellion, see William Cunningham, *The Green Corn Rebellion* (New York: Vanguard Press, 1935).

16. *Selective Draft Law Cases,* 245 U.S. 366, 378 (1918). For a good analysis of the constitutional issues raised by the conscription law, see Alexander M. Bickel and Benno C. Schmidt, Jr., *The Judiciary and Responsible Government, 1910–21* (New York: Macmillan Publishing Co., 1984), pp. 519–522.

17. Bickel and Schmidt, *The Judiciary and Responsible Government,* p. 520.

18. Creel, *Rebel at Large,* pp. 168–169; Mock and Larson, *Words That Won the War,* pp. 72–74.

19. Mary Roberts Rinehart, *Dangerous Days* (New York: George H. Doran Co., 1919), p. 253.

20. Ibid., p. 233.

21. Ibid., p. 394.

22. Ida M. Tarbell, *The Rising of the Tide* (New York: Macmillan, 1919), p. 91.

23. Ibid., pp. 178–179.

24. Ibid., p. 237.

25. On the novel's background and reception, Train commented in his autobiography: "I was forty-five years old and, for family reasons, delayed enlisting for the World War until the summer of 1918, meantime actively occupying myself with propaganda for the Liberty Loan, etc., and the writing of patriotic fiction. . . . 'The Earthquake' had a remarkably enthusiastic press, for even critics were emotional at that tense moment, and was generally bracketed with [H. G. Wells's] 'Mr. Britling Sees It Through.'" See Arthur Train, *My Day in Court* (New York: Charles Scribner's Sons, 1939), p. 348.

26. Arthur Train, *The Earthquake* (New York: Charles Scribner's Sons, 1918), pp. 293–294.

27. Ibid., p. 195.

28. Ibid., pp. 187–188. For examples of other wartime fiction that pursued these Wilsonian themes, see Henry Kitchell Webster, *An American Family* (Indianapolis: Bobbs-Merrill Co., 1918), and Booth Tarkington, *Ramsey Milholland* (New York: Doubleday, Page & Co., 1919).

29. Craig W. Campbell, *Reel America and World War I* (Jefferson, N.C.: McFarland & Co., Inc., 1985), p. 77.

30. Michael T. Isenberg, *War on Film: The American Cinema and World War I, 1914–1941* (Rutherford, N.J.: Fairleigh Dickinson University Press, 1981), p. 88. Although conscription movies and novels emphasized the weakening of class lines, they said little about racial prejudice. African Americans seldom appeared as characters in these narratives, perhaps because they continued to endure flagrantly discriminatory treatment at the hands of military authorities. Black filmmakers nevertheless supported the war effort with such releases as the documentaries *Doing Their Bit* (1918) and *The Heroic Black Soldiers of the War* (1919). On the lighter side, *Spying the Spy* (1917) featured "Sambo Sam" tracking down a German spy, while *Loyal Hearts* (1919) described a battlefield romance between a black nurse and an African-American soldier in war-torn France. See James R. Nesteby, *Black Images in American Films, 1896–1954: The Interplay between Civil Rights and Film Culture* (Washington, D.C.: University Press of America, 1982), p. 67. For a good discussion of the problems faced by early black filmmakers, see also Thomas Cripps, *Slow Fade to Black: The Negro in American Film, 1900–1942* (New York: Oxford University Press, 1977).

31. Campbell, *Reel America*, pp. 62–63. Campbell offers an insightful reading of these wartime films.

32. Quoted in Isenberg, *War on Film*, p. 176.

33. Campbell, *Reel America*, pp. 80–81.

34. Creel, *Rebel at Large*, p. 169. For an excellent discussion of wartime newsreels and documentaries and their propagandistic functions, see Isenberg, *War on Film*, pp. 57–81.

35. Quoted in Steven J. Ross, "Cinema and Class Conflict: Labor, Capital, the State and American Silent Films," in Robert Sklar and Charles Musser, eds., *Resisting Images: Essays on Cinema and History* (Philadelphia: Temple University Press, 1990), p. 83.

36. On the major provisions of these statutes, see Swisher, *American Constitutional Development*, pp. 603–606.

37. *Schenck v. United States*, 249 U.S. 47, 52 (1919).

38. Kennedy, *Over Here*, pp. 75–83.

39. Ibid., pp. 158–160; W. E. B. Du Bois, *Dusk of Dawn*, reprinted in Du Bois, *Writings* (New York: Library of America, 1986), pp. 734–735.

40. Quoted in Roi Ottley, *The Lonely Warrior* (Chicago: Henry Regnery Co., 1955), p. 126.

41. Ibid., p. 146; Patrick S. Washburn, *A Question of Sedition: The Federal Government's Investigation of the Black Press during World War II* (New York: Oxford University Press, 1986), pp. 16–17.

42. Ottley, *Lonely Warrior*, pp. 136–137.

43. Quoted in *Along This Way: The Autobiography of James Weldon Johnson* (New York: Viking Press, 1968), p. 321.

44. Ibid.

45. Washburn, *A Question of Sedition*, p. 17. See also Kennedy, *Over Here*, pp. 160–163.

46. Quoted in Washburn, *A Question of Sedition,* p. 16.

47. Ibid., p. 17. See also Frederick G. Detweiler, *The Negro Press in the United States* (1922; reprint, College Park, Md.: McGrath Publishing Co., 1968), pp. 68–69.

48. "Returning Soldiers" (May 1919), in Du Bois, *Writings,* pp. 1179–81.

49. Viola Gilbert Snell, "To Frank Little," in Joyce L. Kornbluh, ed., *Rebel Voices: An IWW Anthology* (Chicago: Charles H. Kerr Publishing Co., 1988), p. 306. On the early history of the IWW, see Philip S. Foner, *The Industrial Workers of the World—1905–1917* (New York: International Publishers, 1965), and Melvyn Dubofsky, *We Shall Be All* (New York: Quadrangle, 1969).

50. Zane Grey, *The Desert of Wheat* (1919; reprint, Thorndike, Maine: Thorndike Press, 1982), p. 68. Richard Slotkin offers a perceptive analysis of this novel in relation to Grey's other formula Westerns in *Gunfighter Nation* (New York: HarperCollins, 1993), pp. 211–217.

51. Ralph Chaplin, *Wobbly* (Chicago: University of Chicago Press, 1948), p. 247. See also Kornbluh, *Rebel Voices,* pp. 316–325.

52. Chaplin, *Wobbly* , pp. 229–249; Kornbluh, *Rebel Voices,* p. 321.

53. Ameringer, *If You Don't Weaken,* p. 317. See also Samuel Walker, *In Defense of American Liberties: A History of the ACLU* (New York: Oxford University Press, 1990), pp. 14–15.

54. "Address to the Jury," in Jean Y. Tussey, ed., *Eugene V. Debs Speaks* (New York: Pathfinder Press, 1970), pp. 282, 286–287. On Debs's importance as a labor leader, see Nick Salvatore, *Eugene V. Debs: Citizen and Socialist* (Urbana: University of Illinois, 1982). For an insightful reappraisal of Debs's legal radicalism and its enduring significance, see David Ray Papke, "Eugene Debs as Legal Heretic: The Law-related Conversion, Catechism and Evangelism of an American Socialist," 63 *University of Cincinnati Law Review* (Fall 1997): 339–375.

55. The winner of the 1920 presidential election, Warren G. Harding, pardoned Debs on Christmas Day 1921, after the United States Supreme Court had earlier unanimously rejected his appeal. In *Debs v. United States,* 249 U.S. 211 (1919), Justice Holmes acknowledged that Debs's speech had dealt primarily with the growth of socialism, but commented: "If a part of the manifest intent of the more general utterances was to encourage those present to obstruct the recruiting service, and if in passages such encouragement was directly given, the immunity of the general theme may not be enough to protect the speech" (pp. 212–213).

4. Constitutional Conservatism in a Decade of Normalcy

1. *Hammer v. Dagenhart,* 247 U.S. 251, 276 (1918). On the background of the case and the failure of subsequent congressional efforts to regulate child labor in the 1920s, see Stephen B. Wood, *Constitutional Politics in the Progressive Era: Child Labor and the Law* (Chicago: University of Chicago Press, 1968).

2. Quoted in Carl Brent Swisher, *American Constitutional Development* (2d ed., Cambridge, Mass.: Houghton Mifflin, 1954), p. 1.

3. Editorial, "Fiddling," *Saturday Evening Post,* May 22, 1920, quoted in Jan Cohn, *Creating America: George Horace Lorimer and the Saturday Evening Post* (Pittsburgh: University of Pittsburgh Press, 1989), p. 141.

4. For a discussion of the Harris story, see Cohn, *Creating America,* p. 141; see also Booth Tarkington, "Saving the Country," *Saturday Evening Post,* July 5, 1919, p. 81.

5. For a recent perceptive overview of the 1920s, see Ellis W. Hawley, *The Great War and the Search for a Modern Order* (2d ed., New York: St. Martin's Press, 1992).

6. On the Red Scare and its lingering effects, see Paul L. Murphy, "Sources and Nature of Intolerance in the 1920's," in Milton Plesur, ed., *The 1920's: Problems and Paradoxes* (Boston: Allyn and Bacon, 1969), pp. 165–183. See also Samuel Walker, *In Defense of American Liberties: A History of the ACLU* (New York: Oxford University Press, 1990), pp. 42–82.

7. George Kibbe Turner, *Red Friday* (Boston: Little, Brown and Co., 1919), pp. 11, 13–14.

8. Ibid., pp. 241, 243. Compare the criticism of wartime mismanagement in a much better novel by another disgruntled Progressive: "But [Washington] was like some huge engine revolving with much whir and grinding of complicated gears, but without accomplishment, without apparent direction. Just a lot of odds and ends of machinery, mostly new and half installed, whirling madly around in a vacuum. . . . Billions of treasure poured out on this vast project and that, like Pig Island and Muscle Shoals, a huge extravaganza of war industries planned and confusedly started. But no directing mind. Confusion— and intermittent deliverances of grand sentiments from Sinai." Robert Herrick, *Waste* (London: Jonathan Cape, 1924), p. 316.

9. *The Dial,* June 28, 1919, p. 666.

10. Drama critic Burns Mantle, in *The Best Plays of 1919–1920* (Boston: Small, Maynard & Co., 1920), provides the following capsule synopsis of *The Red Dawn:* "On an island off the coast of California an attempt is made by a young visionary to establish a socialistic colony to prove that the theories of socialism are practical. The 'central Soviet of Russia' attempts to gain control of the colony to help along the 'universal revolution.' Five billions in counterfeit money are to be used in financing the scheme, and the aid of a million ex-convicts, three million laborers, and ten million dissatisfied negroes is to be invoked. The scheme is frustrated after the dreamer realizes his mistake. The timely arrival of an off-stage U.S. cruiser helps" (p. 344). The play closed after only five performances. Dixon also helped to produce the movie *Bolshevism on Trial,* which was based on his 1909 novel, *Comrades.* See Raymond Allen Cook, *Fire in the Flint: The Amazing Careers of Thomas Dixon* (Winton-Salem, N.C.: John F. Blair, 1968), pp. 190–192.

For a discussion of *Poldekin* and Tarkington's other anticommunist efforts, see James Woodress, *Booth Tarkington, Gentleman from Indiana* (Philadelphia: J. B. Lippincott Co., 1955), pp. 215–218.

On the films that contributed to the Red Scare, see Craig W. Campbell, *Reel America and World War I* (Jefferson, N.C.: McFarland & Co., Inc., 1985), pp. 133–134, and Lewis Jacobs, "Films of the Postwar Decade," in Arthur F. McClure, ed., *The Movies: An American Idiom* (Rutherford, N.J.: Fairleigh Dickinson University Press, 1971), pp. 70–71.

11. Kammen, *A Machine That Would Go of Itself: The Constitution in American Culture* (New York: Alfred A. Knopf, 1986), pp. 219–222.

12. Ibid., p. 225.

13. Ibid., pp. 223–224.

14. "Program for Promoting American Ideals," *American Bar Association Journal* 8 (September 1922): 587.

15. Kammen, *A Machine That Would Go of Itself*, p. 232.

16. Paul L. Murphy, *The Meaning of Freedom of Speech* (Westport, Conn.: Greenwood Press, 1972), pp. 208–211.

17. Robert S. Lynd and Helen Merrell Lynd, *Middletown: A Study in Modern American Culture* (1929; reprint, New York: Harcourt, Brace & World, Inc., 1956), pp. 198–199.

18. Ibid., pp. 200–201. To the statement, "The white race is the best race on earth," 66 percent of the boys and 75 percent of the girls responded "True." And a whopping 77 percent of the boys and 88 percent of the girls agreed that "[t]he United States is unquestionably the best country in the world" (p. 200).

19. James M. Beck, *The Constitution of the United States* (New York: George H. Doran Co., 1924), pp. 272–273.

20. Ibid., pp. xi, 202, 231, 271.

21. Ibid., p. 202.

22. Quoted in Morton Keller, *In Defense of Yesterday: James M. Beck and the Politics of Conservatism* (New York: Coward-McCann, Inc., 1958), p. 158.

23. Ibid., p. 159.

24. On the background of the Eighteenth Amendment and the constitutional issues it presented, see Alfred H. Kelly, Winfred A. Harbison, and Herman Belz, *The American Constitution: Its Origins and Development* (6th ed., New York: W. W. Norton, 1983), pp. 475–477.

25. Quoted in Russell L. Caplan, *Constitutional Brinksmanship* (New York: Oxford University Press, 1988), p. 66.

26. Quoted in George Wolfskill, *The Revolt of the Conservatives: A History of the American Liberty League, 1934–1940* (Boston: Houghton Mifflin Co., 1962), p. 41.

27. Kirby's cartoon is reprinted in Stephen Hess and Milton Kaplan, *The Ungentlemanly Art: A History of American Political Cartoons* (rev. ed., New York: Macmillan Publishing Co., 1975), p. 147.

28. Keller, *In Defense of Yesterday*, p. 209.

29. For a reprint of Weed's cartoon, see Hess and Kaplan, *Ungentlemanly Art*,

p. 149. "Samuel," which appeared in the St. Louis *Post-Dispatch,* June 29, 1919, is reprinted on p. 216. William E. Leuchtenburg provides a good summary of enforcement problems in *The Perils of Prosperity, 1914–32* (Chicago: University of Chicago Press, 1958), pp. 214–217.

30. A reprint of the constitutional cartoon, which was first published in the Los Angeles *Times,* may be found in *Literary Digest,* April 15, 1922, p. 36.

31. Wolfskill, *Revolt of the Conservatives,* p. 50.

32. Quoted in Keller, *In Defense of Yesterday,* p. 212. Beck made the statement in a 1930 speech attacking prohibition, but his feelings had not changed three years later, when repeal was at last accomplished.

   On the contribution made by the lawyers' committee to the mechanics of ratification, see Wolfskill, *Revolt of the Conservatives,* pp. 51–52. The AAPA formally dissolved on December 30, 1933, but members of the Executive Committee resolved to "continue to meet from time to time and have in view the formation of a group, based on our old membership in the association, which would in the event of danger to the Federal Constitution, stand ready to defend the faith of the fathers" (p. 54). In August 1934 these committeemen founded the American Liberty League to combat the "radical" tendencies of the New Deal and restore the "fundamental principles" of the Constitution.

33. On Hoover's policies and their effects, see Hawley, *The Great War and the Search for a Modern Order,* pp. 83–86, and Morton Keller, *Regulating a New Economy: Public Policy and Economic Change in America, 1900–1933* (Cambridge, Mass.: Harvard University Press, 1990), pp. 36–40.

34. *Maple Flooring Association v. United States,* 268 U.S. 563 (1925). For an assessment of the merger movement in the 1920s, see Leuchtenburg, *Perils of Prosperity,* pp. 189–193.

35. *Adkins v. Children's Hospital,* 261 U.S. 525, 559–560 (1923). On the decision and its repercussions, see William F. Swindler, *Court and Constitution in the 20th Century: The Old Legality, 1889–1932* (Indianapolis: Bobbs-Merrill Co., 1969), pp. 240–243.

36. Melvin I. Urofsky provides a useful account of the Court's treatment of labor issues in *A March of Liberty: A Constitutional History of the United States,* vol. 2 (New York: Alfred A. Knopf, 1988), pp. 626–628.

37. The *Post* published Garrett's work in six installments between December 24, 1921, and January 28, 1922. The book appeared in 1922 under the imprint of E. P. Dutton.

38. Garet Garrett, *The Driver* (New York: E. P. Dutton and Co., 1922), pp. 188–189.

39. Ibid., p. 230.

40. This unsavory character probably represents Garrett's jaundiced view of Louis D. Brandeis, who had abandoned a lucrative corporate practice to become an early public interest lawyer in the prewar years.

41. Garrett, *The Driver,* pp. 263, 271–272.

42. Ibid., p. 78.

43. Two studies provide important insights into Garrett's ideas and influence: Carl

Ryant, *Profit's Prophet: Garet Garrett (1878–1954)* (Selinsgrove, N.Y.: Susquehanna University Press, 1989), and Justin Raimondo, *Reclaiming the American Right* (Burlingame, Calif.: Center for Libertarian Studies, 1993), pp. 51–97. In a related essay, Raimondo has argued, with considerable persuasiveness, that *The Driver* strongly influenced Ayn Rand's more famous novel of a superhuman businessman, *Atlas Shrugged* (1957). The similarities extend even to the name Rand chose for her hero: "John Galt." See Justin Raimondo, "Who Is Henry Galt?" *Chronicles* 16 (August 1992): 47–50.

44. Arthur Train, *The Needle's Eye* (New York: Charles Scribner's Sons, 1924), pp. 129–130.

45. Ibid., pp. 305–306.

46. Ibid., p. 306.

47. Ibid., p. 156.

48. Ibid., p. 376.

49. Ibid., pp. 353–354.

50. "It drives unerringly toward the conclusion that capitalism is right and socialism crooked; it may achieve quite a popularity by that," noted fellow novelist Clement Wood. See *Literary Review*, October 4, 1924, p. 6. Like *The Driver*, Train's novel began as a serial in a mass circulation magazine, *Cosmopolitan*.

51. Edgar Lee Masters, *The Fate of the Jury* (New York: D. Appleton and Co., 1929), p. 112.

52. For an excellent discussion of these early films, see Kay Sloan, *The Loud Silents: Origins of the Social Problem Film* (Urbana: University of Illinois Press, 1988).

53. Lary May's *Screening Out the Past* (1980; reprint, Chicago: University of Chicago Press, 1983) analyzes the replacement of political reform by the "consumer ideal" in the films of the 1920s; see especially pp. 200–236. See also Jacobs, "Films of the Postwar Decade," pp. 72–78, 82–83.

54. Raymond Durgnat and Scott Simmon, *King Vidor, American* (Berkeley: University of California Press, 1988), p. 78.

55. On the antiunion bias of Hollywood films in the 1920s, see Steven J. Ross, "Cinema and Class Conflict: Labor, Capital, the State and American Silent Films," in Robert Sklar and Charles Musser, eds., *Resisting Images: Essays on Cinema and History* (Philadelphia: Temple University Press, 1990), pp. 68–107. Ross notes that a few worker-owned companies managed in the 1920s to produce commercial films that promoted unionism. Some of these films, including the innovative *The Passaic Textile Strike* (1926), reached large audiences. But they had to be shown in union halls, church auditoriums, and an occasional neighborhood theater, since the major studios controlled the large first-run movie houses. State censorship boards posed an additional obstacle to the screening of movies that depicted inhumane working conditions and sympathized with the grievances of strikers. The escalating costs of movie production after the advent of "talkies" in the late 1920s forced the last small independents out of business.

56. On Gray's ideology, see Russel Nye, *The Unembarrassed Muse* (New York: Dial

Press, 1970), pp. 221–222; Lyle W. Shannon, "The Opinions of Little Orphan Annie and Her Friends," in Bernard Rosenberg and David Manning White, eds., *Mass Culture: The Popular Arts in America* (New York: Free Press of Glencoe, 1957), pp. 212–217.

57. Quoted in Leuchtenburg, *Perils of Prosperity*, p. 202.

58. On Progressivism in the 1920s, see Paul L. Murphy, *The Constitution in Crisis Times, 1918–1969* (New York: Harper & Row, 1972), pp. 7–8, 35, 43–44; Kelly, Harbison, and Belz, *The American Constitution*, pp. 472–474.

59. For public reaction to the *Dagenhart* decision, see Alexander M. Bickel and Benno C. Schmidt, Jr., *The Judiciary and Responsible Government, 1910–21* (New York: Macmillan Publishing Co., 1984), pp. 454–456.

60. The cartoon is reprinted in Art Young, *Art Young: His Life and Times* (New York: Sheridan House, 1939), p. 326.

61. *Bailey v. Drexel Furniture Co.*, 259 U.S. 20, 37–38 (1922). See also Wood, *Constitutional Politics in the Progressive Era*, pp. 193–216, 277–294.

62. For press reaction to the *Bailey* decision, see "The Child-labor Law Quashed," *Literary Digest*, May 27, 1922, p. 11. See also William G. Ross, *A Muted Fury: Populists, Progressives, and Labor Unions Confront the Courts, 1890–1937* (Princeton: Princeton University Press, 1994), pp. 190–191.

63. On LaFollette's influence in the 1920s, see Ross, *A Muted Fury*, pp. 194–217, 254–284.

64. Wood, *Constitutional Politics in the Progressive Era*, p. 297; Swindler, *Court and Constitution in the 20th Century*, pp. 237–238.

65. On the opposition to the Child Labor Amendment, see Katharine Du Pre Lumpkin and Dorothy Wolff Douglas, *Child Workers in America* (New York: International Publishers, 1937), pp. 206–209, 233–245.

66. *America*, September 6, 1924, p. 21, quoted in Rev. Vincent A. McQuade, O.S.A., *The American Catholic Attitude on Child Labor since 1891* (Washington, D.C.: The Catholic University of America, 1938), p. 89.

67. Nicholas Murray Butler, "The New American Revolution," *American Bar Association Journal* 10 (December 1924): 845, 846–847, 850.

68. Everett P. Wheeler, "The Labor Amendment Submitted for Ratification," *American Bar Association Journal* 10 (October 1924): 713, 714.

69. Quoted in Swindler, *Court and Constitution in the 20th Century*, p. 239. See also Lumpkin and Douglas, *Child Workers in America*, pp. 205, 209–210.

70. *United States v. Darby*, 312 U.S. 100, 117 (1941). For an excellent discussion of the opinion and its treatment in the press, see Alpheus Thomas Mason, *Harlan Fiske Stone: Pillar of the Law* (New York: Viking Press, 1956), pp. 550–556. See also the entry on the "Child Labor Amendment" in John R. Vile, *Encyclopedia of Constitutional Amendments, Proposed Amendments, and Amending Issues, 1789–1995* (Santa Barbara, Calif.: ABC-CLIO, Inc., 1996), pp. 47–49.

71. *Along This Way: The Autobiography of James Weldon Johnson* (New York: Viking Press, 1968), pp. 329–330; Robert L. Zagrando, *The NAACP Crusade*

against Lynching, 1909–1950 (Philadelphia: Temple University Press, 1980), p. 41; Mary White Ovington, *The Walls Came Tumbling Down* (New York: Harcourt, Brace, and Co., 1947), pp. 147–152.

72. Zagrando, *NAACP Crusade,* pp. 46–50; Ovington, *Walls Came Tumbling Down,* pp. 153–154.
73. Quoted in Zagrando, *NAACP Crusade,* p. 57.
74. Ibid., p. 43.
75. Johnson, *Along This Way,* p. 363.
76. Zagrando, *NAACP Crusade,* pp. 61–64.
77. *City Times* (Galveston, Texas), February 4, 1922, p. 2. A good run of this black newspaper is available on microfilm in the Rosenberg Library in Galveston.
78. Zagrando, *NAACP Crusade,* p. 65; Johnson, *Along This Way,* pp. 366–368.
79. Johnson, *Along This Way,* p. 369.
80. Zagrando, *NAACP Crusade,* pp. 56, 65; Walter White, *Rope and Faggot* (1929; reprint, New York: Arno Press, 1969), pp. 219–220. The guarantee clause is found in Art. IV, sec. 4 of the Constitution.
81. See "Would the Dyer Bill Halt Lynching?" *Literary Digest,* June 10, 1922, p. 14.
82. Ibid.
83. Zagrando, *NAACP Crusade,* pp. 66–69.
84. Zagrando describes the cartoon on p. 78.
85. Ibid., pp. 72, 79, 83–84.
86. Johnson, *Along This Way,* p. 373.
87. Waldo Frank, *The Re-discovery of America* (1929; reprint, New York: Duell, Sloan and Pearce, 1947), pp. 148–150.

5. Symbols of Authority in a Collapsing Economy

1. Quoted in Susan Winslow, *Brother, Can You Spare a Dime? America from the Wall Street Crash to Pearl Harbor* (New York: Paddington Press, 1976), p. 8.
2. On the Agricultural Marketing Act and its effects, see Albert U. Romasco, *The Poverty of Abundance* (New York: Oxford University Press, 1965), pp. 106–124.
3. Quoted in Morton Keller, *In Defense of Yesterday: James M. Beck and the Politics of Conservatism* (New York: Coward-McCann, Inc., 1958), p. 207.
4. For a summary of Hoover's programs, see Ellis W. Hawley, *The Great War and the Search for a Modern Order* (2d ed., New York: St. Martin's Press, 1992), pp. 160–187.
5. Quoted in Roger Biles, *A New Deal for the American People* (DeKalb, Ill.: Northern Illinois University Press, 1991), p. 21.
6. George S. Kaufman and Morrie Ryskind, "Socratic Dialogue," *Nation,* April 12, 1932, p. 403.

7. Biles, *A New Deal,* pp. 21–22.
8. On Hoover's efforts to promote the work of local relief agencies, see Romasco, *The Poverty of Abundance,* pp. 143–172.
9. The advertisement, which originally appeared in the November 21, 1931 issue of *Literary Digest,* is reprinted in Robert Bendiner, *Just Around the Corner* (New York: Harper & Row, 1967), p. 12.
10. Ibid.
11. Quoted in Romasco, *The Poverty of Abundance,* p. 181.
12. On the *Nation's* poll, see Mauritz A. Hallgren, *Seeds of Revolt* (New York: Alfred A. Knopf, 1933), pp. 40–41. John A. Garraty notes that accurate statistics on unemployment did not exist in any industrial nation during the 1930s. See Garraty, *The Great Depression* (Garden City, N.Y.: Anchor Press/Doubleday, 1987), pp. 13, 100–102.
13. Quoted in Hallgren, *Seeds of Revolt,* p. 43.
14. Ibid., p. 14.
15. Biles, *A New Deal,* pp. 22–23.
16. Romasco, *The Poverty of Abundance,* pp. 223–226.
17. Ibid., pp. 226–227, 233.
18. *Literary Digest,* March 21, 1931, p. 6.
19. Reprinted in Milton Meltzer, *Brother, Can You Spare a Dime? The Great Depression, 1929–1933* (New York: Penguin Books, 1977), p. 105. A poem in a small-town newspaper, *The Texas Spur,* of August 14, 1931, expressed similar sentiments:

> Our country first was civilized,
>   And next to that was organized
> And then our nation Christianized
>   But now, oh boy, she's Hooverized.
> . . . .
> Our chief sails high, rides most to the skies
>   And clothes his folks like butterflies
> But fails to hear the moans and sighs
>   Of us poor souls who Hooverize.
> Some men preach rank atheism
>   And others universalism
> And some poor souls preach socialism
>   While a few blame fools preach Hooverism.

Reprinted in Donald W. Whisenhunt, "The Bard in the Depression: Texas Style," *Journal of Popular Culture* 2 (Winter 1968): 376–377.
20. Bruce Kuklick, *The Good Ruler from Herbert Hoover to Richard Nixon* (New Brunswick, N.J.: Rutgers University Press, 1988), p. 42.
21. H. L. Mencken, *A Carnival of Buncombe: Writings on Politics* (Chicago: University of Chicago Press, 1984), p. 262.

22. Reprinted in Whisenhunt, "The Bard in the Depression," pp. 375–376. In some versions the words "Republican Party" or "Depression" replaced "Hoover" at the beginning of the poem.

 The president's supporters, in turn, parodied the willingness of some critics to blame him for all of the nation's ills. One well-wisher sent the following poem to the White House in October 1930:

> I have some corns upon my feet,—
>> Herb Hoover is to blame.
> A recent cyclone wrecked our street,—
>> Herb Hoover is to blame.
> My crop of beans is very small,
> My onions didn't grow at all,
> The rats are in my cellar wall,
>> Herb Hoover is to blame!

 Reprinted in Donald W. Whisenhunt, *Poetry of the People: Poems to the President, 1929–1945* (Bowling Green, Ohio: Bowling Green State University Popular Press, 1996), p. 24.
23. The cartoon, which originally appeared in the Brooklyn *Eagle,* is reprinted in Bendiner, *Just Around the Corner,* p. 7.
24. *Literary Digest,* December 17, 1932, p. 2.
25. Quoted in Meltzer, *Brother, Can You Spare a Dime?,* p. 53.
26. Quoted in Andrew Bergman, *We're in the Money: Depression America and Its Films* (New York: Harper & Row, 1972), p. 28.
27. Quoted in Lawrence W. Levine, *The Unpredictable Past: Explorations in American Cultural History* (New York: Oxford University Press, 1993), p. 235. See also Roger Dooley, *From Scarface to Scarlett: American Films in the 1930s* (New York: Harcourt Brace Jovanovich, 1981), p. 595.
28. Levine, *The Unpredictable Past,* p. 248.
29. Ibid.
30. Ibid., p. 235. For further plot details, see Dooley, *From Scarface to Scarlett,* p. 595.
31. Maxwell Anderson, *Both Your Houses* (New York: Samuel French, 1933), p. 21.
32. Ibid., pp. 174, 177–179.
33. Ibid., pp. 55, 103.
34. Ibid., p. 179.
35. Walter Lippmann, "The Ideal of Representative Government," reprinted in Clinton Rossiter and James Lare, eds., *The Essential Lippmann: A Political Philosophy for Liberal Democracy* (Cambridge, Mass.: Harvard University Press, 1982), pp. 255–256.
36. Rossiter and Lare, *The Essential Lippmann,* pp. 109–110, 152.
37. See, for example, Lippmann's columns "The New Congress" (December 8, 1931) and "The False Gods" (May 20, 1932), reprinted in ibid., pp. 121–

122, 466–468. For a good analysis of Lippmann's evolving thought, see Ronald Steel, *Walter Lippmann and the American Century* (Boston: Little, Brown and Co., 1980).

38. For a sampling of representative reviews, see "Congress Pilloried on the Stage," *Literary Digest*, March 25, 1933, p. 15; "Dramatic Critics Who Disagree," ibid., June 17, 1933, p. 14; Joseph Wood Krutch, "The Minutes Stand Approved," *Nation*, March 29, 1933, pp. 355–356; and Richard Dana Skinner, "The Play: *Both Your Houses*," *Commonweal*, March 22, 1933, p. 582. Anderson's biographer notes that the initial drafts of *Both Your Houses* were more pessimistic and left open no possibility for constructive reform. The dramatist altered the text in a more hopeful direction only late in rehearsals, so that the published version of the play may represent a "compromise . . . between what Anderson felt in his heart about government and what the production staff felt was expedient in order to secure a viable drama." See Alfred S. Shivers, *Maxwell Anderson* (Boston: Twayne Publishers, 1976), p. 100.

39. George S. Kaufman and Morrie Ryskind, *Of Thee I Sing* (New York: Alfred A. Knopf, 1932), pp. 171–172.

40. Ibid., p. 177.

41. Morgan Y. Himelstein, *Drama Was a Weapon* (New Brunswick, N.J.: Rutgers University Press, 1963), pp. 184–185. On the production and its reception, see also Malcolm Goldstein, *George S. Kaufman: His Life, His Theater* (New York: Oxford University Press, 1979), pp. 200–204.

42. Levine, *The Unpredictable Past*, pp. 241, 243; Dooley, *From Scarface to Scarlett*, p. 594.

43. Elmer Rice, *We, the People* (New York: Coward McCann, Inc., 1933), p. 161.

44. Ibid., pp. 247–248.

45. Ibid., p. 253.

46. Rice refers to White's letter in his autobiography. See Elmer Rice, *Minority Report* (New York: Simon & Schuster, 1963), p. 330.

47. Joseph Wood Krutch, "The Prosecution Rests," *Nation*, February 8, 1933, pp. 158–160. In a perceptive conclusion, Krutch pointed to the major challenge facing all dramatists with an unpopular message: "The propaganda play cannot achieve its purpose until it draws in the audience it intends to convince, and it may do this in either of two ways. It may, like the comedies of Bernard Shaw, be so diverting that the bitter is swallowed for the sake of the sweet. It may, on the other hand, be so original, so surprising, so obviously a work of genius, that the enemy comes—either because he is genuinely interested in supreme excellence of any kind or because, snob-like, he must be *au courant* with things artistic and intellectual. Unfortunately, the revolutionary drama of the moment has not found either its Shaw or its Ibsen. One does not have to go" (p. 160).

See also "Two Playwrights, With a Difference," *Literary Digest*, February 11, 1933, pp. 15–16; "Returning to 'We, the People,'" ibid., March 4, 1933, p. 19; Richard Dana Skinner, "The Play: *We, the People*," *Commonweal*, February 8, 1933, p. 411; and Frank Durham, *Elmer Rice* (New York: Twayne Publishers, Inc., 1970), pp. 92–93.

48. Rice, *Minority Report,* p. 329.

49. Burns Mantle, ed., *The Best Plays of 1932–1933* (New York: Dodd, Mead and Co., 1933), p. 271.

50. Fielding Burke [Olive Tilford Dargan], *Call Home the Heart* (1932; reprint, Old Westbury, N.Y.: The Feminist Press, 1983), pp. 285–286. For a good brief account of the Gastonia strike, see Christina L. Baker, "Gastonia Strike," in Mari Jo Buhle, Paul Buhle, and Dan Georgakas, eds., *Encyclopedia of the American Left* (New York: Garland Publishing, Inc., 1990), pp. 255–257.

51. Dorothy Myra Page, *Gathering Storm: A Story of the Black Belt* (New York: International Publishers, 1932), p. 285.

52. Ibid., pp. 327–328.

53. Mary Heaton Vorse, *Strike!* (1930; reprint, Chicago: University of Chicago Press, 1991), p. 46.

54. Horace Liveright published *Strike!* and Longmans, Green brought out *Call Home the Heart.* A good sampling of the reviews for both books may be found in the *Book Review Digest of 1932–33.* Page's novel, in contrast, received few reviews following its publication by International Publishers, a communist press. Other novels dealing with the Gastonia strike include Sherwood Anderson, *Beyond Desire* (New York: Liveright Publishing Corp., 1932); Grace Lumpkin, *To Make My Bread* (New York: The Macaulay Co., 1932); and William Rollins, Jr., *The Shadow Before* (New York: Robert M. McBride & Co., 1934).

55. Whittaker Chambers, "Can You Make Out Their Voices," reprinted in Terry Teachout, ed., *Ghosts on the Roof: Selected Journalism of Whittaker Chambers, 1931–1959* (Washington, D.C.: Regnery Gateway, 1989), pp. 3–21. The quoted material appears on p. 10.

56. Ibid., p. 20.

57. Whittaker Chambers, *Witness* (New York: Random House, 1952), p. 262.

58. Quoted in Jane De Hart Mathews, *The Federal Theatre, 1935–1939: Plays, Relief, and Politics* (Princeton: Princeton University Press, 1967), p. 21.

59. Malcolm Goldstein, *The Political Stage: American Drama and Theater of the Great Depression* (New York: Oxford University Press, 1974), p. 45.

60. Joanne Bentley, *Hallie Flanagan: A Life in the American Theatre* (New York: Alfred A. Knopf, 1988), p. 121.

61. Ibid., pp. 121–122; Goldstein, *The Political Stage,* pp. 45–46.

62. Mary Heaton Vorse, "The Psychology of Demonstrations," in Dee Garrison, ed., *Rebel Pen: The Writings of Mary Heaton Vorse* (New York: Monthly Review Press, 1985), pp. 136, 142.

63. Quoted in Meltzer, *Brother, Can You Spare a Dime?,* pp. 128–129.

64. Vorse, "The Psychology of Demonstrations," p. 141. Mauritz Hallgren provides an informed discussion of farmer militancy and its significance in *Seeds of Revolt,* pp. 137–160.

65. For perceptive accounts of the BEF, see Arthur M. Schlesinger, Jr., *The Crisis of the Old Order, 1919–1933* (1957; reprint, Boston: Houghton Mifflin Co., 1988), pp. 256–265, and William Manchester, *The Glory and the Dream: A Narrative History of America, 1932–1972* (Boston: Little, Brown and Co., 1974), pp. 3–4, 10–18.

66. Quoted in Winslow, *Brother, Can You Spare a Dime?*, p. 43.

67. Manchester, *The Glory and the Dream,* p. 17.

68. Malcolm Cowley, "The Flight of the Bonus Army," reprinted in Cowley, *Think Back on Us: The Social Record,* ed. Henry Dan Piper (Carbondale, Ill.: Southern Illinois University Press, 1967), p. 26.

69. Reprinted in Winslow, *Brother, Can You Spare a Dime?*, p. 45. For a good fictional treatment of the Bonus Army, see John D. Weaver's novel *Another Such Victory* (New York: Viking Press, 1948).

6. Imagining a New Constitutional Order

1. Matthew Josephson, *Infidel in the Temple: A Memoir of the Nineteen-Thirties* (New York: Alfred A. Knopf, 1967), p. 61.

2. Quoted in Arthur M. Schlesinger, Jr., *The Crisis of the Old Order, 1919–1933* (1957; reprint, Boston: Houghton Mifflin Co., 1988), p. 268. On Mussolini's reputation among Americans in the 1920s and early 1930s, see John P. Diggins, *Mussolini and Fascism: The View from America* (Princeton: Princeton University Press, 1972), pp. 77–283.

3. Lewis Mumford, "This Age of Pamphleteers," *The New Republic,* October 11, 1933, p. 249.

4. On the John Day Company, which also published Franklin Roosevelt's *Looking Forward* (1933), a collection of essays outlining his philosophy of government, see Charles A. Madison, *Book Publishing in America* (New York: McGraw-Hill Book Co., 1966), pp. 370–371.

5. Stuart Chase, "If I Were Dictator," *Nation,* November 18, 1931, p. 536.

6. Ibid., p. 537.

7. Ibid., p. 538.

8. Ibid., p. 537.

9. Glenn Frank, "If I Were Dictator," *Nation,* December 23, 1931, p. 690.

10. G. Lowes Dickinson, "If I Were Dictator," *Nation,* November 25, 1931, p. 568.

11. Harold J. Laski, "If I Were Dictator," *Nation,* January 6, 1932, p. 15.

12. Lewis Mumford, "If I Were Dictator," *Nation,* December 9, 1931, p. 632.

13. Ibid., p. 631.

14. Ibid., p. 633.

15. Morris L. Ernst, "If I Were a (Constitutional) Dictator," *Nation,* January 13, 1932, p. 36.

16. Oswald Garrison Villard, "If I Were Dictator," *Nation,* January 20, 1932, p. 69.

17. William Allen White, "If I Were Dictator," *Nation,* December 2, 1931, p. 596.

18. Ibid., p. 597.

19. Josephson, *Infidel in the Temple,* p. 155.

20. William Kay Wallace, *Our Obsolete Constitution* (New York: John Day Co., 1932), pp. 35, 37.

21. Ibid., p. 150.

22. Ibid., pp. 135, 136, 138.

23. Ibid., p. 182.

24. Ibid., p. 189.

25. Ibid., p. 162.

26. Ibid., p. 191. *Our Obsolete Constitution* received respectful attention in the mainstream press. "Even if one agrees with few or none at all of Mr. Wallace's theories, positions or arguments," commented a reviewer in the *New York Times* on November 13, 1932, "any one who has observed modern tendencies and thought much about them will find his book interesting and provocative of thought along new lines" (p. 25). Fabian Franklin, writing in the *Saturday Review of Literature* on December 24, 1932, was less impressed: "While his argument in support of his main contention—that the Constitution is un-suited to our age and ought to be replaced by a wholly different one—is im-pressive, what he says about the actual obsoleteness of the Constitution is ex-travagant and inconclusive" (p. 343).

27. James Cooper Lawrence, *The Year of Regeneration: An Improbable Fiction* (New York: Harper & Brothers, 1932), pp. 54–55.

28. Ibid., p. 39.

29. Ibid., p. 68.

30. Ibid., p. 60.

31. Ibid., p. 78.

32. Ibid., p. 80.

33. Ibid., p. 82. Reviews of Lawrence's work were generally favorable. "An im-probable fiction, indeed," observed Elmer Davis in the *Saturday Review of Lit-erature,* "yet one that many people would find attractive if they could only fig-ure out how to make it real" (July 30, 1932, p. 15). And a reviewer for the *Boston Transcript* was even more positive in his assessment: "The volume is en-tertaining enough as so much fiction, but its value consists less in the political satire here and there indulged in than in the constructive policies which it sug-gests and often strongly recommends" (July 2, 1932, p. 2).

34. Duval McCutchen, *America Made Young: A Plan for a More Perfect Society* (Philadelphia: Humanities Publishing Co., 1932), pp. 26–27.

35. There are echoes of Jefferson's proposed reform of the Virginia educational system in some features of McCutchen's plan. See Thomas Jefferson, *Notes on the State of Virginia,* reprinted in Merrill D. Peterson, ed., *Thomas Jefferson: Writings* (New York: The Library of America, 1984), pp. 271–275.

36. McCutchen, *America Made Young,* pp. 158–159.

37. No reviews of *America Made Young* appear in the 1932 *Book Review Digest,* for example.

38. Charles Elton Blanchard, M.D., *A New Day Dawns: A Brief History of the Altruistic Era (1930 to 2162 A.D.)* (Youngstown, Ohio: Medical Success Press, 1932), p. 152. The concern for a simplified amendment process under popular control recalls Samuel Merwin's Progressive novel, *The Citadel,* discussed in Chapter 2.

39. Blanchard, *A New Day Dawns,* p. 102.

40. Ibid., pp. 170–171.

41. In fact, Blanchard merely reverses Dixon's contention that a single drop of black blood will turn a Caucasian into a jungle animal. From a very different perspective, the civil rights activist Albion W. Tourgée argued unsuccessfully in *Plessy v. Ferguson* that the difficulty of determining questions of racial admixture should prevent a state from imposing Jim Crow restrictions on its African-American population. See "Brief for Homer A. Plessy by Albion W. Tourgée," reprinted in Otto H. Olsen, ed., *The Thin Disguise* (New York: Humanities Press, 1967), pp. 80–103.

42. *A New Day Dawns* is the second volume of Blanchard's "collectivist trilogy," which also includes *Our Altruistic Individualism* and *Our Unfinished Revolution.* For a review of the concluding volume, which summarizes the project, see *New York Times,* April 9, 1933, p. 11.

43. Frederick Palmer, *So a Leader Came* (New York: Ray Long and Richard R. Smith, Inc., 1932), pp. 157–158.

44. Ibid., p. 167.

45. Ibid., p. 181.

46. Ibid., pp. 214–215.

47. Ibid., pp. 282–283. *So a Leader Came* received mixed reviews in major newspapers and magazines. While many critics deplored Palmer's slapdash style and wooden characters, they tended to agree that his ideas were worth considering. "If Mr. Palmer's characters are somewhat sketchy as human beings," observed a writer in the *Saturday Review of Literature,* "they serve sufficiently as mouthpieces for his criticism of our present political 'set-up' and for a program of change which is at least interesting in a time of so many changing values as this" (October 22, 1932, p. 186). See also "A Mussolinian March," *New York Times,* October 23, 1932, sec. V, pp. 18, 21.

48. Ralph Adams Cram, "How Shall We Govern?" *Commonweal,* July 13, 1932, p. 287. For other proposals advocating some form of extraconstitutional presidential rule, see Paul Y. Anderson, "Wanted: a Mussolini," *Nation,* July 6, 1932, pp. 9–10; Frederic A. Ogg, "Does America Need a Dictator?" *Current History* 36 (September 1932): 641–648; and Mauritz A. Hallgren, *Seeds of Revolt* (New York: Alfred A. Knopf, 1933), pp. 286–287.

49. "Shadows of Dictatorship," *Commonweal,* July 13, 1932, p. 278.

50. For Tweed's background, see his obituary in the *New York Times,* May 1, 1940, p. L23. See also the listing in *Who Was Who, 1929–1940,* vol. 3 (London: Adam and Charles Black, 1941), p. 1374.

51. Herbert W. Horwill, "News and Views of Literary London," *New York Times,* March 26, 1933, sec. V, p. 8.

52. "A Leader Comes," *New York Times,* February 12, 1933, sec. V, p. 17.

53. Thomas Frederic Tweed, *Gabriel over the White House: A Novel of the Presidency* (New York: Farrar & Rinehart, 1933), p. 41.

54. Ibid., p. 82.

55. Ibid., p. 121.

56. John Maynard Keynes and other prominent English economists lectured at the Liberal Summer School that Tweed helped to establish in the 1920s. See Tweed's obituary in the *New York Times,* May 1, 1940, p. L23.

57. *Gabriel over the White House,* p. 177.

58. Ibid., p. 191.

59. Ibid., p. 220.

60. Ibid., p. 229.

61. Ibid., p. 106.

62. Ibid., p. 153.

63. Ibid., p. 253.

64. Ibid., pp. 286, 294.

65. Ibid., p. 308.

66. Quoted in Lawrence W. Levine, *The Unpredictable Past: Explorations in American Cultural History* (New York: Oxford University Press, 1993), p. 236.

67. Ibid.

68. Unless otherwise noted, the remaining quotations from *Gabriel over the White House* are taken from the movie's soundtrack. The film is currently available on videocassette, from MGM/UA Home Video.

69. On Hearst's recovery plan and his interest in the movie, see W. A. Swanberg, *Citizen Hearst* (New York: Charles Scribner's Sons, 1961), pp. 429–431, and Greg Mitchell, *The Campaign of the Century* (New York: Random House, 1992), pp. 218–220.

70. Quoted in Levine, *The Unpredictable Past,* p. 236.

71. Colin Shindler, *Hollywood in Crisis: Cinema and American Society, 1929–1939* (London: Routledge, 1996), p. 111.

72. Ibid., p. 112. The referendum suggestion does not appear in the movie, although Hammond refers to "overwhelming popular support" for his program in a radio speech.

73. Quoted in Mitchell, *Campaign of the Century,* p. 219.

74. Quoted in Shindler, *Hollywood in Crisis,* p. 113.

75. Ibid., p. 114.

76. On the film's box-office success, see Andrew Bergman, *We're in the Money: Depression America and Its Films* (New York: Harper & Row, 1972), p. 118. See also Mordaunt Hall, "The Outstanding Pictorial Features of 1933," in *The*

New York Times Film Reviews, vol. 2: 1932–1938 (New York: Times Books and Garland Publishing, 1990), p. 1016.

77. Mordaunt Hall, "The Screen," ibid., p. 923.

78. Quoted in Levine, *The Unpredictable Past,* p. 237. For other assessments, see "A President after Hollywood's Heart," *Literary Digest,* April 22, 1933, p. 13, and William Troy, "Fascism over Hollywood," *Nation,* April 26, 1933, pp. 482–483.

79. Richard Dana Skinner, "The Screen," *Commonweal,* May 5, 1933, p. 20.

80. Quoted in Mitchell, *Campaign of the Century,* p. 219.

81. Quoted in Bergman, *We're in the Money,* p. 118.

82. Quoted in Levine, *The Unpredictable Past,* p. 237.

7. Inauguration Day, 1933

1. Westbrook Pegler, *'T Aint Right* (Garden City, N.Y.: Doubleday, Doran & Co., 1936), p. 283.

2. Krock's comment is quoted in Arthur M. Schlesinger, Jr., *The Crisis of the Old Order, 1919–1933* (1957; reprint, Boston: Houghton Mifflin Co., 1988), p. 1; for Wilson's observation, see Edmund Wilson, "Washington: Inaugural Parade," in *The American Earthquake* (Garden City, N.Y.: Doubleday & Co., 1958), p. 479.

3. For further details, see Morris Markey, "Washington Weekend," in Milton Crane, ed., *The Roosevelt Era* (New York: Boni and Gaer, 1947), pp. 5–9.

4. Numerous accounts describe the inauguration scene. See especially Cabell Phillips, *From the Crash to the Blitz, 1929–1939* (New York: Macmillan Co., 1969), pp. 100–104; William Manchester, *The Glory and the Dream: A Narrative History of America, 1932–1972* (Boston: Little, Brown and Co., 1974), p. 76; and "The New President's Call to Battle," *Literary Digest,* March 11, 1933, p. 5.

5. Quoted in Nicholas Halasz, *Roosevelt through Foreign Eyes* (Princeton: D. Van Nostrand Co., 1961), p. 24. The observer was William Law, M.P.

6. "The Inaugural Address, March 4, 1933," reprinted in Raymond Moley (with Elliot A. Rosen), *The First New Deal* (New York: Harcourt, Brace and World, 1966), p. 121.

7. See Halford R. Ryan, *Franklin D. Roosevelt's Rhetorical Presidency* (Westport, Conn.: Greenwood Press, 1988), p. 82.

8. "The Inaugural Address," p. 122.

9. The editorial comments appear in "The New President's Call to Battle," pp. 6–7.

10. Wilson, *American Earthquake,* p. 478.

11. "The Inaugural Address," p. 122.

12. Ibid., p. 123.

13. Ibid., p. 124. In his column of March 13, 1933, H. L. Mencken cautioned that Congress should go "very slowly in making further grants of its constitu-

tional powers. They will all be made, in form, to the President, but they will be made in fact to a great army of jobholders, some of them intelligent but most of them fools. . . . In brief, all bureaucracies will bear close watching, and none more so than that which comes into power on a wave of popular enthusiasm, and with the avowed purpose of saving the country from ruin." See Mencken, "A Time to Be Wary," in *A Carnival of Buncombe: Writings on Politics* (Chicago: University of Chicago Press, 1984), pp. 273, 274.

14. See "Crowd Mind Read by Mrs. Roosevelt," *New York Times,* March 5, 1933, p. 7. She added: "No woman entering the White House, if she accepts the fact that it belongs to the people and, therefore, must be representative of whatever conditions the people are facing, can light-heartedly take up residence here. . . . One has a feeling of going it blindly, because we're in a tremendous stream, and none of us knows where we're going to land."

15. See "Congress Members Praise Address for Pledge of Action," *New York Times,* March 5, 1933, p. 6.

16. The Dallas *News* statement is reported in "Comment of Press on Roosevelt's Inaugural Address," ibid. For the other quoted material, see "The New President's Call to Battle," p. 6.

17. On press reaction in England and France, see "Bold Action Here Is Urged in Britain," *New York Times,* March 5, 1933, p. 5, and "Roosevelt's Task Impresses Paris," ibid., p. 7.

18. Quoted in Ryan, *Franklin D. Roosevelt's Rhetorical Presidency,* p. 83.

19. Quoted in Detlef Junker, "Hitler's Perception of Franklin D. Roosevelt and the United States of America," in Cornelis A. van Minnen and John F. Sears, eds., *FDR and His Contemporaries: Foreign Perceptions of an American President* (New York: St. Martin's Press, 1992), p. 150.

20. The cartoon is reprinted in "The New President's Call to Battle," p. 5.

21. Quoted in ibid., p. 6.

22. Quoted in Manchester, *The Glory and the Dream,* p. 77.

23. Quoted in Arthur M. Schlesinger, Jr., *The Coming of the New Deal* (1958; reprint, Boston: Houghton Mifflin Co., 1988), p. 1.

24. The poem is reprinted in Donald W. Whisenhunt, *Poetry of the People: Poems to the President, 1929–1945* (Bowling Green, Ohio: Bowling Green State University Popular Press, 1996), p. 83.

25. Quoted in Colin Shindler, *Hollywood in Crisis: Cinema and American Society, 1929–1939* (London: Routledge, 1996), pp. 170–171. For further details on the movie, including Jack Warner's unsuccessful efforts to "borrow" Roosevelt's voice and image for use in the concluding scene, see Giuliana Muscio, *Hollywood's New Deal* (Philadelphia: Temple University Press, 1997), p. 99. *Heroes for Sale* is available on videocassette, from MGM/UA Home Video.

26. Shindler, *Hollywood in Crisis,* p. 40.

27. *The Autobiography of William Allen White* (New York: Macmillan Co., 1946), p. 635.

Index